DIRECTORS' PERSONAL LIABILITY

Other books in the series

The Rights of Shareholders
Peter Xuereb
0 632 02148 9

The Right to Dismiss
Second Edition
Michael Whincup
0 632 01893 3

Contracts of Employment
Vivien Shrubsall
0 632 02145 4

Consumer Credit
Graham Stephenson
0 00 383303 8

Introduction to the Law of International Trade
David Tiplady
0 632 02376 7

The Law of the Investment Markets
Robert R. Pennington
0 632 02372 4

The Law Relating to Credit Cards
Sally Jones
0 632 02146 2

DIRECTORS' PERSONAL LIABILITY

ROBERT R. PENNINGTON
LLD, Solicitor, Professor of
Commercial Law at the University
of Birmingham

BSP PROFESSIONAL BOOKS
OXFORD LONDON EDINBURGH
BOSTON MELBOURNE

Copyright © Robert R. Pennington 1987

All rights reserved. No part of this
publication may be reproduced, stored
in a retrieval system, or transmitted,
in any form or by any means, electronic,
mechanical, photocopying, recording
or otherwise, without the prior
permission of the copyright owner.

First published in Great Britain by
Collins Professional and Technical Books 1987
Reprinted in paperback by BSP Professional Books 1989

British Library Cataloguing in Publication Data
Pennington, Robert R.
 Directors' personal liability.
 1. Great Britain. Companies. Directors. Law. Obligations
 I. Title
 344.106'664

 ISBN 0 632 02619 7 Pbk
    0 00 383294 5

BSP Professional Books
A division of Blackwell Scientific
 Publications Ltd
Editorial Offices:
Osney Mead, Oxford OX2 0EL
 (Orders: Tel. 0865 240201)
8 John Street, London WC1N 2ES
23 Ainslie Place, Edinburgh EH3 6AJ
3 Cambridge Center, Suite 208, Cambridge
 MA 02142, USA
107 Barry Street, Carlton, Victoria 3053,
 Australia

Printed and bound in Great Britain by
Mackays of Chatham PLC, Chatham, Kent

Contents

Preface ix

1 **The Legal Status of Directors** 1
The functions of directors -- British pragmatism – Normal method of appointment – Appointment under contractual arrangements – The power to remove directors – Appointment of managing directors – Functions – Service contracts are not mandatory – Terms of service contracts – Approval by shareholders in general meeting – Decisions of the board – Delegation – Formality and informality – Ideal categorisation – Decisions of the courts.

2 *De Facto* **Directors, Shadow Directors and Group Directors** 25
De facto directors – Status of *de facto* directors – Transactions entered into by *de facto* directors – Shadow directors: definition – Statutory provisions applicable to shadow directors – Directors of groups of companies – Definition of a parent or holding company – Significance of the relationship.

3 **Directors' Basic Fiduciary Duties** 33
Nature of fiduciary duties – Extension of fiduciary duties to company directors – Common law duty of directors – The delimitation of directors' powers – Are directors liable absolutely for exceeding their powers? – Conflicts of interest – Direct personal interest and profits – Exploitation of business opportunities by directors – Competition by directors – Use of corporate information.

4 **The Judicial and Statutory Extension of Directors' Fiduciary Duties** 59
The interests of the company and shareholders as a whole – The interests of employees, creditors and others – The use of directors' powers for the proper purpose – Is there a positive duty for directors to achieve fulfilment of the company's interests? – The rights of the company when its director has an interest – Directors' statutory obligations.

5 **Directors' Duties of Skill and Care** 81
The personal character of the duty of care and skill – Instances of the duty to exercise care and skill – A comparison of American case law.

6 The Termination and Discharge of Directors' Duties   92
When directors cease to be subject to fiduciary duties – Confidential information – Insider dealing – Legality of exoneration provisions – Invalidity of exoneration provisions – Insurance against directors' liability – Indemnity against costs – Powers of the court to give relief – Instances of relief given by the court – The release of directors' liability by a resolution of shareholders.

7 Directors' Duties under the Companies Acts   103
Statutory obligations and prohibitions and their sanctions – Criminal offences under the Companies Act 1985 – Method of analysis – Periodical accounts and reports – Meetings of shareholders – Issues of share and loan capital – Prospectuses – The furnishing of information – Annual accounts and reports – Directors' interests in company transactions – Compromises and arrangements – Investigation of a company's affairs – Directors' declarations in connection with share purchases, liquidations, etc. – Inspection rights.

8 The Enforcement of Directors' Statutory Duties   136
Acquisitions by and disposals to directors – Loans and financial accommodation for directors – Compensation for loss of office – Other statutory remedies – Actions for damages and injunctions – Application to the Companies Acts – Judicial evasion of the question whether breaches of statutory obligation are actionable – Conclusions.

9 Directors' Duties and Liabilities to Shareholders   148
Reason for directors' general immunity – Examples of directors' immunity as regards the company's shareholders – Directors as agents of shareholders – Directors' duty to advise shareholders – Prospectuses containing untrue statements or omissions – Incomplete share subscriptions and Stock Exchange listing undertakings – Preferential subscription rights – Compensation for loss of office.

10 Directors' Duties and Liabilities to a Company's Creditors   173
Immunity of directors as regards the company's creditors and contractors – Exclusive personal liability of directors – Contracts by directors personally – Breach of warranty of authority – Guarantees by directors –   Inadequacy of a public company's initial capital – Sole member of a company – Liability of signatories of negotiable instruments – Persons prohibited from being or acting as directors – Directors' liability to contribute in a liquidation – Directors who are

personally liable by the company's memorandum – Directors' liabilities for fraudulent and wrongful trading.

11 Litigation Concerning Directors' Duties   196
Modes of enforcement by litigation – Other modes of enforcement – Arrangement of subject matter – Litigation in the company's name – Power to sue in the company's name – Proceedings against directors in a company's liquidation – Defendants, contribution and indemnity – Form of litigation – Enforceability by shareholders – The derivative action – Situations where derivative actions lie – *Ultra vires* acts, breaches of the company's constitution and illegal acts – Fraud or oppression of minority shareholders – Breaches of fiduciary duties by directors – The American solution.

12 Shareholders' Remedies for Unfair Treatment and Conclusions   228
Statutory jurisdiction of courts – The present legislation – Conduct by directors meriting relief – The interests of a shareholder seeking relief – The conduct of the petitioning shareholder – Supervision of directors – Investigations and awards – Availability of litigation – Effectiveness and cost of litigation.

Table of Cases   **244**
Table of Statutes   **255**
Index   **265**

Preface

Whether the English as a nation have, like their American cousins, become more litigious in recent years is debatable. What is certain, however, is that litigation brought against directors of companies of all kinds, from the biggest public companies with a Stock Exchange listing for their shares to comparatively small private companies whose shares are held within one family, has increased substantially. Directors are more vulnerable than they have ever been to the cost and trouble involved in defending allegations that they have failed to fulfil their duties fully, either because they have disregarded one or more of the statutory obligations heaped on them by the Companies Acts since 1948, or because they have pursued some interest of their own or their families in a way not permitted by the fiduciary duties imposed on them as directors. Not only has the law become more complex as a result of legislation; it has also become more burdensome on directors as the result of judicial decision.

Additionally, the courts have laid down in recent cases that a shareholder who shows that he has a *prima facie* case for alleging that a director is liable to his company and that there is substantial evidence to support the allegation, may apply to the court in advance of the trial for an order that the whole or part of his costs of litigating shall be borne by the company in any event. This may be the just counterpart of the rule that directors who defend themselves successfully against allegations of breaches of duty are entitled to reimbursement of their costs out of the company's assets if they cannot recover them from the unsuccessful plaintiff, but there is no doubt that the courts' willingness to consider applications by disgruntled shareholders for their costs to be met by the company does encourage litigation.

In this book the duties and liabilities of directors to their companies and to the shareholders and creditors of their companies will be explored. The substantive rules of the Companies Acts and related legislation in this respect will be analysed and related to the underlying principles of common law and equity on which they have been built as an increasingly detailed superstructure. In the first two chapters the legal definition and the legal status of directors and of persons who assume the functions of directors (or who are treated by law for certain purposes as though they were directors) are examined as a basis for the consideration of directors' duties and liabilities which follows. Chapters 3 and 4 are concerned primarily with the fiduciary duties or duties of good faith, fair dealing and loyalty which the courts have imposed upon directors over the years and which have been modified and extended by the Companies Acts. Chapter 5 is taken up with the problematical duty which directors owe their companies to act with proper skill and care, and Chapter 6 with the termination of directors' duties and liabilities. In Chapters 7 and 8 the duties, obligations and liabilities increasingly imposed on directors by successive Companies Acts are surveyed, together with the methods by which such duties and liabilities may be enforced, whether created by the Companies Acts or otherwise.

In Chapters 9 and 10 the growing number of duties and liabilities of directors toward individual shareholders and investors in companies and toward creditors and other persons who deal with companies are classified and considered in detail. The last two chapters of the book are concerned with the various forms and incidents of litigation by means of which the duties and liabilities of directors may be enforced, or reparation for them not being fulfilled or satisfied may be obtained. Consideration is here given to the recently refurbished proceedings which may be initiated by minority shareholders who allege that their companies' affairs are being conducted in a manner which is unfairly prejudicial to them.

Most of the requirements and prohibitions imposed on directors by the Companies Acts are sanctioned by exposure to criminal proceedings as well as enforcement by civil litigation or other means, and the most important of these requirements and prohibitions and the sanctions for their observance are also considered in this book. Directors' criminal responsibility under legislation not primarily concerned with the management and administration of companies (such as the Consumer Protection Acts 1961 and 1971, the Trade Descriptions Act 1970, the Consumer Credit Act 1974, and the Health and Safety at Work Act 1974) is not dealt with, however, since this topic is better dealt with in connection with the legislation to which it relates. It is, nevertheless, not out of place to note that the almost universal practice in modern legislation which creates criminal offences for which companies may be prosecuted, to impose parallel criminal liability on directors and officers of the company who have not taken all practicable steps to prevent the company from committing the offence, makes the possibility of criminal liability a matter of real concern to directors.

The law is given in this book as stated on 1 October 1986, but the provisions of the Insolvency Acts 1985 and 1986, which came into force on 29 December 1986 have also been included. Where appropriate, the law and legislation of other countries, particularly the United States of America, has been mentioned so that useful comparisons with British law may be made.

Robert R. Pennington
University of Birmingham

Chapter 1

The Legal Status of Directors

In one of its definition sections the Companies Act 1985, which now governs all companies, whenever registered, unhelpfully provides that in the Act references to a 'director' include 'any person occupying the position of a director, by whatever name called' (section 741(1)). The Act does not, however, define what the position, status and functions of a director are. It merely imposes obligations and restrictions on directors without attempting to be exhaustive, and without in any way diminishing the duties which directors are under by the rules of common law and equity. All the Act does is to provide that if a person fulfils the functions of a director (whatever they may be), he is to be treated as a director. This is so even though the constitution of the company in its memorandum or articles of association gives him a different name, such as manager, governor or member of the board or council of management.

1.01 The functions of directors

In fact, the law has never attempted to define the distinctive powers and functions which must be vested in one or more persons in relation to a company if they are to be considered to be its directors. In this respect British law differs from the laws of the other Western European countries and the states of the United States of America. The legislation of those countries expressly deputes the management or the direction or the administration of a company's affairs to its directors collectively, if more than one, or to a collegiate body called the board of directors. Such provisions in fact help little, since they leave completely uncertain what powers to act in the name of a company are comprised in its management, direction or administration. Instead, they leave it for the courts to decide whether particular powers or functions of a company are to be exercised by its directors or by its shareholders acting together at general meetings.

British law leaves the division of a company's powers and functions between its board of directors and its shareholders in general meeting to be prescribed by the company's memorandum or articles of association. This is subject to the overriding rule that powers and functions which the Companies Act 1985 vests in the board of directors or a general meeting cannot, unless the Act expressly permits, be vested by the company's memorandum or articles in the other of them. Additionally, any powers which the board of directors cannot exercise automatically belong to the shareholders in general meeting.

In practice, the articles of association of most British companies contain the widest delegation of the companies' powers to their board of directors. Like the standard form of articles set out in the regulations made under the Companies Act 1985, companies' articles of association usually state that 'subject to the provisions of the Act, the memorandum and the articles [of association] and to any directions given by special resolution [of a general meeting of shareholders], the business of the company shall be managed by the directors, who may exercise all the powers of the company'. (The Companies (Tables A to F) Regulations, 1985 (SI 1985/805), Table A, para 70).

This arrangement neatly avoids the problem of designating the powers which belong to the board of directors as powers of management, and the powers which belong to general meetings of shareholders as powers of control or supervision. It does so by vesting all the powers exercisable on the company's behalf in the board, except those powers which are expressly reserved to the shareholders. Nevertheless, under the usual form of articles, control is retained by the shareholders by means of the power reserved to them to override directors' decisions by passing special resolutions by a 75 per cent majority vote. Shareholders also have the ultimate control over directors' decisions by means of their statutory power to remove directors from office by an ordinary resolution passed by a simple majority vote (Companies Act 1985, section 303).

1.02 British pragmatism

British law is essentially pragmatic, and often avoids giving definitions or laying down general principles if it can achieve the results it seeks by other means. The definition of directors is an instance of this pragmatic approach. The nature and functioning of companies require that their affairs shall be conducted continuously by a small group of people, the directors, subject to periodic accounting to the wider body, the shareholders in general meeting, who have clearly defined powers of supervision and control.

In the case of small companies the two groups, directors and shareholders, are usually wholly or largely composed of the same persons. In the case of public companies with a Stock Exchange listing for their shares, the directors may also be the holders of a majority of the company's issued shares, but at least 25 per cent of the company's listed share capital must be available for dealing on the market, and very often the directors collectively hold only a small fraction of it. However interrelated the two groups – directors and shareholders – are, however, they are functionally distinct.

The problems with which company law and the draftsmen of companies' memoranda and articles of association concern themselves are the manner in which directors are appointed and removed and the way in which the board of directors operates, rather than with defining the status of directors. It is because of this that when the courts have been called on to establish the rules for directors' conduct and the measure of their responsibilities, they have done so largely by drawing analogies between directors and other categories of person who act as representatives for the benefit of third parties, such as agents and trustees.

THE APPOINTMENT AND REMOVAL OF DIRECTORS

1.03 Normal method of appointment

British law regards the appointment and removal of directors as a proprietorial function of the shareholders in general meeting. If a company's memorandum and articles were to make no provision for the appointment of directors (which in fact never happens), the directors would be appointed by an ordinary resolution passed by general meetings by a simple majority vote, and they would hold office for such length of time as the shareholders resolved, or if no period were fixed for their appointments, until the shareholders resolved by ordinary resolution to remove them.

Prescriptions of the Companies Act 1985

The Companies Act 1985 prescribes only three matters in respect of the appointment of directors (apart from disqualifications for appointment) namely, that the first directors of a company, whether public or private, must be named in a statement signed by the subscribers of the company's memorandum and articles of association prior to the company's registration (section 10(2)), that every public company must have at least two directors and every private company at least one (section 282(1) and (3)), and that two or more nominees for election as directors at a general meeting of a public company cannot be appointed by a single resolution, unless the meeting has previously agreed to this without a dissenting vote (section 292(1)).

Even with regard to disqualifications from appointment as directors, the Company Directors Disqualification Act 1986 (which supplements the Companies Act 1985) contains only two mandatory provisions, which cannot be avoided by different provisions being inserted in a company's memorandum or articles of association. The first of these is that a person who is an undischarged bankrupt may not act as a director (section 11). Nevertheless, it appears that the appointment of a bankrupt as a director is valid to the extent that he fills a seat on the board, and there is no vacancy because of his bankruptcy. The memorandum or articles may invalidate the appointment of a bankrupt as a director however.

The second mandatory disqualification is that if the court orders that a person shall not hold an appointment as a director of any company at all for a period not exceeding 15 years, as it may do if he is convicted of an indictable offence in connection with the promotion, formation, management or liquidation of a company, or for certain other reasons, that person cannot be appointed a director of any company during the disqualification period without the permission of the court (sections 2 to 6 and sections 8 to 10).

Apart from these basic matters, the Companies Act 1985 leaves it to the memorandum and articles of each individual company to prescribe how its directors shall be appointed and for what period their appointments shall last.

Public companies

In the case of public companies, it is usual for the articles to provide that directors (other than the first directors) shall be appointed by an ordinary resolution passed by a general meeting, that directors so appointed shall hold office for three, four or five years, and that a fraction of the total number of directors shall retire each year at or after the annual general meeting of shareholders for that year. A provision for such staggered retirements means that over the three, four or five year period for which directors hold office, the appointments of all the directors will terminate. Any retiring director (unless disqualified by law or the memorandum or articles of association) may be re-elected on the termination of his appointment, and the articles usually provide that he will be deemed re-elected unless the annual general meeting at which he retires resolves that he shall not be re-elected or someone else shall be appointed in his place.

This machinery for appointing directors is usually accompanied by provisions in the articles of association that the minimum and maximum membership of the board of directors shall be fixed by the shareholders in general meeting. The articles also usually provide that casual vacancies on the board (e.g. by death or resignation) shall be filled by the board itself, and that the new directors shall retire at the next following annual general meeting, but may present themselves for re-election. The articles additionally usually empower the board of directors to appoint one or more managing directors from its number or from outsiders on such terms and with such powers and functions as the board thinks fit. Managing directors usually do not retire by rotation, as ordinary directors do, but are appointed to hold office for a fixed period which is often longer than the period for which an ordinary director is appointed.

These typical arrangements for the appointment of directors of a public company are designed to make them properly accountable to the shareholders in general meeting. Their appointments are not indefinite; they must present themselves for re-election every three, four or five years, although there is nothing to prevent a director making a career of his directorship if he is repeatedly re-elected. On the other hand, the composition of the whole body of directors does not change at any one time, and the fact that only a third, a quarter or a fifth of the directors retire each year ensures continuity in the management and in the business policies of the company.

The one flaw in the effectiveness of the machinery for shareholder control over the appointment and re-appointment of directors is that the incumbent directors control the means for calling general meetings and soliciting proxy appointments from shareholders to vote for the election or re-election of the board's nominees as directors. This, combined with shareholder apathy in attending or being represented at general meetings, makes it possible for the board to become an oligarchical, self-perpetuating body whose membership is only seriously challenged at times of crisis.

In recent years, as a counterbalance, the institutional investors, who now account for more than 70 per cent of the holdings of ordinary shares issued by listed public companies, have made more effort than formerly to monitor the performance of such companies' boards of directors and to lodge effective objections to unwise or hazardous transactions proposed by their boards. Nevertheless, the influence of institutional investors has made itself felt more by way of persuasion of boards of directors rather than direct challenge in proposing nominees for election to the board against the board's own wishes.

Private companies

The appointment of directors to the boards of private companies is in practice very different from that for public companies. This is because most private companies are really incorporated partnerships, whose directors are the only or the principal shareholders. The directors/ shareholders regard the company's assets and undertaking as being in substance 'their' business, despite the fact that in law it is the company which owns the business, and the directors are not proprietors, but the company's officers and agents.

Private companies' articles sometimes do incorporate the same kind of arrangements for the rotation of directors and the partial annual re-appointment of directors as public companies. However, this is usually overlaid by provisions for the appointment of the first directors by name to hold office for life, or until they choose to resign, or at least for a substantial number of years, or for the appointment of one or more managing directors on similar terms.

It is only when a private company's shares are extensively held by persons who are not directors that changes are made in the articles of association to ensure that all directors must present themselves for re-election periodically, or that shareholders or groups of shareholders who are not directors are empowered to nominate a minority of directors to the board. Because of the elasticity which British law permits in framing articles of association, almost any arrangements can be adopted in the articles to cover the appointment of directors and the duration of their appointments without falling foul of the kind of inescapable, mandatory rules which abound in continental systems of law.

1.04 Appointment under contractual arrangements

A question which arises in practice more frequently with private companies than public ones, is whether it is possible for a company or its shareholders to provide by contract for the representation on its board of directors of classes or groups of shareholders, or of individual shareholders or debenture holders or creditors of the company. The company's ability to do this is limited by the fact that directors can be appointed to its board only in a manner which is consistent with its memorandum and articles of association. This is illustrated by the decision of the House of Lords in *James* v. *Eve* (1873) that if the company's articles provide for the appointment of directors by resolution of the shareholders in general meeting, a contract by which the company purports to confer the right to make appointments to the board in any other way is invalid.

However, it is always possible to alter the provisions of the memorandum or articles dealing with the appointment of directors by the shareholders passing a special resolution in general meeting by a three-quarters majority vote (Companies Act 1985, sections 9 and 17(1)). After such an alteration has been made to facilitate appointments of directors under contractual arrangements, the company can enter into a valid contract enabling the shareholders or creditors concerned to make appointments to the board.

Form and enforcement of contracts for appointment

A contract enabling one or more persons to be represented on the board of directors of a company may, if the articles permit, empower those persons to make an appointment to the board directly, so that the appointee becomes a director as soon as he is nominated. Alternatively, the contract may empower the other party to nominate a person for appointment as a director and provide that the company will appoint the nominee. In that case the appointment does not take effect until the board of directors or the shareholders in general meeting, as the case may be, resolve to make the appointment.

The company can be compelled by the court to accept the other party's nominee as a director, unless he is unfit to act, for example, if he has interests which are inimical to or in conflict with the company's, as the court held in *British Murac Syndicate Ltd* v. *Alperton Rubber Co. Ltd* (1915). Except in that case, the court will issue a mandatory injunction to compel the company to allow the nominee to exercise the powers and functions of a director.

If the other contracting party is empowered by the contract only to nominate a director, the proper remedy if the company will not appoint him would be a mandatory injunction compelling the board or the shareholders in general meeting to make the appointment. However, in the one case where such an injunction was sought, *Plantations Trust Ltd* v. *Bila (Sumatra) Rubber Lands Ltd* (1916), Eve J held that he could not compel the company to make an appointment specifically, and because of that he could not issue an injunction to restrain the company from preventing the nominee from acting as a director.

The correctness of this decision is doubtful. It contrasts with the more recent decision of Megarry J in *C.H. Giles & Co. Ltd* v. *Morris* (1972), who held that if a majority shareholder who contracts with a purchaser of his holding to nominate and procure the appointment of a person designated by the purchaser to be a director of the company, the majority shareholder can be compelled to do all acts necessary for that purpose. There seems no good reason why a similar contract made by the company itself should not be specifically enforceable against it in the same way.

Voting agreements

An agreement between certain shareholders to vote at general meetings in a particular way, or as they shall collectively decide by a majority of their number, is perfectly valid, and such an agreement may be enforced by any of the shareholders who are parties to the agreement. They may seek an injunction to prevent another shareholder from voting in breach of the agreement, or alternatively and more effectively, they may apply for a mandatory injunction to compel the shareholder to vote in conformity with the agreement.

In *Puddephatt* v. *Leith* (1916), the court extended the validity of such voting agreements to an agreement between a shareholder and a person who was not a shareholder, and the shareholder's promise to vote for the appointment or reappointment of the other party's nominee as a director was specifically enforced. Consequently, because of the doubts raised by Eve J's decision in *Plantation Trust Ltd* v. *Bila (Sumatra) Rubber Lands* (see above), it is perhaps safer for a third person to be given a power to appoint a director by means of an agreement by the shareholders to elect his nominee and not to vote for his removal from office so long as the third person's interest in the company continues.

On the other hand, shareholders should be conscious of the divisive effect which an agreement of this kind can have on the board of directors. The representation of outside interests on the board may be perfectly legitimate to protect those interests. But the inevitable tendency of an arrangement by which individual shareholders or groups of shareholders or other persons may appoint their representatives to the board is to destroy the cohesion which should exist between directors and to increase the possibilities of dissension between them. What is legally possible is not necessarily in the long-term interests of the company.

1.05 The power to remove directors

The other power by which shareholders in general meeting control the composition of the board of directors is the power to remove directors from the board. This power is valuable if the shareholders consider the performance of the directors to be unsatisfactory or if they wish to replace them by other appointees.

It used to be common for companies' articles of association to empower the shareholders in general meeting to remove a director before his period of office had expired, usually by passing a special resolution by a three-quarters' majority vote. In the absence of such an express power a director could not be prematurely removed, and the shareholders' only sanction against an unsatisfactory director was to resolve that he should not be re-elected when his current period of office expired.

The statutory power of removal

Since July 1948, when the Companies Act 1948 came into force, however, the Companies Acts (now the Companies Act 1985, section 303) have empowered the shareholders in general meeting to remove any director (except a director of a private company who held office for life in July 1945) for any reason by passing an ordinary resolution to that effect. There are, nevertheless, procedural conditions which must be satisfied to ensure that the director has an opportunity to defend himself.

In the first place, the shareholder or group of shareholders who intend to propose a resolution to remove a director must give the company at least 28 days' notice of their intention to do so before the meeting is held at which the resolution is considered (section 303(2) and section 379(1)). On being notified of their intention, the company must inform the director concerned so that he may prepare a written statement of a reasonable length in his defence, and the company must circulate this statement to its shareholders with the notice calling the meeting or separately (section 304(1) and (2)). To give the shareholders sufficient time to consider the matter, the notice calling the meeting must be given to shareholders at least 21 days before the meeting is held (section 379(2)). At the meeting, whether he has submitted a written statement in his defence or not, the director is entitled to address the shareholders who attend the meeting orally (section 304(3)).

When the statutory power of removal is used, there is usually dissension on the board, and a majority of the directors are seeking to get rid of one of their colleagues with the support of the shareholders. Obviously, in such a situation the other directors are likely to be sensitive about the observations of the director whose removal is sought in his defence statement which they are required to circulate. The other directors have no powers of censorship over the contents of the defence statement, however, nor over the remarks made by the director whose removal is sought at the general meeting called to remove him. All the other directors can do is to apply to the court to be relieved from their obligation to circulate the defence statement on the ground that it gives needless publicity for defamatory matter (section 304(4)). The burden of proof that the target director is abusing his right to defend himself rests on those who make the allegation (section 304(4)).

Weaknesses of the statutory power

The statutory power for shareholders to remove an unwanted director looks like an effective mandatory provision to ensure that the shareholders have effective control at all times over the composition of the board. The power cannot be taken away or restricted by the provisions of the memorandum or articles of association or any contract. Nevertheless, the power has a number of weaknesses.

To begin with, a shareholder or group of shareholders who wish to have a director removed have no inherent right to have a general meeting called for the purpose (*Pedley* v. *Inland Waterways Association Ltd* (1977)). They can insist on the board calling an extraordinary general meeting to remove a director only in the same circumstances as they can insist on such a meeting being called for any other purpose. They can do this only if the demand for the meeting is supported in writing by shareholders who between them hold shares carrying voting rights on which there has been paid up at least one-tenth of the total amount paid up on all the company's shares carrying voting rights (section 368(1) and (2)). The board of directors, on the other hand, may call an extraordinary general meeting to remove a director if a majority of the directors vote in favour of doing so at a board meeting.

Secondly, although the resolution by which a director is removed need only be an ordinary one passed by a simple majority vote (so that any provision in the company's articles requiring a special majority would be ineffective), the Companies Act 1985 does not require that the voting rights exercisable at the general meeting should be proportionate to the nominal or paid up value of the company's shares. Consequently, if the company's articles confer multiple voting rights on the director whose removal is sought in respect of shares held by him, the director may be given sufficient voting power to defeat any resolution for his removal. This device was held to be effective by the House of Lords in 1969 in the case of *Bushell* v. *Faith* (1970), despite the fact that the device completely defeats the purpose of the statutory powers of removal.

Finally, the exercise of the statutory power may prove expensive to the company, because a director who is removed under it retains the right to claim damages from the company for the breach of any service contract he has with it, or alternatively, to claim compensation for the premature termination of his directorship to which his service contract or the memorandum or articles entitle him (section 303(5)).

Power to remove a director by the articles

Because of the deficiencies of the statutory power to remove directors, it is common for companies' articles of association to contain express powers of removal. In the case of private companies this power is sometimes exercisable by the board of directors itself without holding a general meeting. Sometimes the power of removal takes the form of a power for the board by a majority vote to call on any of its members to resign, and if the director in question fails to resign within a stated period, the articles provide that he shall be deemed to have done so.

By such a provision for deemed resignation, the company may avoid paying compensation for loss of office to the director under a provision in the articles requiring it to be paid to a director who is removed. However, if the director has a service contract entered into for a fixed period which does not incorporate a provision for his deemed resignation if he fails to resign on request, his deemed resignation under such a provision introduced by an alteration made in the articles after his service contract was entered into will not prevent him from claiming damages from the company for breach of that contract (*Southern Foundries (1926) Ltd* v. *Shirlaw* (1940)).

MANAGING DIRECTORS

1.06 Appointment of managing directors

Both public and private companies' articles of association commonly provide that the board of directors may appoint one or more of its members or, sometimes, one or more outsiders, to be the managing director or directors of the company on such terms and with such powers as the board thinks fit. The managing director or directors are then delegates of the board invested with such of the powers of the board as it confers on them, either concurrently with the board or, more usually to the exclusion of the board.

If a managing director's appointment is for a fixed period, the articles usually provide that he shall not retire by rotation in the manner prescribed for other directors. In that case, if the articles additionally provide that he may exercise the powers delegated to him by the board exclusively, there is an enduring division of the powers of the directors between the managing director (whose power cannot be exercised by or interfered with by the board) and the board itself, which exercises the residual powers conferred on directors by the articles.

The managing director, like any other director, can be removed by the shareholders exercising their statutory power of removal. The board also may remove him from his managing directorship (so that he continues only as an ordinary director) or from his membership of the board completely if power to do either or both of these things is reserved to the board by the company's articles of association, or in the case of his removal from the managing directorship, by the terms of the managing director's appointment.

The purpose of appointing a managing director or directors is to ensure that the day-to-day management of the company's business is conducted by one or a few persons who may be required to devote their whole time and attention to the company's affairs. The remaining powers of the board, which may, following the French and German terminology, appropriately be called powers of supervision and administration, will then be exercised by the board of directors collectively (including the managing director or directors) at board meetings which are held periodically.

The delegation of powers of management to the managing director or directors is not necessarily a permanent feature of the company's constitution, however. Unless the managing director's powers are written into the company's articles of association (which is unusual), he does not exercise his powers as an independent organ of the company, but only as a delegate of the board, and the delegation lasts only as long as the managing director's appointment. Nevertheless, in private companies, where a managing director holds a majority or a substantial fraction of the company's issued shares, his delegated powers may appear to be permanent since he controls the board of directors. In listed public companies this is rarely so, because the managing director is unlikely to have a controlling shareholding, and his accountability to the board, particularly if the board has a power to remove him, is therefore more real.

1.07 Functions

In British practice it is unusual for the board resolution appointing a managing director or the service contract entered into by him with the company upon his appointment (if there is such a contract) to define the managing director's powers in detail. Instead, he is usually empowered to do all things necessary for the management of the company's affairs, or to exercise such powers as the board authorise him to exercise for the time being.

Whether a particular power is a power of management or a power of administration reserved to the board is a question of fact in each particular case. The answer depends largely on the nature and size of the company's business, the powers which the board has allowed managing directors to exercise in the past (so establishing a practical division of function between the managing director and the board), and the seriousness and importance of the transaction contemplated.

It is a function of the board, and not the managing director in the absence of expressly delegated powers, to issue shares of the company, to approve transfers of shares when the company's articles of association empower the board to refuse to register transfers, to call general meetings of shareholders or to call meetings of classes of shareholders for the purpose of consenting to a variation of their rights, and (if the articles empower the board to do so) to present a petition to the court in the company's name to wind the company up.

On the other hand, it is normally within the powers of a managing director to purchase goods or raw materials if the company's business is manufacturing, to receive and pay amounts due to and from the company, to engage and dismiss employees and to borrow and give security over the company's assets. This list of managing directors' normal implied powers is, of course, not exhaustive. The terms of a managing director's appointment rarely attempt a complete list of his powers. Instead, they usually restrict his implied powers by putting limitations on them – for example, by limiting the maximum amount which he may borrow on the company's behalf, or the maximum amount for which he may sign cheques without the concurrent signature of another director.

When a managing director's powers are by the terms of his appointment those which the board of directors delegates to him from time to time, and he has a service contract with the company to the same effect, the managing director cannot claim that there is a breach of his contract if the board resolves to diminish his powers. This is so even if his management of the company's affairs is subjected to the board's detailed control, or even though his remaining powers do not enable him to manage the company's affairs effectively (*Harold*

Holdsworth & Co. Ltd v. *Caddies* (1955). By this means the board may effectively eliminate a managing director without removing him, but of course he retains his nominal appointment and is entitled to his salary or other remuneration.

On the other hand, if the company's articles of association set out the grounds on which a managing director shall cease to hold office and the managing director has a service contract which repeats those grounds and provides that his appointment shall terminate if any of them becomes applicable, it will be a breach of contract on the part of the company entitling the managing director to damages if the shareholders resolve to alter the articles by adding to the grounds on which he will cease to hold office, and the company treats his appointment as having terminated on one of the new grounds (*Southern Foundries (1926) Ltd* v. *Shirlaw* (1940)). The distinction between eliminating a managing director by reducing his powers to a shadow and by terminating his appointment may seem unrealistic, apart from the question of his continued remuneration, pension rights etc., but it is nevertheless material in law.

DIRECTORS' SERVICE CONTRACTS

1.08 Service contracts are not mandatory

It has become increasingly common in recent years for public companies and for private companies whose shares are not held exclusively by their directors to enter into service agreements with their executive directors, whether managing directors, directors who are members of an executive committee with delegated powers to act on behalf of the board between board meetings, or directors who manage and carry responsibility for the various divisions or departments of the company's business. It is less usual, but not unknown, for service contracts also to be entered into with non-executive directors, who are often in a majority on the board and who participate in major policy decisions, but are not full-time directors and are not responsible individually for the management of particular sectors of the company's undertaking.

It is not essential that a service contract should be entered into with any director, and if there is no such contract, the director holds office on the terms set out in the company's articles of association as they stand for the time being, including alterations made in them subsequently to the director's appointment (*Shuttleworth* v. *Cox Brothers & Co. (Maidenhead) Ltd* (1927)). The articles do not normally set out in detail the rates of remuneration of directors and the functions they will individually fulfil in addition to taking collective decisions at board meetings. Consequently, if a director is appointed without a service contract, these matters have to be dealt with by supplementary resolutions passed by the board or by the shareholders in general meeting.

It is, for example, common for articles of association to provide that the directors shall be entitled to such remuneration as the shareholders determine by ordinary resolution. In that case a general meeting may fix the directors' remuneration in advance for one or several years or in arrear at the end of each financial year; it may allocate individual amounts to each director or a global sum which the directors then divide between themselves; and may determine directors' remuneration by any criterion, whether a salary, a commission on the company's turnover or a percentage of its profits.

1.09 Terms of service contracts

Service contracts are valuable in that they are usually entered into for longer periods than the term of office for which directors are appointed under the company's articles without a contract. They therefore provide security of employment for a career director and an assurance of continued service for the company. Moreover, service contracts provide in detail for matters which are not normally dealt with by the company's articles, such as incremental remuneration, pension rights, and participation by the director in a share option or profit-sharing scheme operated by the company. Service contracts also usually prescribe the sector of management for which the director will be individually responsible, if one is assigned to him.

Service contracts must be approved by the board of directors under articles which vest the general powers of the company in the board. A managing director can engage subordinate executive directors and enter into service contracts with them on the company's behalf only if power to do so has been delegated to him by the board under the provisions of the articles.

Service contracts are, of course, ineffective to the extent that their terms conflict with the express provisions of the company's articles at the time they are entered into, because the board has no power to override the articles. However, if under the articles the board of directors can negotiate service contracts on such terms as it thinks fit, and the articles give the board power to dismiss any director or to compel his resignation, the power of dismissal is subordinate to an express term of a service contract with a director that his appointment shall continue for a fixed period. In that case, if the board dismisses the director before the contractual period expires, he may recover damages from the company for breach of contract (*Shindler* v. *Northern Raincoat Co. Ltd* (1960)).

1.10 Approval by shareholders in general meeting

Service contracts with directors are negotiated by the board or by its chairman subject to the approval of the board, and need not be submitted to the shareholders in general meeting for their approval, even though they have an obvious interest in the personality, ability and functions of the director with whom the contract is made and the remuneration awarded to him. Only one feature of a service contract with a director is required to be submitted for shareholder approval, namely its duration.

Whether the service contract relates to the director's employment as a director or in any other capacity (e.g. as a divisional manager or an overseas representative) the duration of the contract must be approved by the shareholders in general meeting by ordinary resolution before the contract is entered into. But this is only if the director's employment will be for longer than 5 years and the contract does not empower the company to terminate it within that period for any reason whatsoever by giving notice to the director (Companies Act 1985, section 319(1) and (3)).

For 15 days before the general meeting at which the resolution approving the duration of the contract is passed, a draft of the contract must be made available for inspection by shareholders and also at the general meeting itself (section 319(5)). The shareholders can therefore examine all the terms of the proposed contract before approving its duration, and if they dislike any of its terms, such as the remuneration to be paid to the director, they may prevent the contract being made by defeating the resolution approving its duration.

If a service contract whose duration requires the shareholders' approval is entered into without its duration being approved by them, the company may terminate it at any time by giving the director reasonable notice (section 319(6)). On the other hand, the director is not expressly empowered to terminate the contract if it has not been approved by the shareholders, but since the term it contains as to its duration is ineffective, it would appear that it must be treated as terminable by either party giving reasonable notice to the other. In all other respects the contract is valid, even though its duration has not been approved by a general meeting.

THE FUNCTIONING OF MANAGEMENT

The traditional idea of the functioning of a board of directors, which still underlies the law on the subject, is that the board is a collective and representative body which makes decisions and enters into transactions on the company's behalf after deliberation at board meetings and, where necessary, the taking of a vote by which the opinion of the majority in number of the directors prevails. This idea is derived from the practice of public companies in the early part of the nineteenth century, and it provides a theoretical ideal to which it is assumed that all companies, large and small, public and private, must conform.

In reality no company's affairs are conducted in that way. Even in the case of public companies whose shares are held by a wide range of investors and whose directors are elected for fairly short terms by the shareholders in general meeting, only major decisions are made by resolution of the board of directors. Most of the decisions required for the daily conduct of the company's business are made by the managing director, by individual executive directors who are responsible for departments or divisions of the company's business, and by subordinate executives who are not directors. In most private companies board meetings are rare events, and management functions are split between the directors in a way which is accepted by all of them, often without any formal delegation of the board's powers at all.

1.11 Decisions of the board

Despite modern practice under which the legal powers of the board are in fact largely exercised by individual directors (whether managing or executive, but usually full-time), the law nominally requires the board of directors to exercise its powers formally. Decisions of the board are required by law to be expressed in the form of resolutions passed by a majority of votes. Articles of association usually assume that this will be the normal pattern, and therefore provide in some detail for the calling and holding of board meetings.

Under typical articles of association, board meetings can be called at any time by any director, and can consider proposals put forward by any director without the need for any advance notice. To ensure that decisions are not taken by only a small number of directors, the articles usually require a quorum of directors to be present at board meetings, though the number of directors who constitute a quorum is usually left to the board to fix itself. Decisions of the board are taken by a majority vote, each director being entitled to cast one vote, but the chairman of the board, who is elected by the board itself, is usually given a second or casting vote in the event of an equal number of votes being cast for and against a proposal.

The attendance, or more accurately, the representation of directors at board meetings is encouraged by a provision often found in modern articles of association by which a director may appoint another director or, with the approval of the board, a non-director to be his alternate with power to attend board meetings, speak and vote and do all other things which the director appointing him may do. An alternate director is simply a substitute for the director who appoints him, and his appointment can be revoked at any time by that director. In law, however, an alternate director is treated in the same way as a director appointed in the normal way, and the statutory and other rules governing directors apply equally to him.

1.12 Delegation

Articles of association nowadays usually recognise that most decisions made in the course of carrying on a company's business are made by individual directors or by their subordinates. Consequently, the articles enable the board to delegate any of its powers to any one or more directors, whether to the exclusion of the board or not. Articles also empower the board to exercise its powers through agents appointed to act in the name of the company.

Often delegations of the board's powers are not formally resolved upon, but simply result from the directors devising or accepting a division of functions between themselves. The court will readily imply that the board has unanimously agreed to such an arrangement from the fact that the directors have operated it, and unanimous consent is treated as the equivalent of a formal resolution.

In its desire to protect outsiders who deal with individual directors who appear to have been invested with delegated powers by the board, the court will recognise transactions entered into by such directors with the tolerance of the board, if the company's articles enable the board to delegate its powers and the outsider knows of the power of delegation and reasonably believes that it has been exercised in favour of the director with whom he deals (*Rama Corpn Ltd* v. *Proved Tin and General Investments Ltd* (1952); *Hely-Hutchinson* v. *Brayhead Ltd* (1968)). Indeed, in one case where it was not necessary to go so far, Diplock LJ ruled that if the articles of association confer power on the board of directors to manage the company's affairs (which articles always do either expressly or by providing that the board may exercise the generality of the company's powers), it is implied that the board may delegate its powers of management generally or any particular powers to any one or more directors (*Freeman and Lockyer* v. *Buckhurst Park Properties (Mangal) Ltd* (1964)). The articles of the company in that case contained an express power for the board to delegate its powers, and the other two members of the Court of Appeal were content to rely on the appearance which the board had created that there had in fact been a delegation of power to the director who negotiated the contract which was the subject of the case.

If Diplock LJ's ruling was correct, it would mean that an outsider could safely deal with a single director who purports to act on behalf of the company if the board tolerates his acting in that way, and it would not matter whether the articles enable the board to delegate its powers or not. Also if Diplock LJ's ruling was correct, every board of directors would have an inherent ability to delegate any of its powers to individual directors without the company's articles expressly saying so. In other words, the board itself would, if it wished, be able to abandon the collective or collegiate management of the company's affairs by the board which the law regards as the norm, and to substitute the management of sectors of the company's business by individual directors.

1.13 Formality and informality

It is true that for most acts of management, modern practice and the necessities of business decisions by individual directors acting in the sector of management which the board has assigned to them or allowed them to assume are treated as effective expressions of the company's will. It is only major decisions, such as the issue of shares or the raising of loan capital or the disposal of major assets of the company, which are in practice taken by the board of directors. Because of this, formal board meetings are normally held only at intervals of one, two or three months by directors of large public companies, and in many private companies it is common for only one formal board meeting to be held each year to approve and sign the annual accounts and the directors' annual report.

Heavy reliance is then put on the increasingly common provision in articles of association that the assent of every director to a proposal shall, if expressed in writing, be the equivalent of a formal board resolution. Even so, unanimous consent is in practice sought only when the decision is a major one, and often the formality of expressing it in writing is omitted.

The informality of management decisions is tolerated by the law because of the undesirability of transactions entered into by companies being treated as invalid when they have not been formally authorised by a resolution of the board of directors. Nevertheless, excessive informality does create difficulties in ascertaining the content of a decision or transaction and the identity of the directors who authorised or assented to it. Also there remains a large area of uncertainty about the kind of decisions which are sufficiently important to require formal board resolutions in the case of a particular company.

To some extent these difficulties are lessened by the wide use by boards of directors of their powers of delegation and the prevalence of the practice of appointing a managing director or directors. It is in smaller and medium-sized private companies that even these precautionary measures are often not taken, and the question whether the company has effectively and legally decided on acts of management or the conclusion of transactions with outsiders is then most difficult to solve.

OFFICE HOLDERS OR EMPLOYEES?

Are directors of companies the holders of offices under the constitution of the company, or merely employees of the company?

An office holder is in law someone who is appointed to fulfil a function which is continuing in character, and for which a succession of appointees will be appointed so long as the function remains to be fulfilled. The office is the personification of the function. An office is therefore contrasted with an employment, where the relationship between the employer and employee is contractual and the employment ends when the contract is terminated, even though the employer may for business reasons enter into a new contract of employment with someone else to do the same or similar work.

The practical distinction made by the law between offices and employments is that an office holder has a sufficient interest in his continued tenure of his office that he may obtain an injunction restraining anyone, whether the person who appointed him or another person, from excluding him from the exercise of the functions of the office. By contrast, an employee has only contractual rights against his employer, entitling him to claim damages from his employer if his contract of employment is broken or improperly terminated, and only in exceptional cases can an employee obtain an injunction against his employer to prevent him from terminating the employment or interfering with the employee in carrying it out.

1.14 Ideal categorisation

Logically, directors of companies should always be treated as holders of offices, namely, their directorships, because the office of director is created by the company's memorandum or articles of association. This office is intended to continue in existence as long as the company exists, and the company is required by law to have at least one director, or in the case of a public company, at least two (Companies Act 1985, section 282(1)). A director may, of course, have a service contract with the company on whose board he serves, or in the case of a director of a subsidiary, a service contract with its parent company. Such contracts are contracts of employment, and insofar as they create rights or obligations for the employing company or the director which do not merely reflect the rights or obligations created by the company's articles of association or by the general law, they are enforceable only as contractual rights and obligations between the employing company and the director. The remedies available to the parties are then confined to claims for payment of liquidated money sums (e.g. salary, percentages of profits, pensions) or damages for breach of contract. The rights and obligations conferred or imposed on directors by the company's constitution, its memorandum or articles of association, on the other hand, should ideally be regarded as incidental to the office of director. They should therefore be enforceable specifically or by means of injunctions directed against the company, the director or third persons who have interfered with the director's exercise of his functions.

1.15 Decisions of the courts

Curiously, the courts have not generally followed this distinction through. Except in one case, *Munster* v. *Cammell Co* (1882), the courts have refused to issue an injunction against a company to restrain it from excluding a director from office or from interfering with the exercise of his functions, in situations where the company was not justified in doing so.

The reasons for the courts' refusal to intervene have been various. The first reason given was that if the court issued an injunction against the company, it would be enforcing specifically the employment of the director by the company, which would be contrary to the rule that contracts of employment are not normally specifically enforceable (*Harben* v. *Phillips* (1883); *Bainbridge* v. *Smith* (1889)).

This deduction, of course, disregards the distinction between a director's contractual rights under any service contract he has with the company and his rights resulting from the company's memorandum or articles of association as the holder of an office under the company, such as his right to attend and take part in board meetings. The treatment of such rights as contractual is perhaps the result of the court holding in other cases that an implied contract arises between the company and a director when he accepts his appointment. Unless he has an express service contract dealing with the matter in dispute (e.g. entitlement to remuneration, duration of appointment), the terms implied in the implied contract to employ the director will be derived from the provisions of the company's memorandum or articles of association in respect of directors (*Re New British Iron Co. ex.p Beckwith* (1898); *Read* v. *Astoria Garage (Streatham) Ltd* (1952)). The implication of a contract on the same terms as the memorandum or articles in such a situation is, however, merely a device to enable the director or the company to sue for a debt or for damages when the other side has failed to honour the terms on which the director was appointed. It does not justify the conclusion that the rights and obligations attached to directorships by the company's constitution cannot be enforced specifically or by injunction.

Enforcement of membership rights

The second reason given by the courts for not enforcing the incidents of a directorship set out in the company's memorandum or articles of association is that rights and obligations set out therein are only enforceable by or against the company insofar as they relate to membership of the company or the holding of shares in it. The rights and obligations attached to a directorship by the memorandum or articles do not fall under this head (*Browne* v. *La Trinidad* (1887)). This reasoning is tenable when the plaintiff sues the company as a member or shareholder, that is, when he is not the director whose rights under the articles he seeks to enforce. It is true that the contractual rights and obligations of members created by section 14 of the Companies Act 1985, to have the provisions of the memorandum and articles adhered to, extend only to rights and obligations relating to their membership or shareholdings. But the reasoning wholly overlooks the fact that when a director seeks to enforce his rights to hold office for the period for which he was appointed under the articles or to exercise the functions which the articles provide a director shall exercise, he does not sue as a member or shareholder, but to assert the rights which are attached to his office as a director of the company.

Non-interference with shareholders' wishes

The final reason given by the court for not protecting a director's right to hold office in accordance with the company's memorandum or articles by issuing an injunction against the company is that the court will not compel the shareholders of the company to accept the services of a director whom they do not want. In two cases, the court declined even to prevent the plaintiff director's fellow directors from excluding him from board meetings unless an affirmative resolution had been passed by a general meeting of shareholders showing that they wanted the plaintiff director to continue to hold office (*Harben* v. *Phillips*; *Bainbridge* v. *Smith* (see above)).

This reasoning accords with the general principle that the court will not interfere with the conduct of a company's affairs when the matter alleged to be irregular can be rectified by a general meeting passing an ordinary resolution. Any director may be removed from office by an ordinary resolution which is properly passed. Nevertheless, the reasoning disregards the other principle established more recently, that directors are not merely agents or representatives of the shareholders, collectively authorised by them to manage the company's affairs subject to the shareholders' direction and control. Directors are in law an independent organ of the company, exercising their powers and functions only subject to such control by the shareholders in general meeting as is prescribed in particular circumstances by the Companies Act 1985, and the company's constitution (*Automatic Self-Cleansing Filter Syndicate Co. Ltd* v. *Cunninghame* (1906); *Gramophone and Typewriter Ltd* v. *Stanley* (1908); *Scott* v. *Scott* (1943)).

This being so, not only the functions of the board of directors, but also its membership must be free from interference by the shareholders in general meeting, except so far as the Companies Act 1985, or the company's constitution otherwise provide. Consequently, individual directors must be able to assert against the company, and against third persons who interfere with the exercise of their functions, the rights and powers which are conferred on them by the company's memorandum and articles of association.

The enforcement of the right of properly appointed directors to function as such and to continue to hold office in accordance with the company's constitution is at present subject to much uncertainty. This will only be cleared away when the courts decide explicitly whether directors are mere employees of the company (and they are clearly more than that), or are primarily holders of offices in the company, which are protected by legal remedies enforceable against the whole world.

Chapter 2

De Facto Directors, Shadow Directors and Group Directors

In addition to directors properly so called, there are certain categories of persons who in law are treated as directors for certain, but not all purposes, mainly so as to impose liabilities on them or the company.

2.01 *De facto* directors

It can happen that a company's affairs are currently being managed by persons who have no legal title to act as its directors. This may be because they have not been appointed in the way prescribed by the Companies Act 1985, in the case of the company's first directors, or in the way laid down by the company's articles in the case of other directors. This situation rarely comes about because outsiders have forcibly usurped the functions of the directors of the company who have been lawfully appointed. More commonly, it happens because the *de facto* directors who are in control of the company's affairs have assumed control on the company's formation without directors being properly appointed at all, or because although steps have been taken to appoint the *de facto* directors lawfully as directors, those steps are insufficient or defective and no proper appointment has been made.

2.02 Status of *de facto* directors

De facto directors are, of course, not really directors at all, and so they cannot claim remuneration as directors, although the court can order the company to pay them the value of the services they have actually rendered (*Craven-Ellis* v. *Canons Ltd* (1936)). Their position is extremely tenuous, however, since they have no right to continue to manage the company's affairs. If they dispose of its assets, they act as wrongdoers, and so unless the shareholders in general meeting resolve to ratify the disposals they have made, they are liable to compensate the company for the value of the assets. Similarly, if *de facto* directors cause the company loss by mismanaging its affairs, they are liable to it for the loss it suffers in the same way as properly appointed directors. It would also appear the during the period they are in control of the company's affairs, *de facto* directors owe it exactly the same duties as directors who have a good legal title to act (*Morris* v. *Kanssen* (1946)).

The one factor which enables *de facto* directors to continue exercising the functions of directors is that only the company can bring legal proceedings against them for an injunction to restrain them from doing so. If an individual shareholder or group of shareholders brings an action in the company's name to restrain them from acting, the action will not be allowed to continue unless it is supported by sufficient shareholders to procure an ordinary resolution that the action shall proceed (*Danish Mercantile Co. Ltd* v. *Beaumont* (1951)). Moreover, individual shareholders cannot bring actions in their own names or by suing on behalf of themselves and the other shareholders of the company, to restrain *de facto* directors from continuing to act. This appears to be so whether the directors were originally lawfully appointed and the period for which they were appointed has expired, or because they were never lawfully appointed at all (*Mozley* v. *Alston* (1847); *Lord* v. *Copper Miners Co.* (1848)).

De facto directors are therefore in the curious position that they can only be compelled to relinquish the management of the company's affairs if the company itself acts against them. While they continue to act they are under the same obligations to the company as if they had been properly appointed as directors. When they are eventually brought to account they are additionally absolutely liable for the value of assets of the company which they have disposed of. Nevertheless, the court would undoubtedly not permit the company both to recover that value from them and to compel them to account for the proceeds of the disposal which they have received on the company's behalf.

2.03 Transactions entered into by *de facto* directors

Although *de facto* directors have no legal status as far as the company is concerned, they can bind the company by transactions which they enter into with outsiders who believe them to have been properly appointed to be directors from the fact that they are in control of the company's affairs. The courts have devised this rule to protect outsiders who act in good faith. The underlying reason for it is that outsiders have no means of ascertaining whether the persons who appear to be the company's directors have been properly appointed or not. The rule for the protection of outsiders applies whether the *de facto* directors have no title to office whatsoever and have simply wrongfully assumed the management of the company, or whether their appointment as directors was merely defective. This could be, for example, because they were appointed at a board meeting or a general meeting of shareholders which was not properly convened, or which was not attended by the necessary number of members to constitute a quorum.

This latter situation, where the *de facto* directors were defectively appointed, is also covered by a provision of the Companies Act 1985, which validates the acts of directors 'notwithstanding any defect that may afterwards be discovered in [their] appointment or qualification' (section 285). Both the rule devised by the courts and the statutory rule only validate transactions for the benefit of third persons who act in good faith, however. The rules in no way protect the *de facto* directors themselves from liability to the company.

Examples of the protection given by the court to outsiders who deal with *de facto* directors in ignorance that their title to office is non-existent or defective are manifold. Where the persons who promoted the company assumed the functions of directors without being appointed at all, and as such made payments from the company's bank account, the court held the bank entitled to debit the account accordingly because it believed that the directors had been properly appointed (*Mahony* v. *East Holyford Mining Co.* (1875)). Where the *de facto* directors borrowed money on the company's behalf on the security of a general mortgage or charge over the whole of the company's assets, the lender, who acted in good faith, was held entitled to treat the mortgage or charge as valid and to enforce it (*Duck* v. *Tower Galvanising Co.* (1901)).

The same legal protection is given to a person who deals with directors who have ceased to hold office but who remain in control of the company's affairs. In a case where the plaintiff was appointed to be an additional director by the board of directors under a power given to the board by the articles, but unknown to the plaintiff, who claimed that his own appointment as a director was binding on the company, the existing directors had all been disqualified from holding office before the appointment was made by their failure to obtain the minimum number of shares in the company which the articles required them to hold, the newly appointed director was held entitled to claim the value of his services from the company (*Craven-Ellis* v. *Canons Ltd* (1936)).

Protection cannot be claimed by directors or persons who act as though they had been validly appointed as directors, however, when the relevant transaction is entered into with themselves and they act on the company's behalf in connection with the transaction. Consequently, when a *de facto* director participated in an allotment of shares to himself by a board of directors, all of whom except one had no legal title to be directors, the *de facto* director was held disentitled to claim that the allotment was valid (*Morris* v. *Kanssen* (1946)). The reason for this was that by acting on the company's behalf in participating in the allotment of the shares, the allottee assumed an obligation to the company to ensure that the allotment was made by persons who had been properly appointed as directors. Consequently he could not, claiming as an allottee, assert a right to overlook the invalidity of the appointments of himself and his fellow *de facto* directors who had made the allotment.

SHADOW DIRECTORS

2.04 Shadow directors: definition

Shadow directors are not real directors at all, and they have no legal powers to act on a company's behalf or to participate in board meetings. A shadow director is purely a statutory concept under the Companies Act 1985. The category of shadow director was created simply so that the Act could extend certain of the obligations and restrictions which it imposes on real directors to persons who exercise the same kind of influence over the board as dominant directors may do.

A shadow director is defined as 'a person in accordance with whose directions or instructions the directors [that is, the real directors] of the company are accustomed to act' (section 741(2)). The question whether a person has such a controlling influence over the board is a question of fact, not entitlement, and so a person is a shadow director if the board habitually conforms to his instructions. He is a shadow director even though there is no contract or other legal relationship between himself and the real directors which requires or compels them to conform to his instructions, and even if the instructions take the form of advice or suggestions which are habitually followed.

On the other hand, a person is not a shadow director merely because he gives professional advice to the company or its directors and they accept that advice and act on it (section 741(2)). Nor is one company the shadow director of another at whose general meetings it can cast a majority of the votes merely because the directors of the other company are accustomed to act in accordance with the first company's directions and instructions (section 741(3)). In this latter situation the first company is the holding or parent company of the other, which is its subsidiary, and by its control over the composition of the subsidiary's board of directors, the parent company is able to determine the subsidiary's business policy. Even if this power is exercised, however, the parent company is not treated as a shadow director of the subsidiary. Nevertheless, there is no reason why the directors of the parent company should not be treated as shadow directors of the subsidiary if the subsidiary's board habitually acts on instructions which they give it on the parent company's behalf.

2.05 Statutory provisions applicable to shadow directors

It is not all of the rules applicable to directors in the Companies Acts 1985 which apply also to shadow directors. The principal rules which do apply to shadow directors are those which (a) oblige directors to notify their personal interest in contracts and transactions with the company to its board of directors; (b) require the approval of the shareholders in general meeting to long-term contracts for the employment of directors by the company, and to contracts for the acquisition by directors from the company of assets of a substantial value and the disposal by them of such assets to the company; and (c) impose restrictions on a company making loans or giving financial assistance to directors and persons connected with them (sections 317, 318, 320 and 330 to 342). Outside the context of the Companies Act 1985, the concept of shadow director has no part to play, and so the equitable fiduciary duties, which are imposed on directors and which are dealt with in Chapter 3, do not extend to shadow directors.

2.06 Directors of groups of companies

A group of companies comprises a parent or holding company at its head and one or more subsidiary companies, including sub-subsidiaries which are themselves subsidiaries of the parent company's subsidiaries.

The legal relationship of parent company and subsidiary is defined by reference to the fraction of the subsidiary's share capital held by the parent company, or the power of the parent company to appoint or remove directors of the subsidiary. This is because the primary purpose of the definition is to enable a company to discover when it is subject to the obligation imposed on parent companies to prepare annual group accounts dealing with the assets, liabilities, profits and losses of all the companies in the group collectively as though they were a single company.

Because the definitions of parent company and subsidiary are formal and primarily accounting definitions, the degree of influence which a parent company in fact exercises over a potential subsidiary and the degree of integration of the potential subsidiary's undertaking or management with that of the parent company are immaterial. The legal relationship of parent company and subsidiary may exist between two companies if the parent company is an industrial holding company which has a majority shareholding in a variety of other companies, but the boards of directors of those companies manage their undertakings independently. The relationship may also exist if the subsidiary is wholly-owned by the parent company and it manages the subsidiary's affairs through directors of the subsidiary who are appointed by the parent company under service contracts which oblige them to conform to the parent company's directions and instructions. The degree of integration between a parent company's undertaking and the undertakings of its subsidiaries and the extent to which the parent company determines the business policy and activities of its subsidiaries are factors which the law leaves wholly out of account in defining the parent company/subsidiary relationship.

2.07 Definition of a parent or holding company

One company is the parent company of another if it holds (by itself or through nominees or other subsidiaries) more than one-half of the subsidiary's issued equity share capital (that is, its issued capital, except preference shares which carry no right to share in the surplus profits of the subsidiary after the fixed preference dividend has been paid, and no right to share in surplus assets of the subsidiary after the repayment of the whole of its paid-up share capital) (Companies Act 1985, section 736(1) and section 744). Alternatively, a company is a subsidiary if the parent company has power by virtue of shares in the subsidiary held by the parent company and its nominees and its other subsidiaries, or by virtue of the subsidiary's articles of association or any contract, to appoint or remove a majority of the subsidiary's directors (section 736(1) to (3)). Additionally, a company is a subsidiary of a parent company if it is a subsidiary of a third company which is the parent company's subsidiary (section 736(1)). Consequently, sub-subsidiaries, sub-sub-subsidiaries etc. are all treated as subsidiaries of the parent company.

In determining whether a company is a subsidiary, the only shareholdings in it and the only powers to appoint or remove its directors which are left out of account are those which are held or are exercisable by the parent company or its nominees or other subsidiaries in a representative capacity on behalf of third persons outside the group, or as security for loans made by them (section 736(4)).

2.08 Significance of the relationship

The Companies Act 1985 often uses the concept of the parent company or subsidiary in connection with its provisions dealing with matters other than group accounts, particularly in connection with the prohibitions and restrictions which it imposes on directors. For example, the same restrictions are imposed on directors borrowing from the subsidiaries of the company of which they are directors as are imposed on them borrowing from the company itself (Companies Act 1985, sections 330 to 342).

On the other hand, the Act does not treat directors of a parent company as a separate category from directors of companies which have no subsidiaries, and it does not impose special duties, prohibitions or restrictions on directors of parent companies which are not imposed on other directors (apart from the duty to prepare annual group accounts and an annual report on the affairs of the group). The special relationship between the directors of a parent company or of a subsidiary with the other companies in the group is therefore left, by the Companies Act 1985, to be worked out by the courts, and the principles which emerge are therefore wholly judge-made.

Up to the present the courts have done little to establish special rules for directors of parent companies and subsidiaries, and have confined the rights and duties of directors to those which they have as regards the company of which they are directors. Consequently, it has been held by the House of Lords that a director of a subsidiary who is employed under a service contract with its parent company, is under no obligation to disclose breaches of duty by him as a director of the subsidiary when he agrees to the premature termination of his service contract with the parent company in return for compensation (*Bell* v. *Lever Brothers Ltd* (1932)). Similarly, the Court of Appeal has ruled that the directors of a subsidiary do not act properly if they cause the subsidiary to guarantee its parent company's debts, or if they give a security for such debts over the subsidiary's assets, in circumstances where only the parent company, and not the subsidiary, can benefit by their doing so (*Charterbridge Corpn. Ltd* v. *Lloyds Bank Ltd* (1970); *Rolled Steel Products (Holdings) Ltd* v. *British Steel Corporation* (1985)).

Nevertheless, the content of a director's obligations toward the company of which he is a director may be affected by the fact that it is a member of a group of companies. The interests of the subsidiary must be to some degree interdependent with those of the group. Furthermore, the rapid expansion in recent years of the common law liability for negligence imposed by the courts on persons whose lack of skill or carelessness results in loss to third persons with whom they have no contractual relationship, may eventually result in the courts holding that directors of parent companies or subsidiaries are liable to other companies in the same group for loss caused by their defaults. In the following chapters, therefore, the extensions or modifications of directors' responsibilities which may or must be made when they are directors of group companies will be taken into account.

Chapter 3

Directors' Basic Fiduciary Duties

Directors are subjected by the rules of common law and equity to a number of duties to the company of which they are directors. These duties are general in character, and are supplemented by the more detailed statutory duties, restrictions and prohibitions which are imposed on directors by the Companies Act 1985 and other legislation. However, these statutory provisions, some of which will be examined in Chapter 7, are not exhaustive. They presuppose the existence of the more general non-statutory duties with which this chapter and Chapters 4 and 5 are concerned.

None of the statutory duties of directors is narrower in terms than their common law and equitable obligations to act or abstain from acting in a certain way in a given situation. Because of this, a company may have a choice of remedies against a director on the facts of a particular case, and it may charge him on the same facts with breaches of both his statutory and his non-statutory duties. However, the company cannot cumulate the damages or compensation or the amount of improper profits which it may recover from the director by suing him for breaches of both kinds of duties. Its right of recovery is limited to the loss it has suffered or the profit the director has improperly made, however many duties, whether statutory or non-statutory, he may have breached.

3.01 Nature of fiduciary duties

The so-called fiduciary duties imposed on directors are the body of duties invented and elaborated by the Court of Chancery in the eighteenth and nineteenth centuries to ensure that persons who hold assets or exercise functions in a representative capacity for the benefit of other people act in good faith and conscientiously protect the interests of those they represent.

The earliest cases decided in Chancery were in respect of trustees, who held property (whether land or investments) in trust for beneficiaries under a trust created by the owner of the property during his lifetime or by his will. The trust was not recognised by the common law, which treated the trustees as the owners of the trust property, but equity treated the beneficiaries as the real owners of the property, and the trustees were compelled to use their legal ownership exclusively for the benefit of the beneficiaries. Consequently, if they employed the trust property for purposes not authorised by the trust (e.g. if they invested trust funds in speculative investments or in carrying on a business when the terms of the trust did not expressly permit them to do so), the rules of equity enforced by the Chancery Court compelled them to make good the assets so applied out of their own pockets. If their breach of trust resulted in profits or gains to themselves, equity compelled them to account to the beneficiaries.

Additionally, equity compelled the trustees to account for personal gains they obtained as a result of opportunities or advantages which came their way as trustees (e.g. commission which a stockbroker who was a trustee charged in connection with the sale or purchase of investments for the trust, the renewal by the trustee for his own benefit of a lease of land which was comprised in the trust), and such gains had to be rendered up to the beneficiaries. Later, from the late eighteenth or early nineteenth century, trustees were compelled in equity to exercise proper care in exercising their functions (e.g in selecting investments for the trust funds), and if they failed to do so, the Chancery Court compelled them to compensate the trust funds for any loss caused by their lack of care. The compensation, when recovered, was held for the benefit of the beneficiaries in the same way as the original trust fund. The duty of care was not a high one, however, and trustees were held liable for loss only if they failed to exercise the standard of care they would be expected to show in dealing with their own private affairs.

3.02 Extension of fiduciary duties to company directors

During the early nineteenth century the Chancery Court extended the fiduciary duties it had imposed on trustees to other persons who acted in a representative capacity, such as agents, company promoters and directors of companies. The extension was by analogy, and the court often referred to these other persons as 'trustees' in the context of the situation with which the court was dealing. This did not mean that other persons who acted as representatives really were trustees, but simply that fiduciary duties similar, or in some cases, identical to those imposed on trustees were imposed on them in equity. The description of directors as trustees was metaphorical.

Sir George Jessel MR observed in this connection in *Re Forest of Dean Coal Mining Co.* (1878):

'Directors have sometimes been called trustees, or commercial trustees, sometimes they have been called managing partners; it does not much matter what you call them as long as you understand what their true position is, which is really that they are commercial men managing a trading concern for the benefit of themselves and of all the other shareholders... they are bound to use fair and reasonable diligence in the management of their company's affairs, and to act honestly.'

Four years later Bowen LJ, in *Imperial Hydropathic Hotel Company v. Hampson* (1882), emphasised the element of analogy when he remarked:

'... when persons who are directors of a company are from time to time spoken of by judges as agents, trustees or managing partners of the company, it is essential to recollect that such expressions are not used as exhaustive of the powers or responsibilities of those persons, but only as indicating useful points of view from which they may for the moment and for the particular purpose be considered – points of view at which they seem for the moment to be either cutting the circle or falling within the category of the suggested kind. It is not meant that they belong to the category, but that it is useful for the purpose of the moment to observe that they fall *pro tanto* within the principles which govern that particular class.'

These are remarks which one would expect to be made by judges who are in the course of working out the precise limits of directors' fiduciary duties to their companies. The rules or principles already established for trustees were largely applied also to directors, but the court reserved the right to apply the rules somewhat differently to the facts of a particular case or to modify the rules in their application to directors.

An example of this is provided by the case of *Re Forest of Dean Coal Mining Co.* mentioned above. There, directors were charged in the liquidation of the company with failing to recover for the company £10,000 which had been improperly paid to its promoters. Jessel MR (at p. 452 of the report) commented:

'But where without fraud and without dishonesty they have omitted to get in a debt due to the company by not suing within time, or because the man was solvent at one moment and became insolvent at another, I am of opinion that it by no means follows as a matter of course, as it might in the case of ordinary trustees of trust funds or of a trust debt, that they are to be made liable. Traders have a discretion as to whether they shall sue their customers, a discretion which is not vested in trustees of a debt under a settlement.'

In more recent cases the court has been less inclined to draw analogies between the duties of trustees and those of directors. This is because there is now a substantial body of case law on directors' fiduciary duties to which the court can refer for guidance, and it is now rarely necessary to refer to judicial rulings on trustees' duties. Nevertheless, the basic, unifying feature of the fiduciary duties of all persons acting in a representative capacity for the benefit of others, that the interests of those others must be the paramount, and often, the only consideration, is still present, and this makes the fiduciary duties of representatives a distinctive and self-contained part of the law.

3.03 Common law duties of directors

The fact that directors owe fiduciary or equitable duties to their companies does not prevent them from also owing duties at common law. The common law duties of directors have not been emphasised strongly in judicial decisions, for the simple reason that most actions against directors for breaches of duty were brought in the Chancery Court in the period up to 1875 and in the Chancery Division of the High Court since then. In many cases this was inevitable, because the question of the directors' liability arose in the winding up of the company or in the course of a receivership initiated by the debenture holders of the company, and both liquidations and receiverships were within the sole jurisdiction of the Chancery Court, and are now assigned to the Chancery Division of the High Court.

Nevertheless, the question remains whether there are any duties owed by directors to their company at common law which have not been absorbed into and completely covered by their equitable duties. The answer to this question is a clear affirmative. In the first place, directors who have service contracts are liable in damages at common if they breach the express or implied terms of those contracts. The measure of damages recoverable by the company for a breach is the same as for any other breach of contract, namely, full compensation for the loss suffered by the company which is a normal, forseeable consequence of the breach. Secondly, it would appear that directors, like agents, owe the company a duty to exercise proper skill and care in fulfilling their contractual functions, and if they have no contract with the company, a non-contractual duty to exercise the standard of care of which they are personally capable or which they hold themselves out as capable of exercising.

Such common law duties of skill and care are imposed on agents, who are also fiduciaries (*Harmer* v. *Cornelius* (1858) 5 CB (NS) 236; *Beal* v. *South Devon Rly Co.* (1864) per Crompton J; *Bagot* v. *Stevens, Scanlon & Co. Ltd* (1966)).

There are, in fact, no decided cases where liability for negligence has been imposed at common law on directors. In all the cases where an action for negligence has been brought against directors in the Chancery Court or the Chancery Division of the High Court, the duty of care relied upon has been the equitable duty of a director to carry out his functions conscientiously and to protect the assets of the company against loss. But there is no logical reason why a director, like an agent, should not be subject to a parallel common law duty of care, whether contractual or non-contractual. As will be shown below, this may offer a means of strengthening the equitable duty of care already imposed on directors, which is little more than an adjunct to their duty to act honestly and in good faith. In this respect, the common law duty to exercise skill and care may call for a higher standard of performance from directors than do the rules of equity.

THE DUTY NOT TO EXCEED DIRECTORS' POWERS

3.04 The delimitation of directors' powers

The first fiduciary duty imposed on directors is not to exceed the powers and authority lawfully conferred on them. If they do, they will be liable to compensate the company for any loss which it suffers in consequence. The powers and authority of directors are circumscribed in four ways.

In the first place, directors must not enter into transactions or dispose of the company's assets in a manner which is prohibited by the Companies Act 1985, or by the general law, or in a manner which is permitted by law only if certain conditions are fulfilled and those conditions have not been fulfilled. For example, if directors apply the company's funds in giving financial assistance to enable a person to acquire shares in the company or its parent company, they contravene the prohibition in the Companies Act 1985, section 151(1), unless the financial assistance falls into one of the exceptional categories in sections 153 or 155, and so is permissible. Except in those cases, the directors are liable to make reparation to the company for funds belonging to it which they have improperly expended in giving such financial assistance (*Selangor United Rubber Estates Ltd.* v. *Cradock (No 3)* (1968); *Wallersteiner* v. *Moir* (1974)).

Secondly, directors must not enter into transactions which are unconnected with the objects of the company set out in its memorandum of association (that is the business which the company was incorporated to carry on). They must not enter into transactions which are not within the powers expressly conferred on the company by its memorandum for the purpose of achieving its objectives, or within the powers implied by law for the company to do things which are incidental to or consequential on achieving its objectives. If directors do enter into such transactions which the company has no power to enter into, they are liable to compensate it for any loss it suffers and, in particular, to restore the amount or value of any of its assets which they have disposed of in connection with the transaction (*Evans* v. *Coventry* (1857); *Land Credit Co. of Ireland* v. *Lord Fermoy* (1869)).

Thirdly, even if a transaction or disposal of the company's assets is within the objects and powers of the company, the directors cannot lawfully carry it out if it is beyond the powers delegated to them by the memorandum or articles of association of the company, or if the memorandum or articles impose a prohibition or restrictions on the directors' entering into the transaction or carrying out the disposal which they then disregard. Consequently, if the articles of association reserve certain powers of the company to the shareholders in general meeting, or require the consent of a general meeting to the exercise of certain powers given to the directors, the directors are liable to compensate the company if they cause it loss by exercising the powers without the approval of a general meeting. Likewise, if directors are authorised to exercise powers conferred on them by the articles only if certain conditions are fulfilled, they are liable to compensate the company if they cause it loss by not ensuring that the conditions are fulfilled. In *Re Oxford Benefit Building and Investment Society* (1886), for example, directors were held liable to make restitution to the company of dividends paid by them out of 'estimated' profits of the company when its articles permitted distributions only out of realised profits. This was so even though the general law at the time permitted the distribution of unrealised profits as dividend if the articles did not otherwise provide.

Finally, an individual director who acts under powers delegated to him by the board of directors or by a general meeting under a provision in the company's memorandum or articles, is guilty of a breach of duty and is liable to compensate the company for any consequential loss if he exceeds the powers delegated to him. An example of this situation is where a managing director who has been appointed by the board under a power conferred on it by the articles, enters into transactions outside the authority delegated to him by the board, or where he exercises powers delegated to him without the board's explicit consent when its consent is required by the terms of his appointment.

3.05 Are directors liable absolutely for exceeding their powers?

In certain early cases, directors who had exceeded their powers were held by the court not to be liable to compensate the company or to make restitution for its assets disposed of by them, if they acted honestly and in good faith, believing that they were acting within their powers and for the benefit of the company (*Pickering* v. *Stevenson* (1872); *London Financial Association* v. *Kelk* (1884); *Studdert* v. *Grosvenor* (1886)). In these cases the directors were required only to prove that they acted in good faith in order to establish a defence, and the court did not require them to prove also that they acted with due care, but nevertheless made a reasonable error as to the extent of their powers.

In two later cases, which must be considered as overruling the earlier ones, however, the Court of Appeal held that the liability of a director to compensate his company for losses caused by exceeding his powers was absolute, and it was no defence for him to show that he acted in good faith under an honest mistake, or that he was not negligent in misconceiving the limits of his powers (*Cullerne* v. *London Suburban General Permanent Building Society* (1890); *Re Sharpe* (1892)). In so concluding, the Court of Appeal was following two earlier decisions of the Court of Chancery to the same effect (*Land Credit Co. of Ireland* v. *Lord Fermoy* (1869); *Joint Stock Discount Co.* v. *Brown* (1869)). Consequently, the three contrary decisions mentioned in the preceding paragraph were departures from a line of authority which the Court of Appeal re-established in *Cullerne's Case*. Those three decisions therefore no longer represent the law.

Liability only for negligence

Nevertheless, there is still one situation where good faith and lack of negligence on the part of a director may still be pleaded by him as a defence. This is where directors have exceeded their lawful powers by proposing or paying a dividend to shareholders when the company has not earned sufficient profits to justify the dividend.

It has been held in three cases, including one decided by the House of Lords, that if after making reasonable enquiry as to the sufficiency of the company's profits available for distribution, directors honestly but incorrectly conclude that the profits available equal or exceed the dividend proposed, they are not liable to make restitution if the dividend is in fact paid out of the company's capital (*Re Kingston Cotton Mills Co. (No 2)* (1896); *Dovey* v. *Cory* (1901); *Lucas* v. *Fitzgerald* (1903)).

Moreover, directors are not liable if in reaching their conclusion that the company's profits are sufficient to cover the dividend, the directors rely on annual accounts of the company audited by an accountant whose competence they have no reason to suspect. On the other hand, if the error made by the directors is one of law (for example, if they misconstrue the provisions of the company's articles defining the part of its profits which may be used to pay dividends), the directors are absolutely liable to restore to the company the dividend which is improperly paid (*Re Claridge's Patent Asphalte Co. Ltd* (1921)). They are also liable if they propose or make a distribution without having any accounts at all prepared showing the amount of the company's distributable profits, or if the accounts on which they rely are clearly inadequate and fail to show how the amount of the company's profits has been calculated (*Re County Marine Insurance Co., Rances's Case* (1870); *Leeds Estate Building and Investment Co.* v. *Shepherd* (1887)).

There has been no attempt in recent years to extend to other situations the exoneration of directors who mistakenly but without negligence distribute a dividend in excess of the company's profits. The reason for this may be that in most other such situations, the directors will have made an error of law in construing the document which defines their powers or interpreting the legislation which imposes restrictions or prohibitions on them. The defence that the directors made an honest mistake without negligence would then not be available in any case. However, it is probable, in the light of the strict decisions at the end of the last century, that directors' liability for exceeding their powers otherwise than by making or proposing an improper distribution of dividends, is truly an absolute one, and that a director must at his peril ensure that he acts only within the limits of his powers and must interpret them correctly if he is to avoid liability.

THE DUTY NOT TO MAKE A PERSONAL PROFIT

3.06 Conflicts of interest

The courts have frequently ruled that one of a director's fiduciary duties is to abstain from putting himself in a position where his duties to his company conflict, or may conflict, with personal interests which he has in the transaction in question. One of the earliest expressions of this principle was given by Lord Cranworth in the leading House of Lords case, *Aberdeen Rly Co.* v. *Blaikie Brothers* (1854), where he said (at p. 471 of the report):

> '... it is a rule of universal application that no one having [fiduciary] duties to be discharged shall be allowed to enter into engagements in which he has, or can have, a personal interest conflicting, or which possibly may conflict, with the interest of those he is bound to protect.'

Similarly, in *Imperial Mercantile Credit Association* v. *Coleman* (1871), Malins VC expressed the rule in a manner which was later approved by the House of Lords. Malins VC said (at p. 563 of the report):

> 'It is of the highest importance that it should be distinctly understood that it is the duty of directors of companies to use their best exertions for the benefit of those whose interests are committed to their charge, and that they are bound to disregard their own private interests whenever a regard to them conflicts with the proper discharge of such a duty.'

Despite the clear assertion in these and other judicial pronouncements that a director is guilty of a breach of duty if he acts on the company's behalf in connection with a matter in which he has a personal interest, it is doubtful whether the rule really goes this far. An indication of the practical limits of the rule is given in the judgment of Lord Upjohn in *Boardman* v. *Phipps* (1967), where he said (at p. 123 of the report):

> 'The relevant role for the decision of this case is the fundamental rule of equity that a person in a fiduciary capacity must not make a

profit out of his trust, which is part of the wider rule that a trustee must not place himself in a position where his duty and his interest may conflict.'

This was supported by the ruling of Lord Herschell in *Bray* v. *Ford* (1896), (at p. 51 of the report) in almost identical words:

'... a person in a fiduciary position... is not... entitled to make a profit; he is not allowed to put himself in a position where his interest and duty conflict.'

These last two passages make it clear that the breach of duty by the fiduciary lies, not in allowing a conflict of interest to arise, because this is something over which he often has no control, but in preferring his personal interests to those of the persons for whom he is a fiduciary. The appropriate remedies in equity, therefore, are an injunction to restrain the fiduciary from pursuing his personal interests instead of not fulfilling his obligations to the persons he represents, an order that he shall account to those persons for any profit he has in fact obtained, and the recovery of compensation for any loss which those persons suffer by the fiduciary preferring his personal interests. If the transaction is one which has not been completed or which can be reversed, the beneficiaries of the fiduciary obligation may also obtain an order rescinding the transaction and ordering the restoration of the parties to their original position.

The most important and most frequently used of these remedies are an injunction, an order for an account and payment over of profits made by the fiduciary, and an order rescinding the transaction in which he has an interest. The remedy of rescission is tied up with the question of the validity of contracts in which a fiduciary has a personal interest when the persons he represents are the other parties, or are interested in the other parties (as a company is in its subsidiary). Rescission will therefore be considered in Chapter 4 in connection with contracts in which directors are interested.

3.07 Directors' personal interest and profits

Many of the decided cases where directors had personal interests in transactions with their companies have involved situations where they blatantly used their positions to make personal gains for which they were compelled to account.

Instances of these comparatively simple situations are where a director placed an order on the company's behalf for the supply of goods or services with a supplier who allowed the director a commission because he was a member of an association to which the supplier also belonged. The fact that the company, which was not a member of the association, would not have qualified for the commission did not prevent it from recovering the commission from the director after he had received it (*Boston Deep Sea Fishing Co.* v. *Ansell* (1888)). Similarly, in another case, a director who was a stockbroker was engaged by a railway company to find subscribers for its debentures in return for a commission of 5 per cent of the issue price of every debenture placed. The director negotiated the subscription of the debentures by the company of which he was a director in return for a commission of 1½ per cent of the issue price, which he paid out of the 5 per cent commission allowed to himself. The House of Lords held that the director was accountable to the company for the balance of 3½ per cent commission which he retained on the debentures subscribed by the company (*Imperial Mercantile Credit Association* v. *Coleman* (1873)).

Share issues

Issues of shares by a company can give rise to conflicts of interests for directors. Directors are free to subscribe for or purchase shares in the company of which they are directors, but when their company issues shares, directors are under a duty to obtain an issue price from subscribers which reflect the market value of the shares at the time of allotment. Consequently, if directors allot shares to themselves at an issue price which is less than the current market value of the shares, they are accountable to the company for the difference as a personal profit obtained by them as a result of the exercise of their power of allotment. Also, if the directors subsequently sell the shares which they allot to themselves at an issue price less than their current market value at the date of allotment, and the price paid to the directors when they sell is higher than the market value of the shares at the date of allotment, the company can recover from the directors the whole difference between the price realised by the directors and the issue price paid by them (*Parker* v. *McKenna* (1874); *Shaw* v. *Holland* (1900)). However, it would seem that if directors make a rights offer of new shares to all the shareholders of the company (including themselves) in proportion to their existing holdings, and the directors subscribe for new shares under the offer in the same proportion as other existing shareholders are entitled to do, the directors are not accountable for any difference between the market value of the new shares they take and the lower issue price they pay for them under the rights offer. The reason for this is that the directors subscribe for the new shares in their capacity as existing shareholders of the company, and they obtain no special advantages for themselves because they are its directors.

Profits obtained indirectly

The strictness of the rule governing directors' accountability is shown by the decision of the House of Lords in *Regal (Hastings) Ltd* v. *Gulliver* (1967). In that case directors subscribed for shares in a company which they promoted in order to expand the business undertaking of the company of which they were directors at a time when that company itself lacked the resources to subscribe for all the shares of the newly formed company.

The directors had negotiated a lease of two properties which their company wished to acquire in order to enlarge its activities, but the owner of the properties was unwilling to grant the lease without the rent and lessee's obligations being guaranteed by the directors personally, unless the issued and paid up share capital of the company which took the lease was at least £5,000. To avoid the need for a guarantee, the directors formed a new company to take the lease, but they considered that the original company could not safely invest more than £2,000 in it, having regard to its other commitments. The directors therefore subscribed the remaining £3,000 of the new company's capital themselves, or found other persons who were willing to subscribe. Shortly afterwards the directors negotiated the sale of the shares they had taken in the new company together with the shares in it which the original company had subscribed at a price more than three times the amount which had been paid on the allotment of the shares. At the same time the shareholders of the original company, including the directors, sold the shares they held in it to the same persons who purchased their shares in the new company, and so control of the original company, as well as the new company, passed to those persons, and new directors of both companies were appointed.

The original company, under the control of the purchasers, then claimed that its former directors who had sold their shares in the new company to the purchasers were liable to account for the profit they had made on selling their shares–namely the difference between the sale price they had received and the issue price they had paid to the new company. The House of Lords held that the directors were accountable for this amount. The opportunity for them to subscribe for shares in the new company had arisen because they were directors of the original company at the time the new company was formed, and they had, whether intentionally or not, preferred their own interests in subscribing personally for £3,000 of the new company's shares. Instead of doing so, they could have raised a loan to enable the original company to subscribe for the whole £5,000 of the new company's capital, or they could have made a rights offer of further shares in the original company to all its shareholders (and not only to themselves) to raise the additional £3,000 which that company needed to subscribe for all the shares in the new company.

The seeming unfairness of the House of Lord's judgment lies in the fact that the profit made by the directors on selling their shares in the new company was provided by the same persons who purchased the whole of the shares of the original company. When those persons acquired control of the original company, they knew of, and must therefore have implicitly assented to, the profit which the directors had made.

The people who were really affected adversely by the directors' sale of their shares in the new company were the other shareholders of the original company, who would presumably have received a higher price for their shares from the purchasers if that company had subscribed for the whole, and not only 40 per cent, of the shares of the new company. If they had retained their shares in the original company, they could in its name have compelled the directors to account to it for the profit the directors made by selling the shares in the new company for which they had subscribed. By selling their shares in the original company, presumably at a reduced price, the other shareholders put it out of their power to call the directors to account, however, and in effect enabled the purchasers of the shares in the original company to recover part of the price they had already paid for the shares of the new company. If the purchasers had purchased the assets of the original company instead of the shares it had issued, the shareholders of the original company would have been able to compel the directors to account to that company (and so indirectly to them) for the difference between the amount they received in respect of their shares in the new company and the issue price they had paid for those shares. This would have increased the amount which the shareholders of the original company would have received in its liquidation, and the purchasers, quite rightly, would not have been entitled to participate in that increase.

Incidental profits

Despite the strictness of the rule that directors must not use their powers for the purpose of making a personal profit, they are not accountable for a profit they make incidentally as a consequence of exercising the powers for a perfectly proper purpose in the interests of the company. In *Hirsche* v. *Sims* (1894), directors had the company's properties revalued by a leading firm of surveyors so as to include the revaluation figures in a prospectus they published in order to raise additional capital for the company. They were held by the House of Lords not to be accountable to the company for the additional price they obtained on selling some of their existing shares because of the increase in the market price of all the company's shares which resulted from the publication of the revaluation figures.

On the other hand, it appears that directors are accountable for a profit they obtain as a direct result of exercising their powers, even though they act entirely for the company's, and not for their own, benefit. In *Albion Steel and Wire Co.* v. *Martin* (1875), a director was held accountable for the profit he obtained by selling to the company goods which it required for the purpose of its business at a price not exceeding the current market price. The profit was the difference between the sale price obtained from the company and the lower price which the director had paid for the goods. It is questionable in the light of later decisions whether a company could now call a director to account this kind of situation, unless the comany can and does rescind the contract of sale and restore the goods to the director. The judicial decisions that the company's right to recover the director's profit depends on the contract first being rescinded will be considered in the section of Chapter 4 which deals with directors' interests in contracts made by their companies.

3.08 Exploitation of business opportunities by directors

A director must not only employ his company's assets exclusively for its benefit and not for his own. He must also pursue and exploit for the company's benefit all business opportunities available to it in the area of commercial activity in which it is legitimately engaged, and must not appropriate such opportunities for himself.

Profits obtained by director-controlled companies

This obligation cannot be avoided by the directors' forming another company in whose capital the original company and its other shareholders have no interest, and by their making the business opportunity available to the other company. Consequently, where two directors, who were the majority shareholders of a company, induced a customer who proposed to place further orders with the company to place them instead with a new company which they had formed and in which they were the only shareholders, it was held that a minority shareholder of the original company could compel both the two directors and the new company to account to it for the profit made by the new company fulfilling the orders (*Cook* v. *Deeks* (1916)). Similarly, in *Thomas Marshall (Exports) Ltd* v. *Guinlé* (1979), a managing director of a company which imported products from abroad for resale in the United Kingdom, solicited orders from the United Kingdom customers of the company and diverted the orders to two new companies he had formed. Those companies also obtained supplies to satisfy orders from overseas manufacturers with whom the director had established a relationship while negotiating supplies for the original company. Megarry VC held that these acts amounted to a breach of the director's fiduciary duties to the original company, as well as a breach of his service contract with it, and he issued an injunction restraining the director from repeating this conduct.

Profits obtained from transactions within the scope of a company's business

A more complex case involving the same principle, *Fine Industrial Commodities Ltd* v. *Powling* (1954), arose from the failure of a director to assist his company to modify its plant used for making a product for which demand had fallen, so as to enable the company to make an alternative product for which there was a demand. The necessary modification was known to the director, but instead of disclosing it to the company, he patented it in his own name and formed a new company to exploit the patent and manufacture the alternative product. It was held that the director held the patent as a trustee for the company. The remedy given in this case is interesting, because the court did not merely order the director to account to the original company for the profit he made from using the patent to make the alternative product. The court also treated the director's knowledge of the practicability of modifying the original company's plant and the patent embodying that knowledge as property which belonged in equity to the company. In this respect the case was decided, not only under the present rule requiring directors to exploit business opportunities for the exclusive benefit of their companies, but also under the rule dealt with in the next section of this chapter by which confidential information acquired by a director in the course of carrying out his functions is treated as property or assets of the company.

In a parallel case, *Cranleigh Precision Engineering Ltd* v. *Bryant* (1964), it was held that a director was in breach of his fiduciary duties to his company when after resigning his directorship, he and a company he formed manufactured a product which embodied an invention he had made in the course of his work for the original company in combination with another patented invention. This director obtained an assignment of the other patent personally from its holder; the assignment of the other patent was essential for the exploitation of the director's own invention, which infringed that patent. The court issued injunctions against both the director and the company formed by him to restrain them from using the invention made by the director and the patent acquired by him. Both of these inventions were held by the director in trust for the original company in consequence of his breaches of fiduciary duty in appropriating them for his own benefit and not for the benefit of the company. The invention by the director was undoubtedly the property of the original company, because the director had made it in the course of his work for that company. The interesting feature of the case, however, is that the court also held that the other patent was acquired by the director as a fiduciary for the company, because the opportunity to acquire it would have been made available to the company if the director had acted properly.

Opportunities not available to the company

The accountability of directors for profits made by exploiting business opportunities has been extended by the courts to profits made by a director exploiting an opportunity which he obtains because of his directorship, even though the company would not be able to do so itself. This is so, however, only if the opportunity arises in connection with an activity which is part of, or related to, the company's legitimate business and the director breaches his obligations of loyalty and honesty in exploiting the opportunity for his own advantage.

Consequently, in the case dealt with at length in [3.07] – where a director availed himself of an investment opportunity which was open to his company, but the company did not have the financial resources to make the investment itself – the House of Lords held that the director was nevertheless accountable for the profit he obtained by acquiring the investment personally and later selling it at a higher price (*Regal (Hastings) Ltd* v. *Gulliver* (1967)).

Likewise, when a managing director of an industrial design and construction company obtained his release from his directorship by means of false representation about his health so that he might obtain a personal contract for design work from a public body, which would not have placed the contract with the company because it preferred to deal with smaller and less independent contractors, Roskill J held that the former managing director was accountable to the company for the profit he obtained from the contract awarded to him (*Industrial Development Consultants Ltd* v. *Cooley* (1972)). The director's disloyal conduct was no doubt heightened by his fraudulent procurement of his release from his directorship, but this was not the ground on which liability was imposed on him. He would have been accountable for the profit he obtained from the contract he made with the public body even if he had not committed fraud.

The only case where a director exploited personally a business opportunity in the company's area of activity but was held not accountable for the resulting profits was *Heyting* v. *Dupont* (1964), a decision of the Court of Appeal. This was a case where there were mutual accusations of such conduct by the two directors and sole shareholders of a private company. The company was formed to engage in a specialised sector of engineering, but lacked the resources to manufacture a product in that sector for which it was necessary to obtain a patent. Both directors formed new companies to manufacture the product for their own benefit, and they brought cross-actions against each other on the original company's behalf for injunctions to restrain each other from doing so.

The Court of Appeal dismissed the action and counterclaim on jurisdictional grounds, but also held that neither director could be sued by the original company, because it had suffered no loss, being unable to engage in manufacturing the product itself because of its lack of resources. It would seem that the Court of Appeal erroneously treated the action and counterclaim as sustainable only if the original company could have sued the directors for compensation for loss inflicted on it by their breach of duty, and the court disregarded the possibility of the company alternatively calling for an account of the profits made by the directors. In such an action for an account, the company's lack of resources would be irrelevant, and for that reason it would appear that the Court of Appeal's decision is inconsistent with the House of Lord's decision in *Regal (Hastings) Ltd* v. *Gulliver*, and is therefore wrong on the question of accountability. The only possible distinction between the two cases is that in *Heyting* v. *Dupont* the profit was made, not from a business opportunity which was open to the company in connection with the business it actually carried on, but from the opportunity to expand the area of its business activities. However, the Court of Appeal did not make this the basis of its decision.

Rejection of opportunity by the company

There is as yet no English decision on the question whether a director is accountable for profits made from a business opportunity which he pursues personally when the board of directors of his company rejects the opportunity for the benefit of the company, and does so in good faith as a matter of business judgment. A logical case can be made out for holding the director accountable to the company if he then pursues the opportunity himself, because it is not an essential feature of the company's case that it could exploit, or that it attempted to exploit, the opportunity itself. On the other hand, it is equally logical to argue that if the company rejects the opportunity, it no longer has any interest in the matter, with the result that the opportunity no longer falls within the company's field of business activity and so is open for exploitation by anyone, including its directors.

This later argument was accepted by the Judicial Committee of the Privy Council in *Queensland Mines Ltd* v. *Hudson* (1978), on appeal from the High Court of Australia, and by a Canadian court in *Peso Silver Mines Ltd* v. *Cropper* (1966), and it probably also represents English law. Normally absolution from a breach of fiduciary duty by a director can only be given by a resolution passed by a general meeting of the company after full disclosure of the facts, but it would appear that in the present circumstances a resolution of the board of directors suffices. This is because the rejection of the opportunity is a business decision made by the board in the course of carrying on the company's business, and its effect is to define the limits of the company's area of interest, so that the personal exploitation of the opportunity by a director cannot thereafter be a breach of his fiduciary duty.

In a similar situation where a business opportunity was open to the trustee of a trust which comprised a controlling shareholding in a family company, the House of Lords held that the solicitors representing the trust could pursue the opportunity for their own benefit only if all the beneficiaries of the trust rejected the opportunity for their own benefit, and not merely all but one of the beneficiaries (*Boardman* v. *Phipps* (1967)). A trust is not comparable to a company in this respect, however, because it is the directors, and not the shareholders, of a company who make business decisions on its behalf. The court would no doubt require clear proof that the rejection of a business opportunity available to a company was decided on by its board in good faith in the interests of the company, and was not merely to accommodate the director who subsequently pursued it himself, and an essential ingredient of the required good faith would be full disclosure to the board of that director's intentions. This is nevertheless far less a restriction on the director's liberty of action than a requirement that he should account to the company for the profit he makes if he exploits an abandoned opportunity.

3.09 Competition by directors

Directors' right to compete

There is only one English decision which has dealt directly with the question whether a director breaches his fiduciary duties to his company by competing with it, or by having an interest in, or being a director of, another company which competes with the original company. In *London and Mashonaland Exploration Co. v. New Mashonaland Exploration Co.* (1891), it was held that there is no breach of fiduciary duty by a director if he does any of those things, and consequently a company cannot obtain an injunction to restrain any of its directors or another company to whose board any of its directors is appointed from giving or accepting his services. In this respect a director's fiduciary obligations are narrower than those of a partner, who is accountable to his fellow partners for the profits which he obtains by carrying on, or being interested in, a business which is of the same nature as the partnership business and actually competes with it (Partnership Act 1890, section 30; *Glassington* v. *Thwaites* (1823); *England* v. *Curling* (1844)).

A director's immunity, however, is a limited one. It extends merely to having an interest in directing a rival concern, and it is an immunity which he may expressly or impliedly agree to forego by his service contract with his company. A director is accountable to his company in equity for profits which he makes by using its assets for the benefit of the rival concern, and this includes its business connection, goodwill, customer lists or trade secrets (*Bell* v. *Lever Brothers Ltd* (1932); *Saltman Engineering Co. Ltd* v. *Campbell Engineering Co. Ltd* (1948); *Horcal Ltd* v. *Gatland* (1984)). Also, as has been shown in the preceding section of this chapter, the director and the rival company may be prevented by injunction from taking advantage of business opportunities which would normally have been available to the original company. Furthermore, if the original company has invested resources in providing the director with special skills, it may be that, like an ordinary skilled employee, he will be restrained from using those skills for the benefit of a rival concern (*Hivac Ltd* v. *Park Royal Scientific Investments Ltd* (1946)).

Contractual provisions

A director's service contract with a company may prevent him from accepting appointment as a director of a rival company, or for that matter, of any other company, whatever its business, while he is a director of the original company. This may be either because of an express prohibition in the director's service contract, which is enforceable by injunction, or because it requires him to devote his whole time and attention to the company's affairs, and so excludes the possibility of his serving as a director of another company. Restrictive contractual provisions of this latter kind are enforceable against the director by a claim for damages for breach of contract, but not by a claim for an injunction or for an account of the profits or gains made by the director from his second directorship, because accepting it is a breach of contract by him, not a breach of fiduciary duty (*Whitwood Chemical Co. Ltd* v. *Hardman* (1891)).

American decisions

By refusing to treat the fiduciary duties of a director as including obligations not to compete with the company and not to be interested in a competing concern, English law limits the occasions when a company may pursue a remedy against a competing director to those where he has diverted to another concern a business opportunity which would normally have been available to the company, and when he has employed the company's assets for the benefit of the other business. The American courts have gone somewhat farther than this in certain cases, and have held that a director is liable to compensate his company if he uses his influence to prevent it from competing effectively with the other concern in which he is interested (*Singer* v. *Carlisle* (1941)), or if he uses his influence to prevent the company from expanding its activities into a related line of business which the other concern already carries on (*Rosenblum* v. *Judson Engineering Corpn* (1954)). In one case a Californian court awarded punitive damages against a full-time director who competed with his company, even though there was no evidence that he used the company's assets to do so or exploited business opportunities which came the company's way for the benefit of his rival business (*Sequois Vacuum Systems Inc.* v. *Stransky* (1964)).

Probably the first of these three cases would be dealt with similarly by a British court, but on the basis that the director had failed to act in the interests of the company of which he was a director, rather than the fact that he obtained a personal profit from the other concern. This facet of a director's fiduciary duties and the question whether directors are under a positive duty to promote their company's interests in all aspects of its business will be dealt with in Chapter 4. The other two American cases would not be followed by a British court in the present state of the law, and the last case would certainly not be considered as one for the award of punitive damages, even if the director had expressly contracted to devote his full time and attention to the company's business.

The three American cases mentioned above go the farthest of any decided by United States courts in defining directors' fiduciary duties in relation to activities carried on in competition with their companies. In most of the American decisions, directors' fiduciary duties are limited in this respect in much the same way as in English law. This is because the United States courts recognise, particularly in the case of part-time directors, that too strict an interpretation of directors' duties of loyalty as part of their fiduciary duties could result in a stifling of enterprise and a bottling up of management talent.

3.10 Use of corporate information

Unpublished and confidential information obtained by a director of a company in carrying out his functions as such a director, or in consequence of his being such a director, must be used by him exclusively for the benefit of the company. If he uses the information for his personal benefit, he is accountable to the company for any profit he obtains, and is also liable to compensate the company for any loss it suffers. This is the result of two overlapping applications of the fiduciary duties imposed on directors.

Information as property

In the first place, it seems reasonably clear that English law will now treat information generated by a company (for example, turnover and profit figures, customer lists, plans decided on for future activities) as property belonging to the company. A director who uses such information for his own purposes misappropriates or misuses assets of the company, and is consequently accountable to it in equity.

This was the approach adopted by the House of Lords in *Boardman* v. *Phipps* (1967), where information obtained by solicitors to a trust in respect of the potential development of the activities of a company in which the trust held shares was held to be property of the trust. It was also the approach of the court in the earlier cases of *Exchange Telegraph Co. Ltd* v. *Gregory and Co.* (1896), and *Exchange Telegraph Co. Ltd* v. *Central News Ltd* (1897), where news items and Stock Exchange dealing prices were obtained promptly by the plaintiff company's reporters and circulated to a limited number of subscribers under contracts which prohibited them from communicating the information to other persons. It was held that the news and dealing prices were the property of the plaintiff company until the information became generally known. An unauthorised third person was therefore enjoined from circulating the information when he obtained it, or could only have obtained it, from one of the subscribers to whom it was circulated.

Confidentially communicated information

More widely, the court will issue an injunction against any person to whom unpublished information is confidentially communicated so as to prevent him from making use of it for an unauthorised purpose (*Saltman Engineering Co. Ltd* v. *Campbell Engineering Co. Ltd* (1948); *Terrapin Ltd* v. *Builders Supply Co. (Hayes) Ltd* (1960)). The court will also issue an injunction in the same terms against a third person to whom such information is passed by a person to whom it was confidentially communicated by the plaintiff, if that third person was aware of the confidential character of the information and the source from which it came when he received it (*Morris Ltd* v. *Gilman (BST) Ltd* (1943)).

The use of information generated by the company by directors for unauthorised purposes, or the use by them for unauthorised purposes of information communicated to them confidentially, or of confidential information obtained by directors from their company, whether directly or indirectly, with knowledge of its source, may be prevented by the company seeking an injunction. Also, since the directors' obligations are equitable, the use of such information may be remedied by an order that the directors shall account to the company for any profits made by their using it for unauthorised purposes, or by the award against the directors of compensation to be paid to the company for the loss it has suffered by such misuse. In all such cases, the directors who use or propose to use the information for their own purposes breach their fiduciary duty not to use their powers or position to obtain a personal profit, and they are liable to account to or to compensate the company accordingly.

Share dealings

One of the uses which directors may make of unpublished information which they obtain in their capacity of directors is to deal advantageously in their company's shares. If they have unpublished figures for projections of the company's future profits, they may buy shares or have their relatives or associates do so in the expectation that if the anticipated profits are higher than is indicated by the current dealing price of the company's shares, the market price of the shares will rise and they will be able to resell at a profit shares which they buy at current prices. Conversely, if the profit projection is pessimistic, directors may contract to sell shares they hold in the company at current prices, and so avoid the loss they would suffer if they retained the shares until the dealing price fell in consequence of the publication of the profit projection. Alternatively, in that situation, directors might contract to sell shares which they do not hold at current prices and buy in shares cheaply to fulfill their contracts after the dealing price has fallen in consequence of the publication of the adverse profit projection.

It is true that such transactions by directors who are in possession of unpublished information which is likely to affect the dealing price of the shares on its publication is made a criminal offence by section 1(1) of the Company Securities (Insider Dealing) Act 1985, if the shares are dealt in on the Stock Exchange or on the 'over the counter market' made by licensed dealers. It is also a criminal offence for a director to communicate such information to a third person so that he may deal in those shares. The third person himself commits an offence if he is aware of the source of the information and that is unpublished, but he nevertheless deals in the shares (section 1(3), (4) and (8)). It is also true that sales or purchases of shares in the company by a director or his relatives or associates in such circumstances would infringe the Model Code for Securities Transactions by Directors of Listed Companies published by the Stock Exchange. The code applies if the company has a listing for its shares on the Stock Exchange, or if its shares are dealt in on the Unlisted Securities Market of the Stock Exchange.

Infringements of the Company Securities (Insider Dealing) Act 1985, and the Model Code do not entail any civil consequences, however. The Act expressly provides that a contravention shall not invalidate any contract for the sale or purchase of shares (section 8(3)). It would also appear that neither the company nor the other party to a prohibited transaction with a director may sue him for damages because of a contravention of the Act. Likewise, the only sanctions for infringements of the Model Code are reprimands administered by the Stock Exchange or, at worst, a suspension of dealings in the company's shares.

The question therefore arises whether a company whose director has used unpublished information obtained by him as a director about the company, its transactions or its prospects to deal at a profit in its shares, may recover the profit from him or obtain an injunction to prevent the deal being carried out on the ground that the director will breach his fiduciary duties to the company by using the information for his own purposes. There are no decisions by English courts on this question, but it would seem to follow from the duty of a director not to use unpublished information he has obtained about the company's affairs for his personal advantage, that the company could seek an injunction to restrain him from engaging in dealings in those circumstances. It would appear also that the company could call on the director to account for any profit he has obtained if the deal has been completed. Several American courts have held that the company can obtain these remedies in those situations, and English law would appear to produce the same results.

American decisions

In *Diamond* v. *Oreamuno* (1969), a decision of the Court of Appeals of New York State, directors sold shares in their company at current dealing prices, knowing that the company was about to publish half yearly profit figures which were poorer than the market expected. The court held that the directors were accountable to the company for the difference between the price at which they sold their shares and the lower market value of the shares after the profit figures were announced.

In *Brophy* v. *City Service Co* (1974), the Delaware Chancery Court held that directors were accountable to their company for the profit they made by buying shares cheaply when they knew that the company would shortly publish an offer to buy in a certain number of its shares at a higher price out of its accumulated profits from holders who wished to sell. Finally, in *Davidge* v. *White* (1974), a Federal circuit court held that where a director of a company resigned immediately before purchasing shares in the company, knowing that the trustee under a bankruptcy reorganisation scheme affecting the company was about to offer to pay the shareholders a greater amount for the purchase of their shares than the price the director paid for his shares, the director was accountable to the company for the profit he made by accepting the trustee's offer.

The nearest English case to this last American decision concerned the promoters of a company which was formed to purchase the insolvent undertaking of an existing company. The promoters were able to purchase debentures issued by the existing company from their holders at depressed prices because the sellers were unaware of the formation of the new company. The promoters received repayment of the debentures in full from the existing company when the purchase of its undertaking by the new company at a generous price was completed. The House of Lords held that the promoters of the new company were accountable to it for the difference between the price paid by them for the debentures and the amount they had received when the existing company repaid them (*Gluckstein* v. *Barnes* (1900)).

The fiduciary duties of promoters and directors are similar, if not identical, in such situations, and it may therefore be concluded that English courts in cases like the American cases outlined above would have given the same decisions as the American courts. There remains, of course, the connected question whether in circumstances such as these the other party to the transaction – the seller or the buyer of the shares – would have a remedy against the director with whom he dealt. This question does not concern directors' fiduciary duties to their companies, however, and so will be deferred to Chapter 9 where the obligations of directors to individual shareholders are dealt with.

Use of information for extraneous purposes

It has so far been assumed that a director who breaches his fiduciary duties by using unpublished information obtained by him as a director, uses it in connection with a private transaction of the kind the company engages in, or at least in connection with a transaction in the company's shares. In principle it would appear to be immaterial whether the offending transaction is one which the company does or could engage in or not, because the company is entitled to have the director use the information exclusively for its benefit, and not his own.

However, in two partnership cases, one of which was decided by the House of Lords, it has been held that a partner is not accountable to his fellow partners for the profitable personal use he makes of information which he obtains as a partner, unless he uses it in connection with a transaction similar to those in which the partnership legitimately engages (*Aas* v. *Benham* (1891); *Trimble* v. *Goldberg* (1906)). If this restrictive application of the fiduciary obligations of partners to each other were applied in respect of the obligation of directors not to use corporate unpublished information for their personal advantage, it would not be possible to compel directors to account to their company for personal profits made by their dealing in the company's shares. This is because a company is precluded by law from subscribing, buying and selling its own shares (Companies Act 1985, section 143(1)).

It is significant, however, that the majority judgments of the House of Lords in *Boardman* v. *Phipps* (1967), did not apply the restriction applied in partnership cases to the fiduciary obligations of solicitors to a trust, and it would seem that the restriction is one which is not recognised outside partnership law. Because of this, it would appear that the obligation of directors to account for profits made by them personally from using unpublished information they have acquired while acting as directors, is a general obligation and that it applies whatever the use to which the directors may put that information. This is logical if unpublished information is regarded as an asset of the company, because any use of the company's assets for a director's personal profit constitutes a breach of his fiduciary duties, even though it is a use which the company itself could not make of the assets.

Chapter 4

The Judicial and Statutory Extension of Directors' Fiduciary Duties

The basic fiduciary duties of directors which were considered in Chapter 3 have been extended by judicial decisions and by statute in a number of ways. In particular, the duty of directors not to promote their own interests which conflict with those of the company has been expanded into an affirmative duty to use their powers in the interests of the company. Also, the law has made contracts entered into by a company in which its directors are interested subject to rescission by the company, or in some cases has required the approval of the shareholders in general meeting as a condition for the validity of the contract.

THE DUTY TO USE DIRECTORS' POWERS IN THE INTERESTS OF THE COMPANY AND FOR THE PROPER PURPOSE

4.01 The interests of the company and the shareholders as a whole

It has been established for over a hundred years by the decisions of the courts in a succession of cases that directors are under a fiduciary obligation to employ the resources of their company and to exercise their powers in order to promote and protect the interests of the company and also the interests of the shareholders of the company as a whole. This duty is quite separate from the duty discussed in the preceding chapter, which compels directors not to use their powers for their own benefit. The latter duty could logically be subsumed under the present one, since it is obvious that if directors pursue their own interests which conflict with those of the shareholders of the company, they cannot be acting in the interest of the shareholders as a whole. Nevertheless, the present rule applies also in situations where directors do not promote their personal interests, but are also not serving the interests of the shareholders either.

Abuse of directors' powers and ultra vires

In some situations the court has treated the acts of directors in pursuing objectives which are not in the interests of the company or its shareholders as a whole as going beyond the scope of the legitimate business which the company was formed to carry on, and therefore as being beyond the powers of the company and consequently totally invalid. The courts have taken this line in cases where the act or transaction in question was not expressly authorised by the objects clause of the company's memorandum of association. The question the court has had to decide is whether a power for the company to do the act or enter into the transaction can be implied because it is incidental to, or consequential on, pursuing the objectives of the company (that is, its legitimate area of business activity) which is set out expressly in its memorandum of association.

For example, in *Hutton* v. *West Cork Rly Co.* (1882), the Court of Appeal held that a railway company whose undertaking had been transferred to another company and whose affairs were being wound up, could not pay gratuitous compensation to its former employees or to its directors for the loss of their employment. There was no express power for the company to make such payments in its memorandum of association, and the power could not be claimed as incidental to carrying out the company's expressed object of running a railway. This was because the payment of compensation to employees and directors would not assist toward achieving that object, which had now become unattainable after the transfer of the company's undertaking. Nor could the payment now reflect any benefit on the company or its shareholders by encouraging employees to work hard in the future and so increase the company's profits, because there were no profits to be earned after the company had ceased to own its undertaking.

The same conclusion was reached by Plowman J, in the more recent case of *Parke* v. *Daily News Ltd* (1962). In that case the company had sold its loss-making newspaper undertaking, and it proposed to distribute the greater part of the proceeds of sale to its employees as gratuitous compensation for loss of employment, despite the absence of an express power to do so in its memorandum of association. Plowman J held that the directors' decision to cease publication of the company's newspaper was justified in the interests of its shareholders, because continued publication would have resulted in even further losses, but the decision to distribute the proceeds of sale among the company's employees who were to be dismissed could not be so justified. The company no longer had an undertaking whose profitability would be improved by encouraging employee loyalty, and the shareholders of the company would certainly not benefit by the payment of gratuitous compensation, because the proposed distribution to the company's employees would disable the company from repaying the company's share capital to its shareholders.

In both *Hutton v. West Cork Rly Co.* and *Parke v. Daily News Ltd* the ground for the courts' decisions was that the proposed payments to the company's employees was beyond the powers of the company, and so if the payments had actually been made, the directors would have been personally liable to make restitution. Nevertheless, the basis on which the court proceeded was that a power for the company to make the payments could not be implied in the circumstances, because it would not have been in the interests of the shareholders of the company as a whole to do so. That is the same criterion as must be applied in equity when testing whether directors have exercised the company's undoubted powers consistently with the interests they are bound to protect.

Misuse of powers vested in directors

Most of the decided cases where the court has held that directors have not acted in the interests of the company and the shareholders as a whole have involved situations where the act or transaction in question was unquestionably within the powers of the company and the directors, but the directors have simply abused or misused their powers.

In *Re European Central Rly Co., Sykes' Case* (1872), for example, the directors exercised a power given to them by the company's articles of association to accept payments of capital unpaid on any of the company's shares in advance of instalments of unpaid capital becoming due. The directors accepted on the company's behalf advance payments of capital on their own shares, and they then used the payment to pay themselves a debt which the company owed them. There was nothing wrong in the directors using the company's resources to pay the debt, because directors act legitimately and, in fact, fulfil their duty to the company to manage its affairs properly by seeing to it that all its debts are duly paid. The breach of duty lay in the directors using their powers to accept advance payments of capital by making payments on their own shares (and so preventing the company from later calling for payment of that capital for its general purposes) when their object in making the advance payment was to pay a particular debt of the company owing to themselves, and not to discharge the company's debts in general.

On the other hand, in *Re Wincham Shipbuilding, Boiler and Salt Co., Poole, Jackson and White's Case* (1878), it was held that directors did act in the interests of the company and its shareholders generally when they accepted advance payments of capital on their own shares under a power in the company's articles, and then used the amounts paid to the company to discharge a debt of the company which they had guaranteed personally to a creditor of the company who was pressing for payment. The directors' purpose here was to discharge the company's liability and so forestall the creditor suing it. The incidental consequence that they also discharged the guarantee which they had given the creditor themselves did not mean that the payment to him was not made in the company's interests and for its benefit.

Fixing directors' remuneration

A number of cases have concerned the exercise by directors of a power given by the company's articles to negotiate service contracts with themselves individually and with senior executives of the company.

In *Re W. and M. Roith Ltd* (1967), directors negotiated a service contract with the managing director of the company, who was already serving under a contract which had some years to run. The managing director was in poor health, and the directors' purpose in negotiating the new contract was to improve the terms on which the company would pay him a pension on his retirement and provide benefits for his dependants in the event of his death. It was held, somewhat ungenerously, that since the directors could have secured the managing director's services for the company for several years without negotiating a new service contract with him, their purpose in doing so was to provide for him and his dependants and not to benefit the company or its shareholders, and the company could therefore rescind the new service contract.

On the other hand, in *Re Horsley and Weight Ltd* (1982), it was held by the Court of Appeal that directors acted properly and in the interests of the company when in exercise of a power in the objects clause of the company's memorandum of association they used the company's funds to purchase an insurance policy under which a pension would be paid to a full-time director who would shortly retire. The directors' purpose was to provide for a director who had worked for the company for many years without a service contract, and who therefore had no contractual right to a pension from the company.

The directors made the provision for the director who was about to retire in the same way as they would for other employees, and they acted in the ordinary course of the company's business, unaware, as was in fact the case, that the payment of the single premium for the pension policy would be so great a drain on the company's resources that it would contribute to its eventual insolvency.

Group transactions

Other cases under the present head have concerned transactions entered into by directors of a company which is a member of a group of companies, when the transaction primarily benefits other companies in the group. The group of companies in this context may be either a group which consists of a parent or holding company and its subsidiaries, or what is sometimes called a horizontal group, namely a number of companies whose shareholders and often also directors are the same, or substantially the same, persons.

In *Charterbridge Corpn. Ltd* v. *Lloyds Bank Ltd* (1970), such a horizontal group of companies was managed as an integrated commercial concern, and one of the companies in the group gave a guarantee and a mortgage of its property to secure a bank loan made to another company in the group so that it might finance the group's operations. Pennycuick J held that the guarantee and mortgage were not given primarily for the benefit of the company which created them, but that it nevertheless did benefit from the loan transaction which was facilitated by the company giving the guarantee and mortgage, because the loan was intended to finance its own activities among other things, and consequently its directors had acted in the interests of the company in creating the guarantee and the mortgage.

On the other hand, in *Rolled Steel Products (Holdings) Ltd* v. *British Steel Corporation* (1985), a guarantee and debenture given by a company to secure the indebtedness of another company to British Steel Corporation was held by the Court of Appeal not to have been given for the benefit or in the interests of the first company at all. The only connection between the two companies was that the majority shareholder and managing director of the first company which gave the guarantee and debenture was the sole shareholder and director of the second company. The two companies' undertakings were distinct and were managed separately, and the second company did not finance the first company's activities, apart from making it a substantial loan with which the first company had acquired additional premises for the purpose of its business. When the first company gave the guarantee and mortgage to British Steel Corporation this loan was repaid out of money provided by BSC and, the second company used the amount it received to satisfy part of its indebtedness to BSC. It was held that the directors of the first company had in fact acted adversely to its interests and had abused their powers, and as BSC was aware of this, the first company could rescind the guarantee and the debenture.

Interests of shareholders

In many of the foregoing cases the court has been able to resolve the dispute by deciding whether or not the impugned transaction was entered into in the interests of the company's business undertaking, and whether the directors sought to secure an advantage or avoid a detriment for the benefit of that undertaking. In such cases, the interests of the shareholders coincide with the company's interests, and can safely be identified with the interests of the company's business undertaking. In certain situations, however, particularly those where the acts of the directors have a direct impact on the shareholders' interests, or a different impact on the interests of different classes of shareholders, it may be obvious that the company's interests have been safeguarded by the directors' actions, but the question still remains whether the directors have acted in the interests of the shareholders as a whole.

Cases where directors have issued unissued shares of the company to persons friendly to the directors in order to defeat an unwanted takeover bid fall into this category. However, consideration of such cases will be deferred until later in this section, because the cases also involve the use of directors' powers for purposes other than those for which they were given, and are therefore best considered under that head.

Decided cases where the directors have acted in a manner which treated certain classes of shareholders adversely as compared with other classes have mostly been concerned with schemes or proposals prepared by directors for the modification or cancellation of the rights of one or more classes of shareholders. The question which has occupied the court has not been whether the directors have acted in the interests of the shareholders as a whole in proposing the changes in shareholders' class rights, but whether the approval of the changes by the classes of shareholders affected has been given at a separate class meeting of each class in the interests of that class, and whether the carrying out of the changes by a resolution passed by a general meeting of all the shareholders of the company has been done in good faith and in the interests of the shareholders as a whole, or, whether, on the other hand, the alteration of the class rights is so unreasonable that no sensible shareholder appraised of the facts would have approved it.

Despite the prevalence of cases involving the alteration of class rights, it is nevertheless possible for situations to arise where the action proposed to be taken is wholly within the powers and discretion of the directors, and they have to choose between alternative courses of action which will have different effects on different classes of shareholders.

For example, directors may have resources of the company to invest in ventures within the company's legitimate field of business. Some of those ventures may be likely to yield generous returns but they also carry higher risks of failure and loss of the resources invested, whereas other such ventures may promise moderate returns but afford greater security. The interest of preference shareholders, who are entitled only to a fixed preference dividend and not to any participation in surplus profits, is clearly to have the company's available resources invested in the more secure ventures, but ordinary shareholders might be better served by investing in ventures offering higher yields, so enabling the company to pay a higher ordinary share dividend.

Again, if the company finances an expansion of its business activities by issuing debentures rather than further ordinary shares, preference shareholders will suffer the risk that their preference dividends may not be paid in full because the payment of debenture interest may absorb most of the company's profits. On the other hand, the ordinary shareholders may benefit by the debenture interest being at a lower rate than the yield which would have to be offered on an issue of further ordinary shares, with the result that profits from the expansion of the company's business will be available to increase the dividend on the existing ordinary shares whilst the preference dividend will, of course, not be increased.

Whichever alternative the directors choose in these situations, the rights of the disadvantaged class of shareholders are not altered, and the consent of that class to the directors' chosen course of action is not required (*White* v. *Bristol Aeroplane Co. Ltd* (1953)). The only limit on the directors' discretion, therefore, is that they must act in the interests of the company and its shareholders as a whole. This involves the exercise of business judgment, and the court will not interfere with the directors' decision, unless there is evidence that they acted in bad faith intending to prejudice the interests of the disadvantaged class of shareholders, or that no sensible board of directors, taking all the features of the alternative choices into account, could reasonably have come to the decision which the directors reached (*Re White Star*

Line Ltd (1938); *Re Smith and Fawcett Ltd* (1942); *Gething* v. *Kilner* (1972)).

4.02 The interests of employees, creditors and others

Originally, the interests to which directors were obliged to have exclusive regard were those of the company and the shareholders of the company, but by the Companies Act 1985, section 309(1), directors must now have regard to 'interest of the company's employees in general, as well as the interests of its members'. Curiously, directors of a company which is a member of a group of companies are not required, or even permitted, to have regard to the interests of the employees of other companies in the group, even though their undertakings are interdependent, or are managed or financed together.

Although the statutory provision is intended to protect employees' interests, they and their representatives (for example, trade unions recognised by the company for collective bargaining purposes) are given no right to enforce the directors' obligation to have regard to employees' interests, or to challenge decisions of the board which disregard them. The Companies Act 1985, section 309(2), provides that the directors' duty 'is owed by them to the company (and the company alone) and is enforceable in the same way as any other fiduciary duty owed to a company by its directors'. Consequently, it is only if a company's employees are also shareholders of the company, or if trustees of a fund held for the benefit of employees (such as a pension fund or a fund set up under a profit sharing scheme) hold shares in the company that they can in their capacity as shareholders enforce the directors' obligation to have regard to the interests of the company's employees.

Extent of the duty to consider employees' interests

There is as yet no case law on the interpretation of the directors' statutory duty to have regard to employees' interests, and any deductions about the practical effect of the duty must therefore be speculative and provisional. The following observations, however, appear to be justified by the words in which the statutory duty is expressed.

First, the directors' duty is to have regard to the interests of the company's employees in general. This must mean that the directors must make their own judgment as to what those interests are, and where there are groups of employees with conflicting interests, what is the predominant interest of the employees in the given situation. Directors must decide what action by the company will best promote that predominant interest and do least harm to other employee interests.

Secondly, although the directors must obviously consider the expressed wishes of employees, or of groups of employees when there are groups with conflicting interests, the directors are not required to give effect to those wishes, even if formally expressed through representative bodies, such as trade unions or works councils. The directors must instead reach their own conclusion as to what is, in fact, the course of action which best promotes or safeguards the employees' interests, and the directors' decision can be impeached only if there is evidence of bad faith on their part, or if their conclusion is so unreasonable that no sensible directors could have reached it in good faith. In this connection there will often be little evidence to support an allegation of bad faith or unreasonableness, because the minutes of board meetings which directors are required to keep under the Companies Act 1985, section 382(1), need not record the discussion which takes place, or the reasons for the decisions reached by the board, or the materials on which it relied in reaching those decisions.

Thirdly, even when the board has reached a conclusion as to the interests of the company's employees, the directors are not bound to give any greater precedence or weight to those interests than they give to what they conceive as the interests of the shareholders of the company as a whole. If they choose to prefer the interests of the shareholders, their decision will be valid and immune from attack, unless the shareholders' interests are so slight and the employees' interests so weighty that the board's decision is manifestly unreasonable and indicative of bad faith. In other words, the interests of the employees generally must be considered, but may be overridden in the interests of the shareholders as a whole.

Power to make provision for employees

In exercising one of their statutory powers, directors may have exclusive regard to the protection of employees' interests and need pay no regard to shareholders' interests. By the Companies Act 1985, section 719(1), directors may make provision for the benefit of employees and former employees of the company or any of its subsidiaries on the cessation or transfer (on sale or otherwise) of the whole or part of the undertaking of the company or the subsidiary. This power cannot be excluded by the company's memorandum or articles of association.

Provision may be made for employees or former employees, even though it is not in the best interests of the company to do so, or even though a provision which is less onerous or expensive could be made (Companies Act 1985, section 719(2)). This presumably means that in making provision for employees or ex-employees the directors may totally disregard the interests of the shareholders. Consequently, the gratuitous payments to employees of compensation for loss of employment which were successfully attacked by shareholders in *Hutton* v. *West Cork Rly Co* (1883), and *Parke* v. *Daily News Ltd* (1962), on the ground that the payments were not in the interest of the company or its shareholders as a whole, could not now be attacked on that ground.

Directors have a choice in making provision for employees and ex-employees when the company's undertaking is sold or closed down, and can therefore provide either cash payments to employees or facilities for them (such as retraining courses to fit employees for other employment, or consultation or information services to help employees to obtain other employment). However, no provision may be made for employees at all unless the company's shareholders in general meeting approve it by an ordinary resolution, or by a resolution passed by a greater majority than an ordinary resolution if the company's memorandum or articles so require (section 719(3)). On the other hand, the memorandum or articles may expressly permit the directors to act on the strength of a board resolution alone without shareholder approval (section 719(3)). A further restricting feature is that provision can be made for employees only out of the company's profits available for distribution as dividends (section 719(4)).

If a company goes into liquidation, the power to make provision for employees or ex-employees is exercisable by the liquidator, and not by the directors, even if they still hold office (section 659(1)). The liquidator requires the approval of a general meeting given by an ordinary resolution or, if the memorandum or articles so provide, by a resolution passed by a greater majority than an ordinary resolution (section 659(2)). The liquidator may meet the cost of any provision he makes for employees only after the company's liabilities have been satisfied in full and the cost of the liquidation has been provided for, but he can apply any part of the surplus which would otherwise be returned to the shareholders, and he is not confined to employing only the accumulated and undistributed profits of the company (section 659(2) and (3)).

Directors' power to consider other interests

Directors must have regard to the interests of the shareholders of the company by the rules of equity and the interest of employees by statute. The question remains whether there are any other interests to which directors may properly have regard in exercising their powers.

The first category of interests which suggests itself as eligible is the interests of the company's creditors, both present and future. The question whether directors may take creditors' interests into account has in fact never come explicitly before the court. The reason for this is that the interests of shareholders in the solvency, earning capacity and profitability of the company usually coincide with the interests of creditors in being paid.

The one situation where creditors' and shareholders' interests may diverge, or at least appear to do so, however, is where directors have to decide whether to exercise a power conferred on them by the articles to present a petition to the court in the company's name for an order that it shall be wound up. The shareholders' interest may be not to present a winding up petition, even though the company is unable to pay its debts already due out of its liquid assets, if there is some reasonable hope of saving the company. The creditors' interests require that a winding up should be initiated immediately so that they will be paid their debts in full, or at least to a greater extent than if a winding up were deferred.

Up to the present the only point on which the courts have ruled in this situation is that the directors may present a winding up petition in the company's name only if the company's memorandum or articles of association expressly empower them to do so, because the power to petition is not implicit in the powers of management usually conferred on directors (*Re Emmadart Ltd* (1970)). The court has as yet given no indication of the way in which the directors' power should be exercised if it is so conferred, and whether directors should have regard exclusively to the interests of shareholders.

On the assumption that directors can legitimately take creditors' interests in general into account, it would seem that the interests of particular creditors can be given effect only if they coincide with shareholders' interests, or at least if there is no conflict between the two sets of interests. There is no British decision on this point, but it has been held in Australia that if directors are expressly appointed to represent sectional interests, such as those of debenture holders or of a particular group of shareholders or creditors, they are justified in acting to protect or promote those interests only if what they do is also for the benefit of the shareholders of the company as a whole (*Levin* v. *Clarke* (1962); *Re Broadcasting Station 2 G.B. (Proprietary) Ltd* (1964-5)). This probably also represents the position in English law.

The public interest

Again there is no explicit decision of an English Court about the extent to which directors may take into account the public interest or the interest of a section or sections of the community, such as consumers, in deciding how to exercise their powers. It would appear that here again such interests may legitimately be considered insofar as they do not conflict with the interests of the shareholders and the company as a whole. On this basis directors may justify making reasonable charitable donations and contributions to causes with a public element out of the company's assets.

The farthest the court has gone in this respect was in *Evans* v. *Brunner Mond and Co* (1921), where the court held that the directors of a major chemical company could lawfully make reasonable grants to universities and scientific institutions to support pure scientific research and to train scientists, even though there was no evidence that the expenditure would reflect benefits directly on the company. The directors' purpose in encouraging scientific research and training was to enable the chemical and pharmaceutical industries in the United Kingdom to keep abreast of innovations and developments in Europe and the United States, and the court held that this was sufficient. However, the court's insistence on a showing of long-term benefits to the industry would seem implicitly to require that the directors must also seek to protect or promote the interests of the company and its shareholders generally. It must therefore be concluded that directors cannot exercise their powers exclusively for the public benefit or in the public interest. Directors may have a social conscience, but only if it is in the interests of the company and its shareholders to do so.

4.03 The use of directors' powers for the proper purpose

In addition to acting in what they reasonably conceive to be the interests of the company and its shareholders as a whole, directors must exercise the powers vested in them by the company's memorandum or articles of association for the purposes for which the powers were conferred. If directors exercise their powers for other purposes, the decisions they take and any resulting transactions will be voidable by the company, and the directors will be liable to compensate the company for any loss it suffers as a result of their decisions being carried out.

Purpose expressed in the memorandum or articles

If the purpose for which a power is conferred on directors is expressed in the memorandum or articles of association, the use of that power for any other purpose is clearly an abuse of the directors' powers. For example, in *Re Bede Shipping Co. Ltd* (1917), the directors were empowered to refuse to register a transfer of shares in a private company if 'in their opinion it is contrary to the interests of the company that the transferee should be a member' of it. The directors were held to have misused their power of refusal when they had no personal objection to the proposed transferee of shares on the ground of character, associations with rival companies or interests which were inimical or conflicting with those of the company. The court held irrelevant the directors' objection that the transfer was to a nominee of the transferor, who retained beneficial ownership of the shares transferred. His purpose in vesting them in a nominee was to split his shareholding between several nominees so as to increase his voting power in general meeting. Likewise, in *Re Cameron's Coalbrook Steam Coal and Swansea and Lougher Rly Co., Bennett's case* (1854), directors who were empowered by the company's articles of association to refuse to register a transfer of shares if they considered it against the company's interests to do so, were held to have used their power for the wrong purpose when they exacted a substantial sum from the transferee as the price of agreeing to register the transfer of shares to him. The directors' abuse of the power was not cured by the fact that the directors intended to use the sum received to pay some of the company's debts.

Where purposes are not expressed

Most powers conferred on directors by a company's memorandum or articles of association are not accompanied by an explicit statement of the purpose or purposes for which the power may be used. The court must then ascertain from the context what the proper purposes were intended to be.

Directors' powers to issue unissued shares of a company are rarely accompanied by express statements in the company's memorandum or articles of the purpose for which shares may be issued. It was at one time thought that the only legitimate purpose which directors could seek to achieve by issuing unissued shares of the company was to raise money which the company needed for its business purposes. Consequently, it was held that an issue of shares made by directors to enable the directors and their associates to gain or retain voting control at general meetings was illegitimate, and could be rescinded by the company (*Fraser* v. *Whalley* (1864); *Piercy* v. *Mills & Co. Ltd* (1920)). It would seem in the light of more recent cases that this is too narrow a view, and that shares may properly be issued for other purposes as well, such as inducing creditors of the company or its debenture holders to accept shares in satisfaction of their claims against the company, to increase the proportionate interest in the company's share capital of another company with which it collaborates in operating its undertaking or from which it wishes to obtain business advantages, such as the preferential supply of raw materials or finished products.

On the other hand, the legitimate purposes for which shares may be issued are limited, even though the court has not attempted to enumerate such purposes exhaustively. In *Howard Smith Ltd* v. *Ampol Petroleum Ltd* (1974), it was held by the Judicial Committee of the Privy Council on appeal from Australia, that an issue of shares cannot be justified if the directors' purpose is to deprive a shareholder or group of shareholders of the voting control in general meetings of the company which they at present have, and to vest that control in a different shareholder or group of shareholders. This is particularly so when two shareholders or groups of shareholders have made concurrent competing takeover bids for the company, and the purpose of the directors in issuing further shares is to give control over general meetings to one of the contending parties, as happened in *Howard Smith Ltd* v. *Ampol Petroleum Ltd*.

This decision had been preceded by two English cases where the court had held that an issue of shares by directors of a company to existing shareholders or other persons who were of like mind with the directors in opposing a takeover bid for the company, was an abuse of the directors' powers to issue shares when their purpose was to ensure that, even if the bidder acquired the shares of all the other shareholders than the directors and their associates, he would still not have control of the company (*Hogg* v. *Cramphorn Ltd* (1967); *Bamford* v. *Bamford* (1970)).

A later decision confirmed the ruling in *Howard Smith Ltd* v. *Ampol Petroleum Ltd* that an issue of shares in the context of competing takeover bids so as to favour one of the bidders will be cancelled by the court (*Heron International Ltd* v. *Lord Grade and Associated Communication Corpn plc* (1983)). The court in that case ruled that in a competitive takeover bid situation, the only interests which directors can properly take into account when issuing further shares are those of the existing shareholders of the company, other than the competing bidders. This means effectively that if the company is the target of a takeover bid, the only purpose for which directors may issue shares while the bid is pending is to raise further capital to meet the company's business needs.

If there are no pending takeover bids, the directors' permissible discretion is wider. In Canada, for example it has been held that directors of a company which carried on a business of the same kind as one of the several businesses carried on by its majority shareholder, could properly issue shares to its other shareholders so as to reduce the majority shareholders' holding to less than a controlling one, and so prevent it from carrying out its intention of closing down the company's business (*Teck Corpn* v. *Millar* (1972)). This decision would probably be followed by a British court, and it is noteworthy that it did not offend the prohibition on directors taking control from a majority shareholder or group and vesting in it a new majority shareholder or group, because the shareholders to whom the new shares were issued acted independently and did not form a collaborating voting unit with the directors.

Nature of the proper purpose rule

The rule that directors must exercise the powers conferred on them for the proper purpose intended is not only more specific than the general underlying rule that directors must act in the interests of the company and its shareholders as a whole, but is also more objective than the general rule in two respects. The general rule is properly expressed as the requirement that directors must act in the way which they reasonably conceive to be in the interests of the company and its shareholders generally. The court interferes only if there is evidence of bad faith on the part of the directors, or if their decision is one which no reasonable board could have reached. The rule that directors must exercise their powers for the proper purposes involves the court in a more objective enquiry, namely, whether the proper purposes for which the directors may legitimately exercise their power include the purpose which the directors intended to achieve in the particular case.

Additionally, the proper purpose rule enables the court to catalogue the permissible purposes for which directors' different powers may each be used and to exclude any other purpose as improper, as the courts have done in the cases where directors have issued shares in a takeover situation. This is, of course, impossible in applying the general rule, when the court must decide whether the directors acted in good faith and in the interests of the shareholders as a whole on the particular facts of each case.

4.04 Is there a positive duty for directors to achieve fulfilment of the company's interests?

In all the cases so far considered, the question which the court has had to decide has been whether action taken by directors was taken by them in the interests of the company and its shareholders as a whole and for the proper purpose. If it was not, the court invalidated the directors' decision to take that action, or ordered the rescission of a transaction resulting from the decision, or compelled the restitution of any assets of the company disposed of because of the decision. The court has never given such remedies where directors have been inactive in pursuing opportunities open to the company on the supposition that they are under a positive duty to achieve the purposes for which the company was formed or to maximise its profits. It is certainly the function of directors to carry on the company's business successfully and to seek ways of increasing its profits, but the sanction envisaged by the court for the directors' failure to do this is not a judicial remedy, but the exercise by the shareholders of their right not to re-elect directors or their power, under the Companies Act 1985, to remove directors from office.

The reason for the courts' unwillingness to impose a positive management duty on directors is that the court will not involve itself in making decisions on questions of business policy or tactics, and this would be unavoidable if the courts were to judge the quality of directors' management performance. On the other hand, when the court is asked to judge the legitimacy of a particular act or series of acts by directors, it is not asked to make a business judgment, but to decide whether the directors acted in good faith, and whether they acted in what they reasonably saw as the best interests of the company and its shareholders, and whether they exercised their powers for the proper purpose for which the powers were given. These questions involve an examination of the factual circumstances and the motives with which the directors acted, but not the making of business judgments.

Although the court will not second guess directors' business judgments and will not impose a positive duty on directors to manage their companies efficiently and profitably, the court does compel directors who cause their company loss by their negligence to compensate it for the loss it suffers. Directors who are guilty of negligence causing loss commit a breach of their fiduciary or contractual duties to act with proper skill and care. These duties are considered in Chapter 5. It suffices at present to note that the enforcement of these duties does not involve the court in prescribing objective standards of adequate management performance. This would be necessary if there were a fiduciary duty imposed on directors to achieve the fulfilment of their companies' interests to the greatest possible extent. In a claim for compensation for directors' negligence the court instead judges whether the defendant directors have acted with the skill and care of which they are individually capable in the circumstances of the case.

DIRECTORS' INTERESTS IN THE COMPANY'S CONTRACTS

4.05 The rights of the company when its director has an interest

Despite the House of Lords ruling in an early case, *Aberdeen Rly Co* v. *Blaikie* (1854), later judicial decisions show that it is not necessarily a breach of a director's fiduciary duties for him to enter into a contract with his company, or to be interested in a contract with his company where the director's interest is derived through a third person, such as another company in which the director holds shares. If the contract is a fair one, for example, a contract by which the company acquires assets or services at the current market price, there is no conflict of interest on the part of the director, and if the contract is entered into for the purpose of the company's legitimate business, there is no breach of the director's duty to ensure that the transaction is for the company's benefit and in its interests.

If on the other hand, the contract is unfair, for example, because the price charged to the company for goods or services is excessive, or because the terms of the contract are disproportionately onerous to the company, it would appear that the director is guilty of a breach of duty if he allows the company to enter into it, either by voting for it at a board meeting or by not warning the board that the contract is unfair. There is no English authority to this effect, but there is ample American authority, which would probably be followed by an English court.

For example, in *Globe Woolen Co.* v. *Utica Gas and Electric Co.* (1918), it was held that a director of the plaintiff company, who was also a director of the defendant company, was guilty of a breach of fiduciary duty to the defendant when he failed to warn its board of directors that a proposed contract under which the defendant would supply electricity to the plaintiff, although apparently fair, would be operated by the plaintiff in a way which would yield the defendant no profit and would probably result in a loss. Had the contract been carried out, the court would have held the director liable to compensate the defendant company for its loss because of his failure to protect its interests.

Company's right to rescind

Although it may not be a breach of fiduciary duty for a director to enter into a contract with his company or to be interested in a contract entered into by his company with a third person, the company is entitled in equity to rescind the contract and to recover whatever consideration it has given to the other party (*Aberdeen Rly Co.* v. *Blaikie* (1854); *North West Transportation Co.* v. *Beatty* (1887)). This is so, even though the terms of the contract are fair to the company. The company is given the right to rescind because of the possibility, not the certainty, that it may have been unduly influenced by the director and thereby induced to enter into a contract which it would not have entered into if the director had not been a member of its board. Nevertheless, if the company is to exercise its right to rescind the contract, it is essential that the company should be able to restore the consideration given by the other party in substantially the same form as before the contract was made (*Burland* v. *Earle* (1902); *Armstrong* v. *Jackson* (1917)). Furthermore, if the contract was made with a third person, such as another company, and the director had an interest in that person, such as holding shares in it, the company may rescind only if the third person was aware of the director's interest at the time the contract was made (*Transvaal Lands Co.* v. *New Belgium (Transvaal) Land and Development Co.* (1914)).

The fairness or otherwise of the contract is not a relevant matter in deciding whether the company may rescind a contract, and the company may rescind even though the contract is perfectly fair in respect of its terms and the consequences it will entail. This clearly shows that the basis of the company's right to rescind is not a breach of fiduciary duty by any of its directors, and that equity gives the company the right to rescind because of the existence of the director's interest, and not because of the abuse of his position.

Moreover, it has been held by the Judicial Committee of the Privy Council in *Burland* v. *Earle* that the company cannot recover any profit obtained by the director from the contract without first rescinding it, and so if the company for any reason cannot rescind, it cannot compel the director to account to it for the profit he has obtained. The inability of the company to recover profits without rescinding, of course, assumes that the director has not been guilty of a breach of his fiduciary duties. If he has done so, by failing to warn the board of the company that the contract is unfair to it (if that is so), or by procuring the contract simply in order to make a personal profit, the director will be accountable for the profit he has obtained, whether the company rescinds the contract or not.

The right of a company to rescind a contract because one or more of its directors are interested in it can be waived or renounced by the company. This may be done by the shareholders passing an ordinary resolution in general meeting authorising the contract before it is made or affirming it afterwards, but it is essential that the shareholders should be made aware of the nature and extent of the director's interest in the contract before the ordinary resolution is passed (*Kaye* v. *Croydon Tramways Co.* (1898); *Tiessen* v. *Henderson* (1899)). On the other hand, an interested director can vote for the authorisation or affirmation of the contract in his capacity as a shareholder, and this is so even if he and his associates hold sufficient shares to ensure that the resolution affirming the contract will be passed (*North West Transportation Co. Ltd* v. *Beatty* (1887)). However, if the contract is unfair to the company, so that the affirmation of the contract by a resolution procured by the interested director's controlling votes would be inequitable to the minority shareholders of the company, the court will disregard any resolution affirming the contract and will treat it as rescinded at the instance of the minority shareholders (*Cook* v. *Deeks* (1916)). The board of directors has no power to waive or renounce the right of the company to rescind a contract in which a director is interested, whether the contract is fair or unfair to the company, and such a power is not delegated to the board by a provision in the company's articles that the board may exercise all the powers of the company which are not vested on its shareholders in general meeting.

The company may alternatively renounce its right to rescind a contract in which one or more of its directors is interested by the provisions of the company's memorandum or articles of association. It is very common for articles of association to permit directors to contract with their companies, or to be interested in contracts to which their companies are parties. The standard form of articles of association in Table A of the regulations made under the Companies Act 1985 contains such a provision, and also provides that directors may hold other remunerated offices under the company or under other companies in which that company is interested (e.g. other companies in the same group), and that directors may retain all profits or gains obtained under such contracts (Companies (Tables A to F) Regulations 1985, Schedule, Table A, articles 85 and 86). The effect of provisions like those in Table A is that a contract made with a director or in which he is interested is not subject to rescission by the company, but articles of association, like Table A, usually make the validation of such contracts conditional on the director disclosing to the board of directors the nature and extent of his interests.

The fact that contracts in which a director is interested can be validated by the memorandum or articles of the company itself shows that the making of such a contract or the existence of a director's interest in it does not amount to a breach of the director's fiduciary duties. If it did, the provision in the memorandum or articles would be void under the Companies Act 1985, section 310(1), which invalidates any contractual provision which exempts a director from liability for breach of duty. However, the memorandum or articles cannot relieve a director from liability for a breach of his fiduciary duties by the director inducing or permitting his company to enter into a contract which is unfair or harmful to it without warning the board of that fact. If such a contract is made with the director, or is made with a third person who is aware of the director's breach of duty, the company can rescind the contract and claim compensation from the director for any loss it sustains from his breach of duty. This is so even though the company's memorandum or articles permit directors to contract with the company or to be interested in contracts made with it.

4.06 Directors' statutory obligations

Notification of interests

The equitable rule enabling a company to rescind contracts in which its directors are interested is supplemented by two statutory provisions. The first obliges a director who has a direct or indirect interest in a contract or proposed contract with his company, or in a transaction or arrangement entered into or proposed to be entered into with it, to disclose the nature of his interest at the first board meeting at which the proposed contract, transaction or arrangement is considered, or if his interest did not then exist, to disclose it at the first board meeting held after his interest arises, whether the contract, transaction or arrangement has by then been entered into or is still only a proposal (Companies Act 1985, section 317(2) and (5)). There is also a more general obligation imposed on a director to disclose his interest in a contract, transaction or arrangement in all cases, and this covers contracts etc. which are not made or approved by the board, but are entered into by individual directors or executives of the company under powers delegated to them by the board. Presumably disclosure must be made by the interested director at the first board meeting after his interest arises (section 317(1) and (5)).

If a director has an indirect interest in all contracts, transactions and arrangements made by the company of which he is a director with another company or partnership of which he is a member, or if a director has an interest in a contract etc. made by the company of which he is a director with a person to whom he is connected in the statutory sense (defined by the Companies Act 1985, section 346), the director may give a general notice in writing to the board of the company of which he is a director (which he must ensure is read out at a board meeting) that he is to be regarded as interested in all contracts, transactions and arrangements thereafter made by the company with such a company, firm or person (section 317(3) and (4)). The failure of a director to give notice to the board of his direct or indirect interest when he is required to do so is a criminal offence punishable by a fine (section 317(7)), but the company cannot rescind a contract, transaction or arrangement simply because a director has not complied with the statutory disclosure requirement, whatever its rights to rescind in equity may be (*Hely-Hutchinson* v. *Brayhead Ltd* (1968)). The statutory disclosure requirements applies also to shadow directors (that is, persons in accordance with whose directions or instructions the directors of the company are accustomed to act (section 741(2)), and notification of their interests must be given in writing to the board of directors.

Approval by general meetings

By the second statutory provision, if a company is to enter into a contract or arrangement with a director of the company or of its parent company, or a person connected with such a director in one of the ways set out in the Companies Act 1985, section 346, and under the contract or arrangement the director or person connected with him on the one hand or the company on the other is to acquire or dispose of assets (other than cash) with a value exceeding 10 per cent of the net assets of the company as shown by its latest balance sheet laid before a general meeting or £50,000 (whichever is less), the proposed contract must be approved by an ordinary resolution of a general meeting before it is entered into (Companies Act 1985, section 320(1) and (2)). If the contract or arrangement is to be made with a director of the company's parent company or a person connected with him, it must also be approved by a general meeting of that company (section 320(1) and (2)).

If a contract or arrangement is entered into by a company without the requisite shareholder approval or approvals being first obtained, the company may rescind the contract and recover the assets or payment which it transferred or made under it (section 322(1)). The company cannot do this, however, if the requisite shareholder approval or approvals are forthcoming within a reasonable period after the contract or arrangement is made and before the company rescinds the contract, or if restitution of any money or asset which has been paid or transferred under the contract is no longer possible, or if the company has already been indemnified for any loss or damage which it has suffered in consequence of the contract or arrangement, or if a third person has acquired an interest in assets which are comprised in the contract or arrangement and the third person acted in good faith without knowledge of the contravention (section 322(1) and (2)).

Furthermore, if the director or the person connected with him who entered into the contract or arrangement did so without the requisite approval or approvals first being obtained, he is accountable to the company for any profit or gain he has made from the transaction (for example, by reselling assets acquired from the company at a profit). The director or person connected with him and all other directors of the company are liable to indemnify the company for any loss or damage it suffers as a result of the transaction (section 322(3)). The statutory provision applies to shadow directors in the same way as it applies to directors (section 320(3)).

The statutory provision requiring shareholder approval for certain transactions with directors enacts in statutory form the rules of equity governing acquisitions and disposals of assets between companies and their directors with the addition of the remedies which equity would give if the director concerned were guilty of a breach of fiduciary duty. The statutory provision is wider than the rules of equity, however, in that the company can recover any profit which is made by the other party and any loss which it suffers without showing that the contract was unfair. Moreover, the company can exercise its rights and remedies not only against its directors, but also against persons who are connected with a director. Furthermore, the company's memorandum or articles or a director's service contract cannot dispense with shareholder approval of an acquisition or disposal of assets in situations where the Companies Act 1985 requires it. A provision in the memorandum or articles that the contract for the acquisition or disposal shall be valid and enforceable even if the shareholders do not approve it, or that the company may not rescind the contract or recover any loss which it suffers or any profits which the director or connected person makes as a result of the contract, will be void as regards contracts and arrangements for which approval is required by the Act.

Chapter 5

Directors' Duties of Skill and Care

Directors owe a fiduciary duty in equity to their companies and probably also a duty at common law to exercise their powers and functions as directors with proper care and appropriate skill so as not to cause the company loss by their failure to do so.

THE STANDARD OF CARE AND SKILL

5.01 The personal character of the duty of care and skill

The Chancery Court has always imposed a duty to act with caution and prudence on fiduciaries. During the eighteenth century a beginning was made on defining the level of caution and prudence required of trustees. Most trustees at that time were individuals who acted gratuitously out of a sense of family or moral obligation, and were consequently required by equity to exhibit no higher level of foresight or punctiliousness in administering a trust than they would be expected to show in dealing with their own personal affairs.

When during the early nineteenth century this duty of care was extended first to agents and later to company directors, the requisite standard of conduct was the same, with the qualification in the case of a remunerated agent, that he was also expected to exhibit the standard of skill and care which is expected of a competent practitioner in his field. This extension of the original fiduciary duty of caution and prudence was largely the result of equity adopting the standard imposed on paid commercial agents by the common law courts, which implied appropriate terms into the agents' contracts of employment. There was no similar development at common law in respect of company directors. This was, first, because until late in the nineteenth century it was uncommon for directors to enter into service contracts which would be subject to the common law. Secondly, it would have been almost impossible for the common law to apply a professional standard of skill and care to directors, who could not be assigned to a recognised category of practitioners like brokers, shipping and forwarding agents and solicitors and accountants.

As a result of the common law courts not being called on to deal with alleged negligence by directors, the rules relating to the skill and care expected of directors have been developed wholly in equity without any significant influence from the common law. The equitable rules have been based on those applied to trustees, where the question whether the defendant has failed to measure up to the degree of caution and prudence expected of him is based on the defendant's own capabilities and the degree of caution and skill which he can be expected to exhibit in dealing with his own affairs, and not upon objective professional standards.

Judicial dicta

In one of the earliest cases decided by the House of Lords in which directors' liability for negligence was in issue, *Overend Gurney & Co. v. Gibb* (1872), the directors of a company formed to take over a private bank were acquitted of negligence. This was so even though the directors failed to investigate the value of the bank's assets and the extent of its liabilities, and even though they agreed that the newly formed company should pay £500,000 for the bank's goodwill in addition to the agreed valuation of its net tangible assets, although, as the directors knew, the bank had insufficient realisable assets to meet its obligations as they fell due and was, in fact, insolvent. The Lord Chancellor, Lord Hatherley, held (at page 487 of the report) that the directors could only be held liable to their company if they exceeded the powers conferred on them by the company's memorandum and articles of association in purchasing the bank's undertaking (which clearly they did not), or if:

> '... they were cognisant of the circumstances of such a character, so plain, so manifest, and so simple of appreciation, that no men with any degree of prudence, acting on their own behalf, would have entered into such a transaction as they entered into... Was the acquiring of that subject matter [the business of the private bank] with the amount of knowledge which the directors had attained an instance of *crassa negligentia*?'

In a later case, *Lagunas Nitrate Co. v. Lagunas Syndicate* (1899), directors of a company formed to purchase a nitrate mining undertaking in Chile were acquitted of negligence in overvaluing it as a going concern. Lindley MR said (at page 435 of the report):

'If directors act within their powers, if they act with such care as is reasonably to be expected of them, having regard to their knowledge and experience, and if they act honestly for the benefit of the company they represent, they discharge both their equitable as well as their legal duty to the company... The amount of care to be taken is difficult to define; but it is plain that directors are not liable for all the mistakes they may make, although if they had taken more care they might have avoided them... Their negligence must not be the omission to take all possible care; it must be much more blameable than that; it must be in a business sense culpable and gross.'

Finally, in *Re City Equitable Fire Insurance Co.* (1925), directors of an insurance company were found not to have been negligent in failing to supervise the company's managing director closely and to check on the accuracy of his periodical reports to the board and on the existence and security of the company's investments, which had been depleted by his fraud. Romer J confirmed what Lindley MR had said a quarter of a century earlier and observed (at page 428 of the report):

'A director need not exhibit in the performance of his duties a greater degree of skill than may reasonably be expected from a person of his knowledge and experience... In respect of his duties that, having regard to the exigencies of business and the articles of association, may properly be left to some other official, a director is, in the absence of grounds for suspicion, justified in trusting that official to perform such duties honestly.'

The absence of a professional standard

In all cases where allegations of negligence have been made against directors, the court's insistence on framing their duties in the circumstances of the case by reference to their own personal abilities and qualifications means that in British law there is no objective standard of skill and care which is applicable to all directors. There is, instead, only a general principle whose application in each case calls for a personal assessment of the individual director. There is a sound reason for this, because directors do not form an homogeneous category and they require different degrees of skill and application to do their work efficiently, depending on the size of the company they serve, the complexity of its operations, the form of its management structure (whether a board of executive directors or a managing director assisted by full-time directors who individually run departments or sectors of the company's business and consult and collaborate only on major matters) and the relative importance to the company of the transactions in respect of which negligence is alleged.

An attempt to establish general standards of conduct for all directors would inevitably fail, and the most the courts can do in seeking to establish objective criteria is to require a minimum degree of specialised competence from directors whose recognised qualifications or experience in the company's area of business make it reasonable to expect them to exhibit a certain level of professional or practical skill. This is a less exacting criterion than the standard of performance expected of a professionally qualified practitioner, namely the level attainable by the average competent practitioner in his field. It is clear from the decided cases, nevertheless, that the less exacting standard is the proper one to apply to directors. This accords with the observations of Neville J in *Re Brazilian Rubber Plantations and Estates Ltd* (1911), where he said (at page 437 of the report):

> 'A director's duty has been laid down as requiring him to act with such care as is reasonably to be expected of him, having regard to his knowledge and experience. He is, I think, not bound to bring any special qualifications to his office. He may undertake the management of a rubber company in complete ignorance of everything connected with rubber, without incurring responsibility for the mistakes which may result from such ignorance; while if he is acquainted with the rubber business, he must give the company the advantage of his knowledge when transacting the company's business. He is not, I think, bound to take any definite part in the conduct of the company's business, but so far as he does undertake it he must use reasonable care in its despatch.'

5.02 Instances of the duty to exercise care and skill

An examination of the facts of cases decided by the courts where it has been alleged that directors have been guilty of negligence helps little toward deciding whether the court would give the same or a similar decision in a new case where the facts were comparable. Consequently, decided cases in this field are useful only as illustrations of the general level of skill or care which the court considers blameworthy or acceptable, and not as indicative of the decision the court would give in a case involving similar facts or where the defendants were directors with similar backgrounds or personal histories.

Another factor which has to be borne in mind is that most of the cases on directors' negligence were decided before the First World War, when most directors served on a part-time basis and their principle function was to attend and participate in board meetings where policy decisions were made, but items connected with the day-to-day management of the company's business were rarely reported or discussed. Such directors were not in daily contact with the company's business, and did not and were not expected to acquaint themselves with the details of running it. They had to depend to a large extent on the honesty and competence of the company's managers and senior executives.

The situation is little different today with regard to part-time directors of large public companies. Nevertheless, such directors do now expect to be supplied with far more detailed information than their predecessors about the company's business operations, its turnover, gross profits, profit margins, projections of future turnover and profits and development plans. On the other hand, the typical full-time director of a public or private company is radically different from his nineteenth century counterpart. This is because of the tendency for a modern full-time director to pursue a career with one company or group of companies, and because in consequence his access to current information about the company's business and day-to-day affairs is immediate and comprehensive. Because he is better equipped to pursue business opportunities on behalf of the company and far better informed about current matters than his nineteenth century counterpart, it would be surprising if the courts did not require him to show a higher level of attention, inquisitiveness and perception and to react more speedily and decisively to business situations than the case law of the nineteenth century would suggest is adequate.

Because most negligence actions brought against directors in the nineteenth and early twentieth centuries failed, there has been a marked disinclination on the part of shareholders to launch such actions in more recent years. The prospects of success are seen as being poor at the outset, and the tendency in the few actions which have been brought has been to present what are really negligence claims as involving elements of deliberateness, self-seeking or bad faith on the part of directors so as to qualify as breaches of the fiduciary duty imposed on directors to act in the interests of their shareholders as a whole or to use their powers for the proper purpose. The normal response of shareholders to incompetent management, however, has been to sell their shares for what they can get rather than to hazard litigation.

Illustrative decisions

In the first of three judicial decisions already cited above, the House of Lords held that directors were not guilty of negligence when they permitted their company to purchase for a substantial price the assets and undertaking of a private bank, the value of whose assets was highly questionable, and which, as the directors knew, was probably insolvent (*Overend and Gurney Co. v. Gibb* (1872)). In another case, the Court of Appeal dismissed a charge of negligence made against directors who used the company's resources to purchase a mining undertaking which they knew had been misdescribed in the contract of sale as being more extensive and valuable than it really was (*Lagunas Nitrate Co. v. Lagunas Syndicate* (1899)).

In a third case, a judge of first instance held that directors were not guilty of negligence when they accepted without question a false and fraudulent report on the extent and output of a rubber plantation prepared by a member of the syndicate which sold it to the company, and when the directors raised share capital from the public by publishing a prospectus which embodied the statements of fact contained in the report without mentioning its authorship (*Re Brazilian Rubber Plantations and Estates Ltd* (1911)). Furthermore, directors have been held not to be negligent when they made a loan out of the company's funds without ensuring that the security which the borrower had agreed to give had in fact been created (*Re New Mashonaland Exploration Co.* (1892)).

In a more recent case, however, Ungoed-Thomas J held that directors had acted negligently when they released company funds to pay a debt and to purchase assets without verifying that the company owed the debt and that the assets had been, or were being, transferred to the company (*Selangor United Rubber Estates Ltd v. Cradock (No.3)* (1968)).

Directors who participate in transactions in the company's name without making enquiries to ensure that the transactions are for the purpose of the company's business and that they have been duly authorised by board resolutions, have been held guilty of negligence. This is so even if a defendant director believes that he is bound to assent to the transaction because his fellow directors want it, or if the director joins in the transaction under protest and the transaction would have been carried out by the other directors in any case (*Land Credit Co. of Ireland v. Lord Fermoy* (1869); *Joint Stock Discount Co. v.*

Brown (1869); *Ramskill* v. *Edwards* (1885)). Directors have also been held liable for negligence when they allowed one of their number to manage a part of the company's business without a board resolution being properly passed for this purpose (*Re City Equitable Fire Insurance Co. Ltd* (1925)).

On the other hand, it was held not to be negligence for directors to delegate their power to manage the company to a properly appointed managing director whose periodic reports and accounts they accepted without checking, with the result that the managing director was able to dispose of the company's investments for his own purposes (*Dovey* v. *Cory* (1901); *Re City Equitable Fire Insurance Co. Ltd* (1925)). These last two cases were decided on the ground that directors may trust managing directors, senior executives and subordinate employees of the company to carry out their functions honestly and competently, unless the directors know or have good reason to suspect that they are not honest or competent. The close supervision of fellow directors or the staff of the company is not a duty of a director, and he is under a duty to supervise them only if the director knows that there is cause for concern. Moreover, in those circumstances it is the director's duty to inform the shareholders of any derelictions of duty he discovers on the part of his fellow directors, and it is not sufficient for him to report the matter to the board or to rest content with a complaint to it (*Joint Discount Co.* v. *Brown* (1869)).

Finally, the court has held that a director is not bound to attend all board meetings or to devote his whole time and attention to the company's affairs, unless his service contract expressly requires him to do so. Consequently, it is not negligent for a director to fail to ascertain what business has been transacted at board meetings which he does not attend, or to ensure that business was legitimate and in the company's interests (*Re Denham & Co.* (1883); *Re City Equitable Fire Insurance Co.* (1925)).

5.03 A comparison of American case law

The American courts have imposed a heavier duty of skill and care on directors than the English courts have done. Probably the tendency of American courts to find that a director has acted without proper care and skill on the facts of a particular case where the English courts would not have done so is indicative of the direction in which the English courts may move in the future, particularly when the director is a full-time director or if he actively participates in day-to-day management.

The American courts have expressed directors' duties of care and skill in two different ways, one adopting a stricter rule than English law and the other much the same kind of rule as the English courts have enunciated. The stricter rule was laid down in *Hun* v. *Carey* (1880), where a New York court held that directors of a small banking company which held deposits of some $70,000 and had capital and reserves of some $25,000, were guilty of negligence in contracting for the erection of an imposing bank building costing approximately $100,000, and were consequently liable in the bank's insolvency for the loss they caused it by entering into this commitment. The court held (at page 83 of the report) that:

'... one who voluntarily takes the position of director, and invites confidence in that relationship, undertakes, like a mandatory [an agent] with those whom he represents or for whom he acts, that he possesses at least ordinary knowledge and skill, and that he will bring them to bear in the discharge of his duties... [The directors' conduct] was not a mere error of judgment... it was a case of improvidence, of reckless unreasonable extravagance, in which [the directors] failed in that measure of reasonable prudence, care and skill which the law requires.'

On the other hand, in *Barnes* v. *Andrews* (1924), where directors who had failed to ensure that their company, a manufacturer of car components, had established an efficient production system before commencing production, and who caused it loss by paying wages, salaries and general overheads which were not matched by output, Learned Hand J observed (at page 630 of the report):

'I cannot agree with the language of *Hun* v. *Carey* that in effect [a director gives] an implied warranty of any special fitness [for his position]. Directors are not specialists, like lawyers or doctors. They must have good sense; perhaps they must have an acquaintance with affairs; but they need not – indeed perhaps they should not – have any technical talent. They are the general advisers of the business, and if they faithfully give such ability as they have to their charge, it would not be lawful to hold them liable.'

Learned Hand J was here speaking of ordinary directors, and not full-time directors with service contracts or the American equivalent of the British managing director – the president of an American company.

Negligence by bank directors

The American cases, whichever rule the courts have applied, reflect the more onerous duty of care and skill in fact imposed on directors by American law. This is particularly so in cases where bank directors have been the defendants.

In *Litwin* v. *Allen* (1940), it was held that directors of a bank who accommodated a corporate customer which had exhausted its borrowing powers, were guilty of negligence when they entered into a sale and repurchase arrangement by which the corporate customer sold investments to the bank at the current market price and took an option to repurchase the investments at the end of the accommodation period. The option entitled the customer to repurchase the investments at the price at which he sold them plus interest, and the bank's only remuneration for providing the accommodation was a modest commission. The bank's risk lay in the certainty that the customer would not exercise his repurchase option if the market price of the investments fell, which in fact happened, and the fact that the bank entered into a second agreement with its own subsidiary under which the subsidiary undertook to purchase the investments at the original sale price if the customer did not exercise its repurchase option, was held to be no defence.

In *Atherton* v. *Anderson* (1938), bank directors were held guilty of negligence in failing to check on large loans made to the bank's president, many of which were beyond the powers of the bank to make by the terms of its constitution. They were also held negligent in appointing an auditor who was nominated by the president and paid a salary decided on by the president. The auditor, not wholly surprisingly, collaborated with the president in concealing from the directors the true state of the bank's loan portfolio. Similarly, in *Francis* v. *United Jersey Bank* (1981), an inactive bank director was similarly held negligent in leaving the whole management of the bank to his co-director without supervision, when the co-director over an extended period misappropriated $10 million of the bank's funds.

Directors of non-banking companies

The duty to exhibit care and skill imposed by the American courts on directors of companies other than banks has been somewhat lighter, but nevertheless heavier than the duty exacted by the English courts.

A director who failed persistently to attend board meetings was held liable to compensate the company when decisions were taken in his absence to employ the company's assets for improper purposes.

Because of his persistent absence from board meetings, he failed to discover that this had happened. It was held to be no defence in the circumstances that the director resided a considerable distance from where board meetings were held, or that he was elderly and infirm (*Dinsmore* v. *Jacobson* (1928); *Gamble* v. *Brown* (1929)). In *Kavanaugh* v. *Commonwealth Trust Co.* (1918), directors of an investment trust company were held liable for losses caused by the president of the company making improvident investments in companies in which he was interested, when the directors left the investment of the company's funds to the president's unfettered discretion and exercised no supervision over him.

On the other hand, in *Graham* v. *Allis-Chalmers Manufacturing Co.* (1963), directors of a manufacturing company were held not liable to indemnify the company against damages it had to pay to third parties because of illegal price-fixing agreements entered into by the company's senior executive, when there was no evidence either that the directors knew or had reason to believe that such arrangements had been made, or that they were negligent in appointing the senior executive.

Finally, in *Burt* v. *Irvine Co.* (1965), a director was held to have been negligent when he did not check the accuracy of accounting calculations and valuations of the company's assets and liabilities made by the other directors for the purpose of determining the price at which the company would repurchase their shares, and the repurchase was consequently made at an excessive price.

A comparison of the English and the American case law on the question of the duty of care and skill imposed on directors is interesting, not only because of the greater strictness of the American courts in applying rules which are similar in principle to the English ones, but also because of the different origins of the principle in the two systems. The English rules originated in the fiduciary obligations imposed on directors, and were shaped by equity on lines analogous to the duties imposed on trustees. The American rules governing directors' liability for negligence have never been considered part of the law governing trusts. They have always been treated as an application of the common law rules governing agent's implied contractual duties of skill and care and the liability in tort of persons who undertake to provide services, whether under a contract or not, if they cause loss by their negligence.

There can be no doubt that the standard of care called for by the common law of negligence has become stricter in recent years. Since the courts have now ruled that duties of care in contract and tort can co-exist, so that a defendant who has entered into a contract to provide services can now be made liable under both heads, the way has been open to the courts to impose heavier duties of skill and care on directors for negligence than the rules of equity have done in the past.

There are signs that this is already happening. In *Dorchester Finance Co. Ltd* v. *Stebbings* (1977), unreported but summarised in (1980) 1 *Company Lawyer* 38, Foster J held that two directors of a moneylending company who were chartered accountants had been negligent in leaving the negotiation of loans wholly to the discretion of the third, professionally unqualified, director without supervision, and also in drawing cheques on the company's account to make loans without enquiring for what purpose the loans were made, what security (if any) was taken and what were the terms for repayment of the loans.

The duties of care and skill exacted of accountants and auditors have been sharply increased in recent years by the court's more rigorous enforcement of their obligations in contract and in tort. A similar development could follow with regard to directors' duties without the general rules expressing those duties being changed, but simply by the courts adopting the approach of the modern common law, instead of equity, in enforcing directors' duties more strictly on the facts of individual cases.

Chapter 6

The Termination and Discharge of Directors' Duties

THE TERMINATION OF FIDUCIARY AND OTHER DUTIES

6.01 When directors cease to be subject to fiduciary duties

A director's fiduciary duties toward his company come to an end when he ceases to be a director. He then no longer has any legal power to influence the conduct of the company's affairs and the transactions it enters into, and the corollary of this is that he ceases to owe it the duties of a director in connection with the future conduct of its affairs.

It may be, however, that a former director still in fact controls or, at least, influences decisions of the board, and he may be a person 'in accordance with whose directions or instructions the directors of the company are accustomed to act', and so qualify as a shadow director (Companies Act 1985, section 741(2)). In that case certain statutory obligations, prohibitions and restrictions will continue to apply to the former director under the Companies Act 1985, but the fiduciary duties imposed by the rules of equity will not. There are various ways, nevertheless, in which a former director may continue to be under liabilities for breach of fiduciary duties to the company on whose board he formerly served.

Initiation of breach of duty

If a director makes preliminary arrangements to commit a breach of fiduciary duty while he is still a director and consummates the breach after resigning his directorship, he remains accountable to the company for any profit he obtains from the transaction or series of transactions taken as a whole.

In *Cranleigh Precision Engineering Ltd* v. *Bryant* (1964), in the course of his work in designing the company's products, a director discovered the existence of a patent which impeded the company from adding a refinement to its products so as to make them more marketable. He thereupon resigned his directorship, purchased the patent from its owner and formed a new company controlled by himself to manufacture the product with the addition of the patented refinement. The director was held accountable to the original company for the resulting profit. Similarly, in *Industrial Development Consultants Ltd* v. *Cooley* (1972), a managing director negotiated a personal contract to do work for a public body of the same nature as his company undertook. The director then fraudulently induced the board of the company to accept his resignation of his managing directorship before the normal expiration of his service contract, and after he ceased to be a director carried out work for the public body under the contract he had negotiated. Roskill J held that the former managing director was accountable to the company for the profit he made by carrying out the contract for the public body after his resignation took effect, because he had commenced to carry out his scheme to obtain a profit illicitly before his resignation, and the fact that the profit was earned afterwards was immaterial.

On the other hand, it was held in *Nordisk Insulinlaboratorium* v. *Gorgate Products Ltd* (1953), that an agent is not accountable to his former principal for a profit made after his agency has terminated (in that case by the outbreak of war) when the profit is obtained by the agent exploiting a business opportunity which arises after the termination of the agency. The fact that the agent avails himself of the opportunity by relying on non-confidential information which he obtained during the agency was held not to affect his immunity. There have been no similar cases affecting directors, but the rule would undoubtedly be the same for them. It would protect them from liability, however, only if no part of the acts done by them which could constitute a breach of fiduciary duty if they had remained directors was done by them before they ceased to be directors.

Cessation of directorship

A director's fiduciary duties continue right up to the time when he ceases to be a director of the company, and his duties do not terminate simply because steps are taken to bring his directorship to an end. For example, in *Thomas Marshall (Exports) Ltd* v. *Guinlé* (1979), it was held that a director who wrongfully repudiates his service contract does not terminate it automatically, but merely gives the company the right to terminate it if the company wishes. Until the company exercises its right of termination, the director remains bound by the terms of the contract and by his fiduciary duties. On the other hand, if a director's service contract is terminated by the occurrence of an event which by the terms of the contract causes its automatic termination (for example, the failure of a director to attend board meetings held during a certain period of time, or the failure of the director to resign when called on to do so by the board), or if the director's service contract is terminated by law (for example, by the court ordering the company to be wound up or appointing a receiver of the company's assets on the application of its debenture holders, or by the court making an order disqualifying the director from being a director of any company without leave of the court), the director ceases to hold office immediately and his fiduciary duties terminate forthwith (*Reid* v. *Explosives Co.* (1887); *Measures Brothers Ltd* v. *Measures* (1910)).

6.02 Confidential information

Although a director's fiduciary duties come to an end on the termination of his appointment, he remains under an equitable obligation not to disclose or use for his own or a third person's benefit any confidential information which he obtained while he was a director. This obligation terminates only when the company releases him from it or when the information is published or becomes generally known (*Morison* v. *Moat* (1851); *Merryweather* v. *Moore* (1892); *Robb* v. *Green* (1895)).

This duty is quite independent of the director's fiduciary duties, and extends to any person to whom unpublished information is communicated confidentially, or by whom it is obtained while a relationship of confidence exists with the originator of the information or the person entitled to the benefit of it. The duty terminates, not with the ending of the confidential relationship, but with the publication of the information. If this occurs only after the confidential relationship has ended, for example, by a director resigning or being dismissed, the person who has obtained the information confidentially remains bound in the meantime by the duty not to disclose or use it for an unauthorised purpose (*Franchi* v. *Franchi* (1967)).

6.03 Insider dealing

The criminal offences created by the Company Securities (Insider Dealing) Act 1985 apply to the use or communication or use of unpublished price-sensitive information in respect of securities listed or dealt in on a recognised stock exchange or in respect of advertised securities dealt in on the 'over the counter' market. These offences were dealt with in detail in Chapter 3. They are committed when the information is used or communicated by a person who is, or has within the preceding six months, been connected with the company. A director is treated as connected with the company of which he is a director and all other companies in the same group (sections 1, 4 and 9).

The definition of 'connected' is used only for the purpose of the criminal offences created by the Act. Consequently, a director who has ceased to hold office for more than six months is no longer a person connected with the company by reason of his directorship, even though the price-sensitive information is still unpublished and is protected by the confidentiality rule of the civil law. Because of this the use or communication by him of unpublished price-sensitive information after that period has elapsed is no longer a criminal offence, nor is the use of such information by a person to whom he communicates it after that time.

EXONERATION PROVISIONS IN A COMPANY'S CONSTITUTION

6.04 Legality of exoneration provisions

Before the Companies Act 1928 was enacted, provisions in a director's service contract or in the memorandum or articles of association of the company of which he was a director which exonerated him from liability for breaches of duty as a director, or entitled him to an indemnity from the company against such liability, were valid, and could be relied upon by a director who had breached any of his fiduciary or statutory obligations. The only exception was where the director was guilty of fraud or acted wilfully, knowing that he was committing a breach of duty, or reckless whether he was doing so or not (*Re Brazilian Rubber Plantations and Estates Ltd* (1911); *Re City Equitable Fire Insurance Co. Ltd* (1925))

6.05 Invalidity of exoneration provisions

By the Companies Act 1985, section 310(1) and (2) (re-enacting the Companies Act 1928, section 78), however, no provision contained in any contract or in the company's articles of association (or seemingly in its memorandum) can now validly exempt or indemnify any officer (including a director, manager or secretary (section 744), or an auditor of the company from 'any liability which by virtue of any rule of law would otherwise attach to him in respect of any negligence, default, breach of duty or breach of trust of which he may be guilty in relation to the company'; nor can any such provision validly entitle him to be indemnified against any such liability. Consequently, a director is answerable and accountable for all his breaches of fiduciary or other duties and also for all breaches by him of the Companies Act 1985, which make him liable to the company. Any constitutional or contractual attempt to exonerate him is void.

The statutory invalidation of exoneration clauses has never been subject to judicial interpretation, but it is generally accepted that the statute cannot be evaded by specifying exhaustively in a director's service contract or in the company's articles of association the duties which a director shall be under and ensuring that the specified duties are less onerous than those imposed by law. It is clear that the duties inescapably imposed on a director are those defined by the general law, and whilst those duties may be increased by the terms of the company's articles or a director's service contract, they cannot be diminished. Because of this, it would seem that a resolution passed by the shareholders in general meeting relieving a director from any of his fiduciary or statutory duties in the future would be void, because the articles themselves cannot entitle a director to commit breaches of duty with impunity, and so a resolution passed under the articles could not do so either.

6.06 Insurance against directors' liability

Some concern has been voiced as to whether the statutory invalidation of exoneration clauses also invalidates insurance policies which companies or directors take out to cover liabilities incurred by a director if he commits breaches of his duties. Probably the section does not affect insurance policies, even though they are contracts of indemnity. This must certainly be so if the company takes out insurance for its own protection against loss caused to it by its directors' breaches of duty.

The invalidation by the statutory provision of indemnity clauses which would, apart from the statute, be effective to prevent the company from suing a director for breach of duty is intended to cover clauses which have the same effect as exoneration clauses. The purpose of the enactment is to prevent directors from relying on provisions which purport to exonerate them from liability, whether expressed directly or indirectly by placing an obligation on the company to refund to the director the amount of damages, compensation or costs which the director would be liable to pay to the company under the general law. A true indemnity contract is one by which a third person agrees to compensate the director for the loss he suffers by having to make good his liability to the company, and this is precisely what an insurance policy against liability taken out by a director is. Insurance cover obtained by a director would therefore appear to be outside the statutory invalidation, and its validity would appear to be subject only to the general rule of insurance law that a person cannot insure against his own wilful or fraudulent wrongdoing. It would also seem that a policy taken out by a director is not invalidated by the fact that the company pays or agrees to pay the premiums under the policy. The company does not thereby agree to indemnify the director against his liability to it, but merely to meet the expense of procuring an undertaking from a third person, the insurer, to do so.

6.07 Indemnity against costs

Although the Companies Act 1985 invalidates exoneration and indemnity clauses in articles of association and directors' service contracts, section 310(3) of the Act empowers a company which has such a clause in its articles, or which is a party to a contract which contains such a clause, to indemnify a director against costs which he incurs in successfully defending any civil or criminal proceedings brought against him, or against the costs incurred by a director who successfully applies to the court for relief from liability under the statutory provision dealt with below.

This statutory concession in effect interprets an invalid exoneration or indemnity clause as though it validly empowered the company to give a different kind of indemnity, not against liability, but against costs incurred by a director who proves that he has not committed a breach of his fiduciary or other duties, or who is relieved from liability by the court exercising its discretion in his favour. An express provision in a company's articles or in a director's service contract empowering or obliging the company to indemnify a director against the costs incurred by him in such circumstances would, of course, be equally valid. Furthermore, the court may always award a director his costs in such circumstances under its general jurisdiction to order the payment of costs in litigation.

THE RELIEF AND RELEASE OF DIRECTORS FROM LIABILITY

6.08 Power of the court to give relief

In contrast to its invalidation of exoneration clauses in articles of association and service contracts, the Companies Act 1985, section 727(1) gives the court a discretionary jurisdiction to relieve an officer (including a director, manager or secretary (section 744)) or an auditor of a company from liability which he has incurred by his negligence, default, breach of duty or breach of trust. Relief from liability may be given completely or partially. It can, however, be given only if it appears to the court that the applicant for relief is or may be liable, 'but that he has acted honestly and reasonably, and that having regard to all the circumstances of the case (including those connected with his appointment) he ought fairly to be excused'.

If an action is brought against a director, the court may give relief in that action on the defendant applying for it, and the court can decide whether the conditions for giving relief have been satisfied and whether it should exercise its discretion in the defendant's favour without necessarily first deciding whether he is guilty of the breaches of duty alleged against him (section 727(3)). This enables the court to shorten the proceedings when the extenuating circumstances are so strongly in favour of relief being given that the court will give it in any event. If, in such a case, the court decides that the relief should not be given after hearing both the defendant and the plaintiff on that question, however, it will then have to decide whether the breaches of duty alleged by the plaintiff have in fact been committed by the defendant.

As an alternative to seeking relief in an action brought against him, a director may take the initiative himself and apply to the court for relief when he has reason to apprehend that a claim will or may be brought against him, even though no action has in fact yet been brought, and the court may then give him relief against liability in the same way as if an action had been commenced (section 727(2)). In that situation the director has to admit the breaches of duty which may be alleged against him for the purpose of seeking relief. The admission is made only for the purpose of his application, however, and so if relief is refused by the court, there is nothing to prevent the director from denying that he has in fact been guilty of any breaches of duty if an action is later brought against him. All that he is prevented from doing by reason of his unsuccessful application for relief is to ask the court for relief from liability for the same breaches of duty in any later action, because there is already a judicial decision against him on that question.

6.09 Instances of relief given by the court

The court has jurisdiction to give relief to a director for any breach of fiduciary duty and for any breach of the obligations, prohibitions and restrictions imposed on directors by the Companies Act 1985. The fact that the director has disposed of any of the company's assets or has caused the company loss by a transaction which was not connected with its legitimate business, or which was beyond the objects and powers of the company as set out in its memorandum of association, or beyond the powers of its directors as set out in the company's articles, does not prevent the court from giving relief (*Re Claridge's Patent Asphalte Co. Ltd* (1921)).

Although the wishes of the company's shareholders and, if the company is in liquidation, its creditors will be taken into account by the court, the fact that they are opposed to the court giving relief to a director does not prevent the court from giving it if it considers that the director should be excused (*Re Gilt Edged Safety Glass Ltd* (1940)). On the other hand, the court cannot give relief to directors from liability which they incur personally to persons other than the company (*Customs and Excise Commissioners* v. *Hedon Alpha Ltd* (1981)), and it would therefore seem that directors cannot be relieved in those cases where they incur personal liability to shareholders or creditors of the company, although they may be relieved from liability to the company on the same facts.

The court can relieve directors against criminal liability, and so preclude a prosecution from being brought against them (*Re Barry and Staines Linoleum Ltd* (1934)). However, this may be done only in respect of criminal offences committed by directors under the Companies Act 1985 or, possibly, under related statutes (such as the Company Securities (Insider Dealing) Act 1985 and the Prevention of Fraud (Investments) Act 1958), but certainly not under unrelated legislation, such as legislation imposing personal liability on directors for taxes payable by the company (*Customs and Excise Commissioners* v. *Hedon Alpha Ltd*).

The court has never given relief from liability lightly in exercise of its statutory power. In the case of remunerated and full-time directors particularly, the court has insisted on their taking all practicable steps to make good their breaches of duty short of paying damages to the company out of their own resources before the court will give relief

(*Re Windsor Steam Coal Co. Ltd* (1929)). Furthermore, relief is rarely given to directors who have been guilty of serious dereliction of duty over a long period, such as conforming automatically to instructions given by the majority shareholder of the company without verifying the legality or propriety of those instructions (*Selangor Rubber Estates Ltd* v. *Cradock (No.3)* (1968)). On the other hand, the court has given relief to a director who followed the established practice of his fellow directors in drawing a monthly amount as remuneration from the company in anticipation of the remuneration which the shareholders would vote to the directors at the next annual general meeting in exercise of the power given to them by the company's articles to fix the directors' remuneration in arrear. But, in the same case, the court refused relief to the director for such monthly drawings made by him in excess of the amount fixed by the board. The court also refused to give the director relief against his liability to repay compensation which the board had paid out of the company's resources to an incompetent director to induce him to resign when the board had not considered whether he could have been dismissed without payment of compensation because of breaches of his obligations under his service contract (*Re Duomatic Ltd* (1969)).

The relief of directors from liability to compensate the company for breaches of fiduciary duties is the most frequent use made by the court of its power to give relief under the Companies Act 1985, section 727, although it is rarely given against the liability of directors to account for personal profits which they have improperly obtained. On the other hand, the power of the court to give relief from liability incurred by directors for not fulfilling their statutory obligations under the Companies Act 1985, or under related statutes is also of importance, particularly when the breaches of statutory duty are technical, or where the statutory liability is absolute and the directors have acted with as much care as could reasonably be expected of them in the circumstances. The problems associated with directors' statutory obligations will be considered at lengh in Chapter 7.

Relief cannot be given to a director by the court validating a transaction in which a director is interested and which the company is entitled to avoid, except in certain specific instances in the winding up of a company.

6.10 The release of directors' liability by a resolution of shareholders

The Companies Act 1985 contains no provision establishing a

procedure for the formal release of directors from liability to their company for breaches of their fiduciary or other duties to it, although the Act does contain a number of provisions governing particular statutory obligations or restrictions imposed on the company or its directors under which a general meeting may resolve to approve action taken by directors without such approval and so release the directors from liability for not obtaining the approval beforehand. The only general provisions which the Act does contain governing releases of office holders from liability are in respect of trustees for debenture holders (section 192(2)). In omitting to provide expressly for the release of directors from liability, British companies legislation differs from that of most states of the USA and the countries of western Europe. These countries have provisions for the release of directors from liability for fully disclosed breaches of duty by the shareholders passing a resolution by a simple majority vote at a general meeting, or in the case of many states in the USA by the board of directors resolving to release individual directors.

The result of the Companies Act 1985 containing no provision for the release of directors from liability for breaches of fiduciary duties is that a formal release extinguishing the company's right to sue a director can only be given at common law by the company executing a deed of release under its seal, or entering into a contract with the director to release him from liability in return for valuable consideration. Such consideration may take the form of the payment of an agreed sum as compensation by way of a compromise of the company's claim against the director, or a promise to pay such a sum. Also in equity the company may prevent itself from suing a director for a breach of fiduciary duty by inducing him to believe that it will not do so, but the director must act in reliance on that belief so that it would be inequitable for the company to assert its claim later (*Hughes v. Metropolitan Rly Co.* (1877)).

A resolution passed by the board of directors of a company purporting to release a director from liability for a breach of duty is ineffective, because it would, if valid, amount to a gift to him of an asset of the company (its claim against the director) and directors have no power to make gifts to themselves (*Re George Newman & Co. Ltd* (1895)). If the board resolved to release the director in return for a payment or other consideration given by him to the company, the release would be a contract in which the director was interested, and so even if the directors had an implied power to enter into compromises with one of their own number (which is doubtful), the contract and therefore the release would be voidable by the company and so could not be relied on by the director.

A resolution passed by a general meeting of shareholders releasing a director from liability after he has made full disclosure of the facts would appear to be valid, unless passed by the controlling voting power of the director who is released (*Ammonia Soda Co. Ltd* v. *Chamberlain* (1918); *Regal (Hastings) Ltd* v. *Gulliver* (1967); *Cook* v. *Deeks* (1916)).

Curiously, the resolution of a general meeting purporting to release a director from liability does not operate to discharge him from liability in the absence of a formal deed of release or a contract entered into with the director for valuable consideration given or promised by him. Nevertheless, such a resolution will have the effect of preventing any shareholder from bringing an action in the company's name or on its behalf to enforce the company's claim against the director. This is because a shareholder cannot institute such an action unless the shareholders in general meeting resolve that he may do so, and the resolution purporting to release the director precludes a general meeting from passing a subsequent resolution that such an action shall be brought (*Marshall's Valve Gear Co. Ltd* v. *Manning, Wardle & Co. Ltd* (1909); *Airways Ltd* v. *Bowen* (1985)). By this indirect means, the shareholders may effectively release a director from liability by a resolution passed by a general meeting, except where the resolution is passed as a result of the director's votes as a controlling shareholder. If he abstains from voting, however, it would appear that a resolution releasing him, or a resolution that no action shall be brought against him for his breach of duty, is effective if passed by a majority of the votes cast by the other shareholders.

Chapter 7

Directors' Duties under the Companies Acts

NATURE OF THE OBLIGATIONS AND METHODS OF ENFORCEMENT

7.01 Statutory obligations and prohibitions and their sanctions

The contents of the Companies Act 1985 and the other legislation relating to companies in the United Kingdom have rarely been subjected to a structural analysis. Textbook writers as well as the courts have been content to take the statutory provisions one by one, to relate them to the underlying rules of common law and equity which they supplement, modify or supersede, and to present them as a body of substantive law and procedural rules without examining how the underlying principles and detailed contents of the legislation are made to work. The mechanism of the legislation and the methods employed to ensure compliance with it have attracted little attention, apart from the frequent complaints about the low percentage of companies which comply with the filing requirements of the Companies Acts and the low level of enforcement action taken by the Registrar of Companies to compel compliance.

Prevalence of criminal sanctions

It is true that Parliament has paid little attention to the question of enforcement when imposing new statutory obligations and prohibitions on companies and their directors. It has become standard form for new statutory obligations and prohibitions to be attended automatically by a provision that in the event of non-compliance the company and every officer of it who is in default shall be liable to a fine, or in the case of more serious contraventions by directors or officers, to imprisonment or a fine or both. The one exception to this is where the enactment provides a facility which the company may use only if certain conditions are complied with (such as the conversion of a private company into a public one, or *vice versa* (Companies Act 1985, sections 43 to 47 and sections 53 to 55)), or where the legislation prescribes a procedure which must be followed in order to achieve a certain result (such as the procedure for authorising a private company to purchase shares it has issued by using assets representing its issued share capital (sections 171 to 176)). Criminal sanctions are then omitted, apart from sanctions for making false declarations or filing false returns or no returns at all at the Companies Registry. Here the company can only attain the result it presumably desires to achieve by conforming to the statutorily prescribed procedure and fulfilling the statutorily prescribed conditions, and the implied sanction is that the desired result will not be attained in law if this is not done. It is only in connection with statutory provisions of this kind that criminal sanctions are omitted from the Companies Act 1985, because they are not required as an inducement to ensure compliance.

In other contexts the almost universal employment, in the Companies Act 1985, of criminal sanctions obscures the possibility of using other and possibly more effective means of compelling or inducing compliance which may be available. In fact, the imposition of criminal sanctions can raise doubts whether other sanctions which are available at common law or equity are intended by Parliament to be excluded.

The most obvious example of this is the doubt, which persisted for years, whether the statutory prohibition on companies from giving financial assistance for the acquisition of shares issued by them, made contracts which contravened the prohibition illegal and void, or whether the only sanction intended was the fine imposed by the enactment on the company and its officers, leaving the contravening contract intact (see Companies Act 1929, section 45(1) and Companies Act 1948, section 54, now Companies Act 1985, sections 151 to 158).

In early cases it was held that a contract for the purchase of shares was not invalidated by the fact that the purchase price was to be paid out of funds provided by the company which issued the shares (*Spink (Bournemouth) Ltd* v. *Spink* (1936)), and that a loan made by a company to finance a purchase of its shares was valid and recoverable (*Victor Battery Co. Ltd* v. *Curry's Ltd* (1946)). It has only been in recent years that the court has held that both the contract to purchase shares which is financed by a loan made by the company and the loan itself are invalidated by the contravention of the statutory prohibition (*Selangor United Rubber Estates Ltd* v. *Cradock (No. 3)* (1968); *Heald* v. *O'Connor* (1971); *Carney* v. *Herbert* (1985)).

Examples of criminal sanctions

Criminal sanctions are imposed by the Companies Act 1985:

(a) to enforce prohibitions on companies or their directors or other officers from doing certain acts or entering into certain transactions (e.g. the financing of share acquisitions with financial assistance provided by the company (section 151) and the provision of loans and other financial accommodation by public companies for their directors and persons connected with them (sections 330 and 342));
(b) to compel companies and their directors and officers to comply with the mandatory requirements of the Act (e.g. the requirements that every company shall call an annual general meeting of shareholders each year (section 366) and that every company shall lay copies of its annual accounts and directors' and auditors' reports before a general meeting of shareholders within certain time limits each year and, if the company is a limited one, that it shall deliver a copy of those documents to the Registrar of Companies within the same time limits (sections 277, 235, 238, 239, 241 and 243)); and
(c) to penalise companies and their directors and other officers who enter into transactions or who do acts permitted by the Act, when the conditions specified in it are not fulfilled or the procedure required by the Act to be followed is not followed (e.g. the exercise by a public company of its statutory power to issue shares for a consideration other than cash, but only if the consideration has been valued by a qualified valuer and a copy of the valuation report has been delivered to the person to whom the shares are to be allotted before allotment takes place (section 99(1) and sections 103, 108 and 114), and the exercise by a company of its statutory power to purchase or otherwise acquire shares issued by it if the acquisition is for one of certain authorised purposes, but not otherwise (section 143)).

7.02 Criminal offences under the Companies Act 1985

There are altogether 202 criminal offences created by the Companies Act 1985 for contravention of its provisions, some of which have now been re-enacted in the Insolvency Act 1986. All of these offences are punishable by a fine, and 37 of them are also punishable by imprisonment with or without a fine as well. Of the offences punishable by imprisonment, all but 10 can be committed only by a company or by the directors or officers of a company, and any of the remaining 10 offences may be committed by directors or officers of a company as well as by other persons.

Additionally, the legislation enacted at the same time as the Companies Act 1985 – namely, the Companies Consolidation (Consequential Provisions) Act 1985, the Company Securities (Insider Dealing) Act 1985 and the Business Names Act 1985 – create 8 further criminal offences, all of which are punishable by a fine, and 4 of which are also punishable by imprisonment with or without a fine. Two of these further offences can only be committed by a company or the directors or officers of a company, and the remaining 6 offences may be committed by such directors or officers as well as by other persons.

Penalties

By the Companies Act 1985, section 730(1) and (2) and Schedule 24, the more serious offences created by the Act may be tried on indictment or summarily, that is either by a Crown Court or by a magistrates' court. There are altogether 87 such offences, and so the remaining 115 offences created by the Act can only be tried summarily.

The maximum punishment which may be imposed on conviction depends on whether the accused is convicted on indictment or summarily. There are 35 offences for which the convicted accused can be sentenced to imprisonment; the normal maximum period of imprisonment is 2 years on indictment and 6 months on summary conviction, but 10 of the more serious offences carry a maximum sentence of 7 years imprisonment on conviction on indictment. The maximum fine which may be imposed on indictment is unlimited, but on summary conviction it is limited to £400, except in respect of 94 of the more serious offences, when the maximum fine is £2,000 (Companies Act 1985, section 730(3) and Schedule 24, applying Magistrates' Courts Act 1980, section 32 and the Criminal Penalties etc. (Increase) Order 1984 (SI 1984/447)).

Additionally, many offences under the Companies Act 1985 are continuing in nature (e.g. directors failing to lay copies of the company's annual accounts before a general meeting of shareholders and to deliver a copy of the accounts to the Registrar of Companies within the appropriate time limits (section 243(1)). Most of these continuing offences are punishable on a second or subsequent conviction by a default fine for each day that the offence has been continued since the first or previous conviction, as an alternative to the fine which may be imposed for committing the crime on the first occasion (section 730(4)). Default fines are mostly imposed for continuing offences which are triable only summarily, and the daily default fine then cannot exceed £40, except in four instances where the maximum daily default fine is £200. There are additionally 12 continuing offences which are triable either summarily or on indictment, and on a second or subsequent conviction for any of those offences a daily default fine not exceeding £200 may be imposed by a magistrates' court (Companies Act 1985, section 730(4) and Schedule 24, applying Magistrates' Courts Act 1980, section 32 and Criminal Penalties (Increase) Order 1984).

Under the three Acts of Parliament passed at the same time as the Companies Act 1985, 4 criminal offences are created which are triable only summarily, and each of these offences is punishable by a maximum fine of £400 with a daily default fine on a second or subsequent conviction for a continuation of 3 of these offences. There are also 4 more serious offences which may be committed under one of these supplementary Acts, the Company Securities (Insider Dealing) Act 1985. These offences are triable summarily or on indictment, and carry a maximum penalty on conviction on indictment of imprisonment for not more than 2 years and an unlimited fine or both, and on summary conviction by a maximum penalty of imprisonment for not more than 6 months and a fine not exceeding £2,000 or both.

Persons who may be convicted of offences

It is obvious that where, under the Companies Act 1985, the penalty of imprisonment may be imposed on conviction for an offence, the punishment may be imposed only on an individual, who may be, but need not necessarily be, a director or officer of the company concerned. Even though an offence is punishable by imprisonment in the case of an individual, the only punishment which may be imposed on the company if it, too, by the terms of the Act may be convicted of the offence, is a fine not exceeding the amount prescribed by the Act, or in the case of the conviction of the company on indictment for certain offences, an unlimited fine.

Certain offences under the Companies Act 1985 can be committed only by the company concerned itself (e.g. a company failing to comply with a direction of the Secretary of State for Trade and Industry that it shall change its name because its existing name is misleading (section 32(1) and (4)). In that situation, any director, manager or secretary or similar officer of the company who consented to, or connived at, the company's offence, or to whose neglect the company's offence was attributable, is also guilty under the Act of the same offence and is punishable accordingly (section 733(2)). In most situations where a company commits an offence under the Companies Act 1985, however, the statutory provision creating the offence expressly provides that the offence is also committed by every officer of the company who is in default. In that case, any officer of the company who knowingly and wilfully authorises the default or contravention which constitutes the company's offence is guilty of the same offence as the company, and is punishable accordingly (section 730(5)).

Where a director or other officer of a company is convicted of an offence for which he is made criminally liable by the Companies Act 1985, and a continuation of the offence after a first conviction is punishable by a daily default fine, such a fine may be imposed on him as well as on the company (if the offence is one of which it may be convicted), but the default fine may be imposed only if that director or officer (and not merely the company or another officer) has already been convicted of the same offence and the offence has been continued by him since his previous conviction (section 730(4)).

7.03 Method of analysis

Although criminal sanctions predominate as the means by which the Companies Act 1985 seeks to compel conformity to its requirements and prohibitions, a proper analysis of directors' statutory obligations to their companies calls for an examination of their principal statutory duties and of the means employed by the Companies Act 1985 (in addition to the imposition of criminal liability) to induce them to fulfil those duties. Furthermore, it is necessary to examine the remedies other than criminal prosecution which may be available to a company, its shareholders and creditors to compel compliance by directors with the Companies Act 1985, or to obtain reparation if they cause the company loss by their failure to comply.

It will not, of course, be possible to examine all the statutory obligations of directors in this book. An attempt to do this would result in an unwieldy presentation of most, but not all, of the various elements of company legislation, but with the omission of the underlying rules of law and equity which provide cohesion to the British system of company law. The statutory obligations of directors which are dealt with in this chapter and the sanctions available for their enforcement (dealt with in Chapter 8) have been selected, either because they are the most important obligations of directors and therefore the ones which give rise to the most significant practical problems, or because the remedies available for their enforcement are distinctive or particularly effective or inadequate. For directors' statutory obligations which are not mentioned in this chapter, the reader is director to the standard practitioners' manuals on company law and practice.

PRINCIPAL STATUTORY OBLIGATIONS IN RESPECT OF ACCOUNTS, REPORTS AND SHAREHOLDERS' MEETINGS

7.04 Periodical accounts and reports

Companies are required to keep proper accounting records. These are records which are sufficient to explain their current transactions and financial position and to enable their directors to prepare an annual profit and loss account and balance sheet to be laid before their shareholders (Companies Act 1985, section 221(1) and (2)). A company's accounting records are open to inspection by its directors at all times (section 222(2)), and the directors are individually responsible for ensuring that the records are properly kept. Every director and officer of a company who is in default in respect of the proper keeping of accounting records is guilty of a criminal offence, and may be convicted and punished by a fine or, in serious cases, by imprisonment with or without a fine, unless he proves that he acted honestly and that in the circumstances the default was excusable (section 223(1)).

Annual and group accounts

Each year the directors of a company must prepare annual accounts comprising a profit and loss account and a balance sheet and, if the company is a parent or holding company, a group profit and loss account and a group balance sheet, setting out the profit or loss and the assets and liabilities of the parent company and all its subsidiaries taken together as though they were a single company (section 227(1) and section 229(1)). Annual and group accounts must be prepared by reference to the company's or parent company's annual accounting reference period, which is synonymous with its financial year, provided that it is borne in mind that the annual reference period may be longer or shorter than 12 months if the company changes the accounting reference date (i.e. the date on which its financial year ends) which it currently employs.

Consequently, an annual or group profit and loss account will show the profit or loss of the company or group for the period from the company's incorporation or the end of its last complete accounting reference period until the end of the current period. An annual or group balance sheet will also show the assets and liabilities of the company or group as at the end of its current accounting reference period (that it, on the accounting reference data for that period) (section 224(1), (4) and (6)). A company's accounting reference date is chosen by the board of directors and, subject to certain restrictions, may be changed from time to time (section 224(3) and section 225(1) and (4)). A company's annual and group accounts (if any) must be laid before a general meeting of its shareholders within 7 months after the end of the accounting reference period (that is, the financial year of the company) to which they relate, or within 10 months after the end of that period if the company is a private one (section 242(1) and (2)).

The form and contents of annual accounts are governed by two quite different but complementary rules. The paramount rule is that annual or group balance sheets must give a true and fair view of the state of the company's or group's affairs at the end of the accounting reference period to which they relate, and annual or group profit and loss accounts must give a true and fair view of the company's or group's profits or loss for the same period (section 228(2) and section 230(2)). Secondly, annual accounts and group accounts must contain the amount of detail about the constituent items included in them that Schedule 4 of the Companies Act 1985 requires. The accounts must also be framed in accordance with one of the alternative forms prescribed for balance sheets and profit and loss accounts which are set out in the same Schedule (section 228(1) and section 230(1)).

The purpose of requiring annual and group accounts to be in one of the alternative standard forms and the separate items included in them to be set out under standardised headings giving a certain minimum amount of detail (which often may or must be embodied in notes to the accounts), is to ensure that shareholders and others who use the accounts are presented with the company's or group's financial position and results in sufficient detail and with sufficient elucidation. If this is done they should be able to comprehend how the company or group stands financially at the end of each accounting period, and also to see how efficiently and successfully the business of the company or group has been conducted in financial terms. The significance and reliability of the items which are included in annual and group accounts is enhanced by the accounting principles and valuation rules set out in Schedule 4 of the Act. These require standard accounting assumptions and methods of valuation to be employed, for example, in valuing current assets (such as stock in trade, raw materials and semi-finished products) and in providing for the depreciation or diminution in value of fixed assets (Schedule 4, paras 10 to 34).

Notes to accounts and directors' report

The figures included in annual and group accounts, even if calculated strictly in accordance with the rules in the Companies Act 1985, are not sufficient by themselves to convey an accurate and adequate picture of the company's or group's resources, liabilities, earnings and earning potential. Supplemental factual information is required for this purpose, and also to disclose the extent to which the management of the company or group (that is, its directors and senior executives) have financial or other interests in the company or group and stand to benefit by its success. The Companies Act 1985 requires the most significant items of such supplemental material to be included in the notes to the company's or group's accounts when the material has a direct bearing on its financial position or results, or in the director's report if it is of a more general or background character (e.g. information about the company's or group's employees, or donations made by it for charitable or political purposes).

The directors' report must be laid annually before the shareholders in general meeting and communicated to the Registrar of Companies at the same time as the annual and group accounts. The report is intended primarily to contain a statement of, and the directors' comments on, the development of the business of the company and its subsidiaries (if any) during the accounting period to which the acompanying annual accounts and group accounts (if any) relate, and to review the financial position of the company and those subsidiaries at the end of that accounting period (section 235(1) and (2)). The directors' report must also contain details of the persons who have been directors of the company during the relevant accounting period and particulars of the interests of directors and their families in shares and debentures of the company and its subsidiaries at the end of that period (section 235(2) and (3) and Schedule 7).

The notes to the annual accounts must contain particulars of amounts paid or payable in respect of directors' remuneration, pensions and compensation for loss of office during the accounting period and particulars of dealings by those persons with the company and its subsidiaries during the same period (including loans made to them and financial assistance given to them by the company or its subsidiaries and the amounts repayable by them) (section 231(1) and (2), section 232(1) to (3) and Schedules 5 and 6). The directors' report must additionally contain other general information, in particular, information about the company's and the group's workforce and about likely future developments in the business of the company or the businesses of the group (section 235(3) and Schedule 7).

Signing and circulation of accounts

When a company's annual accounts have been prepared, they must have certain other documents annexed to them before the company's own balance sheet is signed on behalf of the board by at least two of its directors. These annexed documents are the directors' report, the group accounts prepared by the company if it is a parent company, and a report by the auditors of the company on the company's own accounts and the group accounts (if any) stating whether in the auditors' opinion they have been properly prepared and give a true and fair view of the company's and (where appropriate) the group's financial position and results (section 236, section 238(1) and (3) and section 239).

The purpose of having the other accounts and documents annexed to the company's balance sheets before it is signed on behalf of the board is to ensure that the directors collectively are made responsible for the accuracy and completeness of all the accounts and reports which are laid before a general meeting of the company and copies of which are delivered to the Registrar of Companies. At least 21 days before the general meeting is held at which a company's annual accounts are laid before its shareholders, the company must send copies of the accounts and the group accounts and reports annexed to them to each of its shareholders and debenture holders. This requirement can be waived, however, with the consent of all the shareholders who are entitled to attend and vote at the meeting, provided that accounts and reports are circulated before the meeting is held (section 240(1) and (4)).

Criminal offences

The statutory requirements in respect of companies' accounting records and annual and group accounts and directors' and auditors' reports are enforced by criminal sanctions against the company and its directors and officers. If a company fails to deliver to the Registrar of Companies a copy of its annual accounts with copies of its group accounts (if any) and directors' and auditors' reports annexed within the time allowed by the Act, the Secretary of State for Trade and Industry may recover by civil proceedings (in addition to the fine which a magistrate's court may impose), a progressively increasing penalty depending on the duration of the default, with a maximum penalty of £450 if the default continues for more than 12 months (section 243(3) and (4)).

This penalty is recoverable only from the company, and not from its directors personally, but in the event of the company's default in filing copies of its annual accounts etc., the Registrar of Companies or any member or creditor of the company may, after giving 14 day's notice to the directors to remedy the default, apply to a court which has jurisdiction to order the winding up of the company (that is the High Court or, if the company's paid-up share capital does not exceed £120,000, the county court in whose locality the company's registered office is situated) for a default order. This is an order requiring the company and its directors or officers or any of them to make good the default within the time specified by the court order, and failure by any director to comply with such an order made against him personally is punishable as a contempt of court (section 244(1) and section 713(1)).

Apart from the criminal and other sanctions imposed on companies and their directors and officers for failing to lay annual accounts, group accounts and directors' and auditors' reports before a general meeting of shareholders, or for failing to deliver copies of such accounts and reports to the Registrar of Companies, the Companies Act 1985 imposes criminal sanctions on directors of a company if they lay or deliver copies of such accounts 'which do not comply with the requirements of [the] Act as to the matters to be included in, or in a note to, the accounts' (section 245(1) and (2)). This offence is confined to the omission from annual accounts or group accounts or the notes to them of the detailed entries which the act requires them to contain. It does not extend to the laying or delivery of accounts which are correct in form and contain the requisite amount of detail, but give inaccurate figures or information. The Act creates a similar offence in respect of omissions from, or inadequate detail in, directors' reports annexed to annual accounts (section 235(7)).

The far more serious offence of presenting or using false accounts or reports which contain inaccurate information or figures, is governed, not by the Companies Act 1985, but by the Theft Act 1968, section 19(1). This makes it an offence punishable on indictment by imprisonment for not more than 7 years for an officer of a body corporate (including a director) to publish or concur in publishing 'a written statement or account which to his knowledge is or may be misleading, false or deceptive in a material particular' if he does so 'with intent to deceive members or creditors of the [company] about its affairs'. It will be noticed that it is not a criminal offence for directors to prepare, present to a general meeting or to file at the Companies Registry annual or group accounts which do not give a true view of the company's financial position or results if the other elements for an offence under the Theft Act 1968 section 19(1) are not present.

Interim reports

In addition to their obligation to lay accounts and directors' and auditors' reports before a general meeting of shareholders each year, the directors of a public company whose shares or debentures are listed on the Stock Exchange must prepare and publish interim reports on the company's activities and profits or losses during the first 6 months of each of its financial years (i.e. accounting reference periods) (The Stock Exchange (Listing) Regulations 1984 (SI 1984/716), para 3(1) and (2) and Interim Reports Directive, article 2). An interim report must show the company's net turnover and its profit or loss (before tax) for the 6 months period, and if the company has paid or intends to pay an interim dividend, the company's profit for that period after the deduction of corporation tax and the interim dividend. The interim report must also set out the corresponding figures for the first 6 months of the company's preceding financial year and an explanatory statement about the company's activities during the first 6 months of its current financial year so as to enable investors to assess its activities and profit or loss (Interim Reports Directive, article 5(1), (2) and (4) to (6)).

The Stock Exchange rules require the information contained in a company's interim report to be supplemented by certain additional information relating to the same 6 months period (The Stock Exchange: *Admission of Securities to Listing*, Section 5, Chapter 2, para 25(b)). Interim reports must be published either in the form of an advertisement in two national daily newspapers, or by the company sending copies of them to the holders of its listed shares and debentures, and making copies available to the public at its registered office (Interim Reports Directive, article 7(1); The Stock Exchange: *Admission of Securities to Listing*, Section 5, Chapter 2, para 24).

No sanctions are expressly enacted against the failure of a listed company or its directors to publish proper interim reports. Nevertheless, it would appear that directors owe a duty to their company to ensure that such reports are properly prepared and published as part of their general obligation to conduct the company's affairs with care and skill. Consequently, it appears that they will be liable in damages to the company for any loss it suffers in consequence of their failure to do so (e.g. the loss caused to the company by the suspension or termination of its listing, or the expense to which the company is put to end such suspension).

7.05 Meetings of shareholders

The Companies Act 1985 places on the directors of a company the primary responsibility to call the general and class meetings of its shareholders which the company is obliged to hold under the Act, and to ensure that the shareholders are provided with facilities to record their votes, express views which may be opposed to those of the board, and to initiate proposals of their own for consideration at shareholders' meetings. The sanctions for the directors' failure to satisfy these requirements is usually the imposition of a fine on the company and on every director and other officer who is in default. In reality, however, the punishment of the company is merely the imposition on it of vicarious liability for the directors' defaults, since all the duties imposed by the Act in respect of shareholders' meetings are active duties, and they can only be fulfilled by human agents. In certain respects, other remedies are also provided for breaches of such duties as well as the imposition of fines, and these alternative remedies encourage a measure of self-help on the part of shareholders who are adversely affected by the directors' defaults.

Annual general meetings

Directors are required by various provisions of the Companies Act 1985 to call general meetings of shareholders. Every company must hold an annual general meeting at least once in every calendar year, and not more than 15 months may elapse between one annual general meeting and the next. If, however, the company holds its first annual general meeting within 18 months of its incorporation, it need not hold any other annual general meeting for the first two calendar years of its existence (Companies Act 1985, section 366(1) to (3)).

The business to be transacted at the annual general meeting of a company is not prescribed by the Companies Act 1985, but it invariably includes the laying of the company's annual accounts, group accounts (if it has subsidiaries) and directors' and auditors' reports before the shareholders, although the Act permits these documents to be presented at any other general meeting, provided that the presentation is made within the proper time limits mentioned in the preceding section of this chapter (section 239, section 241(1) and section 242(1) and (2)). Additionally, the general meeting before which the company's annual accounts are laid must appoint an auditor or auditors from appropriately qualified persons to hold office until the conclusion of the general meeting before which the company's next annual accounts are laid (section 384(1)). Again, because in practice annual accounts are laid before annual general meetings, the appointment or re-appointment of auditors, too, is made at such meetings.

The other business usually transacted at annual general meetings includes the re-election or replacement of directors whose terms of office expire at or before the end of the annual general meeting under the provisions of the company's memorandum or articles of association; the declaration of dividends to be paid to shareholders; the passing of resolutions for the capitalisation of profits under powers conferred by the articles and the authorisation of the directors to issue bonus shares paid up by the capitalisation to shareholders in proportion to their existing holdings; and other incidental matters which arise periodically (such as the renewal of the directors' authority to issue unissued shares of the company (section 80(1))), or matters which can conveniently be settled at an annual general meeting (such as the approval by shareholders of proposed service contracts with directors which will continue for more than 5 years (section 319(1) and (3)) and the approval by shareholders of substantial dispositions of assets between the company and its directors (section 320(1) and (2)). None of these matters are required to be dealt with at an annual general meeting, however, and so they may all be transacted at extraordinary general meetings held between annual general meetings.

Because of the permissive character of the rules governing business which may be transacted at annual general meetings, directors commit a criminal offence only if they are in default in failing to call and hold an annual general meeting at all during a calendar year and within 15 months of the preceding annual general meeting (section 366(4)), or in failing to present the company's annual accounts and related documents to a general meeting (whether an annual or other general meeting) within the prescribed time limits (section 241(1) and (2)). Directors are not punishable for failing to include the appointment or re-appointment of directors or auditors on the agenda of the general meeting at which the company's annual accounts are presented.

However, if an annual general meeting is not held during a calendar year within 15 months since the last one was held, the Secretary of State for Trade and Industry may call or direct the calling of such a meeting on the application of any shareholder. If the Secretary of State directs that an annual general meeting shall be called, the directors commit an offence punishable by a fine if they fail to call it accordingly (section 367(1) and (3)). Furthermore, if no auditor is appointed by the general meeting at which a company's annual accounts are presented, the company must notify the Secretary of State and he may appoint an auditor or auditors. If the company fails to give such a notification, the company and its directors and officers who are in default are guilty of an offence punishable by a fine (section 384(5)).

Extraordinary general meetings

The Companies Act 1985 does not require general meetings other than annual general meetings to be held at periodic intervals or on the occurrence of particular events. The one exception to this is that the directors of a public company are obliged to call an extraordinary general meeting within 28 days after they discover that the company's net assets have fallen to one half or less of its called-up share capital (i.e. its paid-up share capital plus unpaid calls already made on its shares plus instalments of the issue price of its issued shares which are payable by fixed amounts and at fixed times in the future) (section 142(1)). The extraordinary general meeting must be called for a date not more than 56 days from the discovery by the directors of the company's financial situation, but curiously the directors and the company are not required by law to take or to propose to shareholders at the extraordinary general meeting that any remedial steps should be taken to improve the company's position (section 141(1)). Instead, the agenda for the meeting can be confined to 'considering whether any, and if so what, steps should be taken to deal with the situation', so apparently leaving it to the shareholders to make proposals. If the statutory requirement that an extraordinary general meeting of a public company must be called if the company loses half of its capital is disregarded, every director who knowingly or wilfully authorises or permits the default, or who allows the default to continue after the last date by which the meeting should be held, is guilty of an offence punishable on indictment by an unlimited fine and on summary conviction by a fine not exceeding £2,000 (section 142(2), section 730(1) and Schedule 24).

Shareholders' rights

The provisions of the Companies Act 1985 about annual and extraordinary general meetings other than those already dealt with, confer limited rights on shareholders or groups of shareholders to insist on extraordinary general meetings being called and held; to require resolutions which they propose to be put on the agenda of annual general meetings; to have circulars prepared by them with regard to any items of business at any general meeting circulated by the company to the other shareholders; and to have the voting rights conferred on them by the company's articles or by law duly recognised and to have their votes recorded.

Requisition of extraordinary general meeting

For example, shareholders who between them hold not less than one-tenth of the paid-up capital of the company carrying voting rights at general meetings, may require the directors to call an extraordinary general meeting within 21 days after the shareholders' written requisition is delivered to the company. If the directors fail to send out notices calling the meeting within the 21-day period, the requisitionists, or those of them who hold between them at least one-half of the total voting rights exercisable by them all, can call the extraordinary general meeting themselves to be held on a date within 3 months after the delivery of the original requisition to the company (section 368(2) and (4)).

The written requisition calling on the directors to convene an extraordinary general meeting must specify the business to be transacted at it (e.g. a resolution for the appointment or removal of a director), and if the requisitionists call the meeting themselves on the directors' failure to do so, the agenda of the extraordinary general meeting cannot include matters which did not appear in the original requisition (*Patent Wood Keg Syndicate Ltd* v. *Pearse* (1906)). Curiously, no criminal offence is committed by directors who fail to call an extraordinary general meeting which has been requisitioned by the proper fraction of shareholders, and the only sanction available against them is that the expenses incurred by the requisitionists in calling the meeting themselves are recoverable by them from the company, which in turn can recover the same amount from the directors who were in default by deduction from their remuneration (section 368(6)).

Requisition in respect of resolutions at annual general meetings

The other rights of shareholders to have proposals prepared by them considered and voted on at a general meeting are created by a provision of the Companies Act 1985, which enables the holders of shares carrying at least one-twentieth of the total voting rights exercisable at an annual general meeting, or 100 or more shareholders who have paid up an average of at least £100 on their shareholdings (i.e. a total of at least £10,000), to require the company to give notice to its members of any resolution which they intend to move at the next annual general meeting. On receiving the requisition the directors must circulate the proposed resolution either with the notice calling the annual general meeting or in the same manner as notice of that meeting may be given (section 376(1) to (3)).

A requisition that the proposed resolution shall be included in the agenda of the next annual general meeting must, however, be given to the company in writing at least 6 weeks before the meeting is held, but if the requisition is delivered to the company before the meeting is called (and only 21 days' notice need be given of an annual general meeting (section 369(1) and (2)), the fact that less than 6 weeks elapses between the delivery of the requisition and the holding of the meeting is immaterial (section 377(1) and (2)). Moreover, the requisitionists must pay or tender to the company a sufficient sum to recover the expenses of complying with the requisition, but this should present no difficulty if the requisition is delivered in good time, because the additional expense of including the requisitionists' resolution in the agenda of the annual general meeting should be minimal (section 377(1)).

If the directors of a company fail to comply with a requisition for the inclusion of a resolution on the agenda of an annual general meeting when the requisition has been properly presented, every director and officer of the company who is in default is liable to a fine (section 376(7)). There is, however, no statutory provision enabling the requisitionists to send out a notice of the resolution and of their intention to support it at the next annual general meeting and then to move the resolution and possibly to procure its adoption at that or any other general meeting.

Circulation of shareholders' opinions

The same fraction of shareholders who may require a company to circulate a resolution which they intend to move at an annual general meeting, may also require the company to circulate to its members a statement by the requisitionists not exceeding 1,000 words in length in respect of any resolution or business to be proposed or dealt with at any general meeting. If the directors or any other persons consider that the statement gives needless publicity to defamatory matter, they may apply to the court for an order that the statement need not be circulated (section 376(1) and (2) and section 377(3)).

A written requisition and a copy of the statement to be circulated must be deposited with the company at least 7 days before the meeting is held, and must be accompanied by a sufficient sum to cover the cost of circulating it (section 377(1)). This may be a substantial amount if the requisition is delivered after notices calling the general meeting have been sent out, because a second set of mailing expenses will then be incurred.

If a requisition is properly delivered, the directors and officers of the company who are in default in failing to circulate it are liable to a fine (section 376(7)). This is not the only remedy available, however, because there is nothing to prevent shareholders who are entitled to requisition the circulation of a statement prepared by them, or who have in fact delivered such a requisition which has not been acted on, from circulating the statement themselves.

Application to class meetings

The statutory requirements that a resolution proposed by the holders of a fraction of a company's shares should be included on the agenda of an annual general meeting, or that a statement relating to business on the agenda of any general meeting should be circulated at the request of the holders of the same fraction of shares, apply also to a class meeting of the holders of shares of a particular class which is called to consent to an alteration of the rights attached to shares of that class (section 125(6)). The relevant fraction of shares which the requisitionists must hold is the same fraction of issued shares of the class in question, and a requisition that a proposed resolution should be included in the agenda of a class meeting may be delivered in respect of any meeting of the class at which the consent of the class is sought to an alteration of the rights of the class. Likewise, the directors and other officers of the company who are in default in not complying with the requisition are liable to the same fine as if the default were in respect of a general meeting.

Proxy appointments

The final statutory provisions relating to general meetings relate to the notification of shareholders entitled to attend it of their right to be represented and to cast their votes by proxies of their own choosing, whether members of the company or not. In the notice calling a general meeting sent to each shareholder there must be included a statement of his right to appoint another person to attend and vote at the meeting on his behalf as his proxy, or in the case of a public company, a statement of his right to appoint one or more proxies, either in respect of different parts of his holding or in the alternative, so that if one proxy does not attend the meeting, another may do so (section 372(1) to (3)). If the required statement about the appointment of proxies is not included in the notice calling a general meeting, the notice is not invalidated and the meeting may be held, but the directors and other officers of the company who are in default are punishable by a fine (section 372(4)). The statutory provisions in respect of the appointment of proxies to represent shareholders at general meetings apply equally to appointments of proxies to attend meetings of classes of shareholders (section 372(7)).

A further requirement in relation to proxy appointments for general meetings and class meetings is that if a company invites shareholders to appoint persons named in the invitation as their proxies (e.g. if the company invites shareholders to sign proxy appointment forms in which the names of the directors' nominees are already filled in as the proxies to be appointed), the same invitation must be circulated to all shareholders who are entitled to be sent notices of the meeting (section 372(6) and (7)). Nevertheless, this does not prevent a company from furnishing any shareholder on request with a list of persons who are willing to be appointed as proxies, provided that the list is equally available on request to all other shareholders who are entitled to vote at the same meeting (section 372(6) and (7)). If this provision is disregarded, the directors or officers of the company who are in default are punishable by a fine.

PRINCIPAL DISCLOSURE OBLIGATIONS ON ISSUE OF CAPITAL

7.06 Issues of share and loan capital

The Companies Act 1985 prescribes several conditions which must be fulfilled and procedures which must be followed when a company issues shares and certain kinds of debentures. The Act also requires that invitations issued by the company to the public to subscribe for its shares or debentures should contain a certain minimum amount of information about the company, and the Act imposes liability on the company's directors if such invitations contain misstatements of fact. Compliance with most of the provisions of the Companies Act 1985 in respect of the issues of shares and debentures is sanctioned by the imposition of criminal liability on directors. However, this is not universally so. Several provisions are enforced only by directors being made liable to pay damages or compensation to persons who suffer loss as a result of contraventions, or by the imposition on directors of an obligation to restore amounts paid to the company on the allotment of shares or debentures. A full treatment of the requirements of the Companies Act 1985 with regard to the issue of share and loan capital would go beyond the purpose of this book, and so the statutory provisions will simply be summarised with an indication of the remedies which the Act itself creates for contraventions.

Authorisation to issue shares

Directors may not allot shares of a company comprised in its unissued share capital unless the company's articles of association or an ordinary resolution passed by its shareholders in general meeting authorise them to do so. Such an authorisation must specify the maximum number of shares which the directors may issue and the date on which the authorisation will expire, being not more than 5 years from the company's incorporation if the authorisation was contained in the company's articles when it was originally registered, and 5 years from the date of the resolution conferring the authorisation in any other case (Companies Act 1985, section 80(1) to (4) and (8)). The same provision applies also to the creation by the directors of any right to subscribe for shares or to convert any security into shares of the company, and so an appropriate authorisation is needed if directors are to issue options to subscribe for shares, or if they are to issue debentures which carry the right for the holder to convert them into, or exchange them for, a specified number of fully paid shares or to subscribe in cash for new shares in proportion to the number of debentures held (section 80(2)). When such options, conversion rights or subscription rights are exercised, however, there is no need for further authorisation to be given to the directors to issue shares to satisfy those rights, because the authority to issue those shares is inherent in the authorisation originally given to create the right to call for them to be issued.

If directors issue shares without proper authorisation, even if the person to whom they are issued is aware of this, the allotment is valid and the allottee has a good title to the shares and is bound to pay their issue price (section 80(10)). The only sanction for contraventions is that the directors who knowingly and wilfully issue or permit the issue of shares or rights to acquire shares when no authorisation is currently in force are liable to a fine (section 80(9)).

Shareholders' preferential subscription rights

When a company proposes to issue equity shares or securities for a cash payment or payment by cash instalments, it must first offer the shares or securities to its existing holders of equity shares in proportion to their holdings at a certain issue price before it may offer or allot the securities in any other way at the same or a lower price (for example, by allotting the shares to outsiders, or to existing equity shareholders, but not in proportion to their existing holding) (section 89(1) and (4)). All shares and rights to subscribe for or to convert securities into shares are equity securities for this purpose, unless they are shares (or the right to acquire shares) which carry a right to participate only up to a specified amount on a distribution of profits of the company and in a distribution of the company's assets in a liquidation or on a reduction of capital. A typical non-equity share is a preference share which entitles its holder to a dividend of a fixed amount in priority to the payment of dividends on ordinary shares, and also entitles its holder to repayment of the capital paid up on the share in the company's liquidation in priority to repayment of its ordinary share capital. Other shares, such as ordinary and preferred ordinary shares, are equity shares, and a right to subscribe for them or to convert another security into them is an equity security.

A company's obligation to offer equity securities which it proposes to issue for cash to its existing equity shareholders in proportion to their existing holdings means that offers by the company to issue equity shares or equity securities (such as convertible debentures) must be made by way of rights offers in the first instance. The company can allot only the shares or securities which are not taken up by its equity shareholders in exercise of their rights to other persons or in any other way. There are, nevertheless, several statutory exceptions to the company's obligation to offer equity securities by rights offers. The most important of these are that a private company may exclude or modify the obligation by its memorandum or articles of association, and a general meeting of any company may waive or modify its equity shareholders' preferential subscription rights in respect of a particular issue of securities by passing a special resolution to that effect (section 91(1) and section 95(1) and (2)).

The honouring of existing equity shareholders' preferential subscription rights on an offering of equity securities is obviously a responsibility of the directors of the issuing company. If they fail to fulfil this responsibility, they do not commit an offence under the Companies Act 1985, however, although they may be guilty of a criminal conspiracy to defraud the equity shareholders to whom a proper offer is not made. On the other hand, the Companies Act 1985 does provide that every director and other officer of a company who knowingly authorises or permits the allotment of its equity securities in disregard of the existing equity shareholders' subscription rights, shall be liable to compensate all shareholders to whom an offer should have been made for any loss, costs or expenses which they have sustained or incurred by reason of the contravention (section 92(1)).

Curiously, no statutory liability is imposed on directors to compensate the company itself against expenses to which it is put, for example, in dealing with, settling and compromising claims by equity shareholders for the allotment of new equity securities for which they have the right to subscribe. Undoubtedly, however, the company could recover such expenses from its directors who were actively involved in the issue of equity securities in disregard of the equity shareholders' statutory preferential subscription rights. Even if the court held that the Companies Act 1985 imposed no statutory duty on the directors toward the company in this respect, they would still be liable to it for their negligence in failing to fulfil their functions properly.

Public offerings of shares and debentures

Subject to the preferential subscription rights of equity shareholders, when a company issues equity securities for cash, the company may offer its unissued shares or debentures for subscription in whatever manner it chooses, but a private company may not offer such securities to the public, whether directly or by procuring a merchant bank or other intermediary to offer the securities to the public for purchase after having agreed to subscribe for them itself (Companies Act 1985, section 81(1)). For this purpose, an offer of securities is made to the public when it is made to the public generally, or to a section of the public, howsoever selected. However, an offer is not considered to be a public one if only the persons to whom it is addressed individually may accept it without being able to transfer the benefit of the offer to other persons, or if the offer is a matter of domestic concern between the company and the recipients (i.e. if the offer, although transferable, is made to a restricted number of persons, or if the offer is limited to existing shareholders or employees of a private company or members of their families, or to existing debenture holders of the company, and the benefit of the offer may be transferred only to other persons in the same category) (section 59(1) and section 60(1) and (3) to (6)).

If a private company offers its shares or debentures for subscription to a wider range of persons than is permitted by these provisions, both the company and its directors who are in default are guilty of an offence punishable by a fine, but the illegality of the offer does not invalidate the issue of shares or debentures under it (section 81(2) and (3)). Consequently, the only sanction against directors of a private company making a public offering of its shares or debentures is a criminal one, and there is no possibility of the company or the persons to whom the securities are issued claiming damages from the responsible directors, because none of them can possibly suffer any loss in consequence.

7.07 Prospectuses

A public company which offers its shares or debentures for subscription by the public or a section of it, either directly, or by a merchant bank or other intermediary subscribing for them and offering them for sale to the public, must deliver to the Registrar of Companies a copy of the document by which the offer is made (a prospectus) signed by all of the directors of the company and on behalf of the intermediary (if any) before the prospectus is published (section 58(1) and (2) and section 64(1) and (2)). If this is not done, the company and every person who is knowingly a party to the issue or publication of the prospectus (including the directors of the company) is guilty of an offence punishable by a fine, and if the offence is continued after conviction by the copy prospectus still not being delivered to the Registrar of Companies, every such person is also liable to a daily default fine (section 64(5)).

Obligatory contents of prospectuses

Unless a prospectus is issued only to existing shareholders and debenture holders of the company, it must contain detailed information about the company, its capital, financial history, business and directors and any business or assets which the company intends to acquire with the proceeds of the securities offered, in accordance with the requirements of Schedule 3 of the Companies Act 1985 (section 56(1), (2) and (5)). A criminal offence punishable by a fine is committed, however, only if a prospectus which should, but does not, contain that information in a complete and accurate form is issued together with a form of application for the securities which are offered (section 56(1), (2) and (4)). Even in that situation, any person responsible for the issue of the prospectus and the application form may escape conviction if he shows that he was unaware of any matter which should have been disclosed in the prospectus, or if he shows that the misstatement or omission complained of resulted from an honest mistake of fact on his part (section 66(1)).

Criminal liability for the issue of a defective prospectus together with an application form in respect of the securities offered is not imposed on directors of the issuing company as such, but on the persons who issue or publish those documents. Nevertheless, directors will always be caught by this provision, because if the company issues the prospectus itself, they will act on its behalf in doing so, and if the prospectus is issued by a merchant bank or other intermediary who offers the securities for sale to the public, the directors will be statutorily liable in the same way as if the company had issued the prospectus itself (section 58(2)).

The court has expressed the opinion in two cases that a director or other person who is responsible for the issue of a prospectus which does not set out all the information called for by Schedule 3 of the

Companies Act 1985 may be liable in damages to anyone who is thereby induced to subscribe for the securities offered, or who is induced to purchase them from the intermediary who offers them for sale to the public (*Re South of England Natural Gas and Petroleum Co. Ltd* (1911); *Lynde* v. *Nash* (1928), overruled on another ground (1929)). If directors are, in fact, subject to a liability in damages to subscribers, and the company is also secondarily or vicariously liable to subscribers for the directors' wrongdoing under the general principles of liability, it would seem that the responsible directors would also be obliged to indemnify the company if subscribers recover damages from it. It may also be that directors are liable directly to the company to compensate it for any loss it suffers under their general obligation to conduct the company's affairs with reasonable skill and care.

There is only one decided case where a company has been held entitled to recover damages from a person who was responsible for causing it to issue a false prospectus, with the consequence that the subscribers for the shares offered by it exercised their right to rescind the issue of shares to them and so deprived the company of the capital it needed. In that case, *Re Leeds and Hanley Theatre of Varieties Ltd* (1902), the persons responsible for the prospectus were promoters of the company. They were held liable to the company for the loss caused to it by the rescission of allotments by the subscribers, because by publishing a prospectus which they knew to be false the promoters had breached their duty to conduct the flotation of the company with proper care. If a promoter is liable to the company in these circumstances, a director must be liable, too, if he participates in the issue of a prospectus knowing that it contained false statements. A director would probably also be liable to the company if by the exercise of reasonable care he could have discovered that the prospectus was false or that it omitted information required to be included in it by law, even though he did not in fact know that the prospectus was false or defective.

Prospectuses in respect of listed securities

The provisions of the Companies Act 1985, dealt with above apply when a company offers shares or debentures to the public for subscription or for purchase through an intermediary, but after their issue the securities will only be dealt in on the Unlisted Securities Market of the Stock Exchange, or on the 'over the counter market' made by dealers in securities who are licensed by the Department of Trade and Industry, or by private dealings between investors. If a company offers securities which are to be listed on the Stock Exchange, however, the form and contents of the prospectus by which they are offered (the listing particulars) are governed, not by the Companies Act 1985, but by the Stock Exchange (Listing) Regulations 1984.

These regulations incorporate the Listing Particulars Directive issued by the Council of Ministers of the European Communities to harmonise the national laws of the member states in respect of prospectuses offering securities which will be listed on a stock exchange (Regulations, para 2(1) and para 3(1)). The disclosure requirements of the Listing Particulars Directive are more exacting than Schedule 3 of the Companies Act 1985, and in addition to its detailed requirements, the Directive requires listing particulars to contain all the information which 'is necessary to enable investors and their investment advisers to make an informed assessment of' the company, its financial position and the securities offered (Listing Particulars Directive, article 4(1)). Listing particulars must state the names of the persons who are responsible for their contents, that is the directors of the issuing company and the merchant bank or other intermediary (if any) who are offering the securities for sale to the public, and those persons must expressly declare in the listing particulars that to the best of their knowledge the information given therein is accurate and complete (Listing Particulars Directive, article 5(1) and Schedules A and B, para 1.2). Furthermore, listing particulars may not be published until they have been examined and approved by the Stock Exchange authorities (Listing Particulars Directive, article 18).

The additional safeguards designed to ensure the completeness and accuracy of listing particulars do not necessarily or logically exclude the normal obligations under the Companies Act 1985, of the directors of the issuing company and other persons who are responsible for their contents, nor do they necessarily exclude the liability of such persons for defective listing particulars under the Companies Act 1985. However, the Stock Exchange (Listing) Regulations 1984 do expressly exclude the whole, or at least some, of the obligations and liabilities imposed by the Companies Act 1985, in respect of prospectuses in their application to listing particulars (Regulations, para 7(1)(b)).

The vagueness of the drafting of the exclusion provision makes it difficult to ascertain which obligations and liabilities of directors, imposed by the Companies Act 1985, do apply when the prospectus takes the form of listing particulars, and which obligations do not apply. All that is certain from the Regulations is that a company and its directors commit a criminal offence punishable by a fine if they publish listing particulars without first delivering a copy of them to the Registrar of Companies (Regulations, para 7(7)). Whether directors are liable in damages to subscribers or purchasers of the securities offered by prospectuses published in the form of listing particulars if the particulars are defective, is not stated in the Regulations, nor is the question of any liability which the directors may incur to the issuing company dealt with there.

The result is that directors may be liable in damages to subscribers and purchasers of securities for breaches of statutory duty if the courts interpret the Regulations as imposing such a liability by implication. If such a liability does arise, it may be that the issuing company is also liable to subscribers and purchasers of securities in the same way, and in that case the company would undoubtedly have an indemnity claim against the responsible directors. It may also be that the responsible directors will be liable directly to the issuing company for any loss it suffers on the ground that they have failed to exercise proper skill and care in preparing and publishing the listing particulars. None of these questions has yet come before the courts for decision.

Material false statements in prospectuses

Directors incur liability under the Companies Act 1985 if they publish prospectuses which contain material false statements of fact, or if they allot shares under a prospectus before all the shares offered by it have been subscribed, or in the case of the first prospectus published by a company, if they allot shares under it before the minimum subscription specified in the prospectus has been subscribed (Companies Act 1985, sections 83 to 85 and sections 67 to 69). The remedies in these situations are primarily given to the persons who subscribe for or purchase securities under such prospectuses, however, and so are dealt with below in Chapter 9 in connection with directors' liabilities to shareholders. Nevertheless, it should be borne in mind that the publication of a prospectus containing material false statements also involves participating directors in criminal liability.

PRINCIPAL DISCLOSURE OBLIGATIONS

7.08 The furnishing of information

Directors are extensively required by the Companies Act 1985 and the Insolvency Act 1986 to provide their company and other persons and public authorities with information about themselves and their acts and activities, and about the transactions and interests of themselves and of members of their immediate families which may be of concern to the company or the public. Some of this information must be recorded by the company in registers or records which are open to inspection by shareholders and also by the public. Other information is embodied in accounts or reports which the company or its directors are required to publish or circulate. Other information still is exacted for a particular purpose, such as an investigation into the management of a company's affairs. The sanction for fulfilment of the directors' obligation to notify or inform the company or any other person or authority of such matters is liability to a fine, or in some situations where information is suppressed or false information is provided, liability to a fine or imprisonment or both.

7.09 Annual accounts and reports

The notes to the annual accounts of a company must give a considerable volume of information about the company's relationships to its subsidiaries and associated companies, and also detailed information about its directors' remuneration and about pensions and compensation for loss of office paid or payable by the company or its subsidiaries to the company's present and past directors (Companies Act 1985, section 231(1) and (2)). To ensure that information about directors' remuneration, pensions and compensation payments is correctly given, all present directors and all persons who have been directors within the preceding five years are required to furnish details of the remuneration, pension payments and compensation received or receivable by them for the financial year to which the annual accounts relate, and their failure to do so is punishable by a fine (section 231(4)).

Similarly, the directors' annual report which accompanies its annual accounts must show the number of shares and debentures issued by the company or any other company in the same group in which its directors and their spouses or minor children were interested at the beginning and end of the company's financial year (section 235(3) and Schedule 7, Part I). Information about such interests must be notified to the company by the director concerned when an interest is acquired or disposed of, and the notified information must be recorded by the company in a register which it must keep (sections 324, 325 and 328). Failure of a director to give a notification of an acquisition or disposal of an interest in such securities or the giving of a notification which the director knows to be false, is an offence punishable by imprisonment or a fine or both (section 324(7)). Furthermore, directors collectively commit an offence punishable by a fine if they fail to include the necessary information about the interests of each of them and their families in the directors' annual report, but it is a defence for a director to show that he took all reasonable steps to ensure compliance (section 235(7)).

7.10 Directors' interests in company transactions

The obligation of directors and shadow directors to disclose their interests in contracts and transactions and proposed contracts and transactions with their companies at the first board meeting at which the matter is discussed, or at the first board meeting after the directors' interest arises, has already been mentioned in [4.06] (section 317(1) and (5)). If the director has a continuing interest in contracts or transactions between the company and another company or firm of which he is a member, or between the company and a particular person with whom he is connected in one of various ways, he may give a general notice to the board of directors that he is to be regarded as interested in all contracts and transactions between the company and that other company, firm or person, and he need not then disclose his interest again when such a contract or transaction is proposed or entered into (section 317(3) and (4)). The failure of a director to disclose his interest in a contract or transaction with his company is an offence punishable by a fine (section 317(7)), but the failure to disclose does not affect the validity of the contract or transaction, although it may be voidable by the company under the rules of equity discussed in Chapter 4 (*Hely-Hutchinson* v. *Brayhead Ltd* (1968)).

A particular interest which a director must disclose is the promise of a payment to him of compensation for loss of office on his retirement or removal from his directorship when a takeover or general offer is made to acquire the company's issued shares from their holders. If the director does not disclose the proposed payment to the shareholders to whom the offer is addressed as well as to the board of directors, he commits an offence punishable by a fine, and is accountable to the shareholders who accept the offer for any payment he receives (section 314(3) and section 315(1)).

7.11 Compromises and arrangements

A company may propose a compromise or arrangement with its shareholders or creditors or any class of them, and if the compromise or arrangement is approved by separate meetings called by the court of all the different classes of shareholders or creditors affected, and is also sanctioned by the court after the class meetings have approved it, the compromise or arrangement becomes binding on the company and all its shareholders and creditors concerned (section 425(1) and (2)).

With the notices calling the class meetings the company must send to the shareholders and creditors a statement explaining the effect of the compromise or arrangement, and the statement must in particular explain its effect on any material interests of the directors, with a full disclosure of the nature and extent of those interests (section 426(2)). To enable the company to prepare and circulate the explanatory statement, every director must give the company all relevant information about any interest he has and the effect of the proposed compromise or arrangement on it, and if he fails to do so, he commits an offence punishable by a fine (section 426(7)).

7.12 Investigation of a company's affairs

The affairs of a company may be investigated by inspectors appointed by the Secretary of State for Trade and Industry if it appears to him that the company's affairs have been improperly conducted, or if a certain fraction of the company's shareholders request an investigation, or the court orders it to be held (sections 431 and 432). The present and past directors of a company subject to such an investigation must produce to the inspectors all books and documents relating to the company which are in their possession or power. They must also give the inspectors all the assistance which they are reasonably able to give, including answering questions put to them by the inspectors on oath if the inspectors require it. They must also at the inspectors' request produce all documents in their possession relating to their own or other persons' bank accounts if the inspectors have reasonable ground for believing that money of the company has been paid into such bank accounts in connection with undisclosed or improper transactions (section 434(1), (3) and (4) and section 435(1)). If a directors fails to fulfil any of these obligations of disclosure and refuses to comply on the inspectors requiring him to do so, the inspectors may certify the matter to the court, which may punish the director in the same way as though he had been guilty of a contempt of court (i.e. by fine or imprisonment or both) (section 436(2) and (3)).

In addition to ordering a formal investigation of the company's affairs, the Secretary of State for Trade and Industry may, if he thinks there is good reason for doing so, require any company to produce to his officers such books and papers of the company as he specifies (section 447(1) and (2)). If the directors of the company fail to produce the books and papers called for, or if any present or past directors fail to explain them or their contents when required to do so, they are guilty of an offence punishable by a fine (section 447(6)). Furthermore, any director who destroys, mutilates or falsifies any document relating to his company, or makes a false entry in it, or knowingly makes a false statement in respect of a document which he is required to produce to an officer acting on behalf of the Secretary of State, is guilty of an offence punishable by imprisonment or a fine or both (section 450(1) and (3) and section 451).

7.13 Directors' declarations in connection with share purchases, liquidations, etc.

Directors are required to disclose information about the company's affairs or to make declarations about them in connection with several different legal actions and transactions which a company may take or enter into and which may affect its capital or status. Since the transaction is based upon the directors' declaration, criminal sanctions are imposed if the declaration is false or unfounded.

Share purchases

If a private company proposes to provide financial assistance out of its profits to enable a person to acquire shares in it or in its parent or holding company, or if a private company proposes to purchase or redeem shares in itself out of assets representing its capital, the transaction must be approved by a special resolution passed by a general meeting based on a statutory declaration made by the directors of the company that there will be no ground on which the company will be unable to pay its debts (including contingent and prospective debts) as they fall due during the year following the date on which the financial assistance is given or the shares in the company are purchased or redeemed by it (section 155(6), section 156(2) and (3) and section 173(3) and (4)). The statutory declaration must state that the directors have made full inquiry into the affairs and prospects of the company, and the declaration must be supported by a report by the auditors of the company that they too have enquired into the financial condition of the company and that they are not aware of anything which indicates that the opinion as to the company's present and future solvency expressed in the directors' statutory declaration is unreasonable (section 156(2) and (4) and section 173(3) and (5)).

A director who makes a statutory declaration as to the company's present and prospective solvency without having reasonable grounds for expressing the opinion that the company is and will remain solvent for 12 months, is guilty of an offence punishable by imprisonment or a fine or both (section 156(7) and section 173(6)). Moreover, if a private company which purchases or redeems its own shares out of assets representing its share capital goes into liquidation within one year thereafter, every director who joined in making the statutory declaration about the company's solvency may be required to contribute to the company's assets a sum equal to the assets so applied. He may, nevertheless, escape this liability by showing that he had reasonable grounds at the time for expressing his opinion about the company's present and continuing solvency in the statutory declaration (section 504(1) to (3)).

Declaration of solvency

Somewhat similar to the statutory declaration which directors make in connection with a private company's purchase or redemption of its own shares out of assets representing its capital is the statutory declaration which the directors of any company, whether public or private, must make if a general meeting of the company is about to pass a resolution that it shall be wound up voluntarily, and that the liquidation shall be a members' voluntary winding up controlled by the shareholders, and not by the creditors of the company (sections 577 to 582 and sections 584 and 585). The statutory declaration must be made by all the directors or by a majority of them if they are more than two in number. It must state that the directors making the declaration have made full inquiry into the company's affairs, and that they have formed the opinion that the company will be able to pay its debts in full within 12 months after the winding up resolution is passed; and the declaration must embody a statement of the company's assets and liabilities at the most recent practicable date (Insolvency Act 1986, section 89(1) and (2)).

If the company's debts are not paid in full within the 12 month period, the directors who made the statutory declaration are guilty of an offence punishable by imprisonment or a fine or both, unless they prove that they had reasonable grounds for expressing the opinion that the company was solvent and able to discharge its debts in full within the 12 month period (section 89(4) and (5)). However, no personal liability is imposed on the directors to pay or contribute toward the company's debts if their opinion in the statutory declaration proves to be unfounded.

Statement of a company's affairs

There is no equivalent to the directors' statutory declaration of solvency when a company is ordered to be wound up by an order of the court on the petition of a creditor, a shareholder or the company itself. When a winding up order has been made, however, one or more of the directors and the secretary of the company must within 21 days after being required to do so by the official receiver (an official of the Department of Trade and Industry) prepare and submit to him a statement of the company's affairs verified by affidavit and containing details of the company's assets and liabilities, the names and addresses of its creditors, and particulars of mortgages or other securities held by creditors of the company for their debts, and if any shares of the company are not fully paid, the names and addresses of the holders of those shares and the amounts paid up and remaining unpaid on their respective shareholdings (Insolvency Act 1986, section 131(1), (2) and (4)). The directors' statement of the company's affairs is used as the basis of the official receiver's inquiry into and report on the company's affairs and the cause of its failure (if it is insolvent) which he is required to make (section 132(1)), and the directors' statement of the company's affairs is also used by the liquidator together with other information he possesses or obtains as a guide to the way in which the liquidation should be conducted.

If directors fail to submit a statement of affairs to the official receiver within 21 days after he calls for it, they commit an offence punishable by a fine, and on a second or subsequent conviction for a continuation of the default, they are liable to a daily default fine (section 131(7)). If directors knowingly give false information in a statement of affairs, they commit an offence punishable by imprisonment for not more than 7 years or by an unlimited fine or by both (Perjury Act 1911, section 2). Furthermore, if a director makes a material omission in a statement of affairs he is also guilty of an offence punishable by imprisonment for not more than 7 years or by an unlimited fine or by both, but it is a defence for him to prove that he had no intent to defraud (Insolvency Act 1986, section 210(1), (4) and (5)). No statutory liability is imposed on directors to pay or contribute the amount of debts of a company if they fail to disclose them fully in a statement of the company's affairs, or if they misrepresent the extent of the company's assets.

7.14 Inspection rights

None of the provisions of the Companies Act 1985 which require directors to furnish information to a company or to notify or publish information, expressly empowers the company or any interested person to obtain an order for the court compelling the disclosure or notification of that information. It is only an apparent exception to this that in certain circumstances interested persons can obtain orders compelling the company to allow them to inspect certain registers and documents which the company is required to keep, such as its registers of shareholders and of debenture holders and its registers of directors and of directors' interests in shares or debentures issued by it or other companies in the same group, and copies of directors' service contracts and of contracts by the company for the purchase of shares issued by itself (section 169(4), (5) and (8), section 191(1), (2) and (5), section 288(1), (3) and (5), section 318(1), (7) and (9), section 325(1) and (5), section 326(6) and section 356(1), (3), (4) and (6)). These provisions are not in fact exceptions to the omission from the Companies Act 1985, of express provisions for the enforcement of directors' obligations of disclosure or publicity. All of them enable third persons to compel the company to disclose information in the company's possession which may well have been provided to the company by its directors, but none of them establish machinery by which the company or an interested person may compel a director to supply information directly.

Chapter 8

The Enforcement of Directors' Statutory Duties

The principal means for enforcing directors' obligations under the Companies Act 1985 is the prosecution of delinquent or defaulting directors under the Act or other legislation, such as the Insolvency Act 1986, the Theft Act 1968 or the Perjury Act 1911. Alternative remedies for breaches of directors' statutory obligations to their companies or the infringement of statutory prohibitions imposed on them are rarely specified expressly in the Companies Act 1985. On the few occasions when the Act does create a specific remedy, it most frequently takes the form of a power for the company to rescind an offending transaction; or to recover funds of the company which have been improperly expended; or to require a director who has improperly benefited to account to the company for the value of the benefit he has obtained; or to recover damages or compensation from a director responsible for the contravention if the company has suffered loss in consequence.

There are, nevertheless, certain obligations of directors which the court is expressly empowered to enforce specifically by the Companies Act 1985. There are also certain situations where express authority is given by the Act for interested persons to fulfil an obligation which directors have failed to fulfil. These statutory remedies will first be examined. The general questions will then be considered whether a company can obtain an order of the court compelling specific fulfilment of directors' statutory obligations when no express statutory remedy is provided, and whether a company can alternatively recover damages or compensation from directors who breach or fail to fulfil their statutory obligations when the Companies Act 1985 is silent on the availability of such a remedy.

STATUTORY REMEDIES

8.01 Acquisitions by and disposals to directors

If a director of a company or its parent or holding company or a person connected with him enters into a contract or arrangement with the company under which the director or the person connected with him is either to acquire from the company or to transfer to it assets (other than cash) exceeding a certain value, the contract or arrangement must be approved by a general meeting of the company by ordinary resolution, and if the director is a director of the company's parent company, it must also be approved by a general meeting of the parent company by ordinary resolution, as indicated earlier in Chapter 4 [4.06] (Companies Act 1985, section 320(1) and (2)).

If the necessary approval or approvals of the contract or arrangement are not given before it is entered into or within a reasonable time afterwards, the company which enters into the contract or arrangement may rescind it and recover any assets which have been transferred under it. However, the company may not rescind if restitution is no longer possible, or if the company has already been indemnified for any loss or damage it has suffered in consequence of entering into the contract or arrangement, or if a third person has acquired rights under the contract or arrangement or in assets transferred under it for value in good faith and without knowledge that the contract or arrangement had not been approved by the appropriate general meeting or meetings (section 322(1) and (3)).

Additionally, if the contract or arrangement is not approved before it is entered into by a general meeting of the company and (where necessary) its parent company, the director or person connected with him who is the other party to the contract or arrangement, and any other director of the company who authorised the contract or arrangement or any transfer of assets under it, are liable to indemnify the company for any consequential loss or damage it suffers, and they are also accountable to the company for any gain which he makes directly or indirectly from the contract or arrangement (section 322(3)).

The company's remedies are nominally cumulative, and the Companies Act 1985 expressly provides that it may recover damages for its loss and compel the director or other party to account to it for his gain, whether or not it has rescinded the contract or arrangement (section 322(4)). Nevertheless, the company is expressly precluded from rescinding if it has recovered the full amount of its loss (section 322(2)), and it would not be able to rescind and also recover any gain made by the other party, because this would prevent the parties from being restored to their original position under the process of restitution. The result of this is that rescission and restitution on the one hand and the recovery of damages or gains on the other are alternative, and not cumulative, remedies. These provisions apply to shadow directors in the same way as they do to directors (section 320(3)).

8.02 Loans and financial accommodation for directors

Identical remedies are given by the Companies Act 1985, when there is a breach of the statutory prohibition on companies making loans or quasi-loans to any of its directors or to a person connected with any of them, or if there is a breach of the statutory prohibition on companies entering into credit transactions with any such director or other person.

The Act imposes a general prohibition on a company making a loan to a director of itself or its parent or holding company, and also a general prohibition on a company which is a public company or which belongs to a group which includes a public company, making quasi-loans to, or entering into credit transaction with, a director of itself or its parent company, or making loans or quasi-loans to a person connected with such a director or entering into credit transactions with such a person (section 330(2) to (4)). Shadow directors are treated in the same way as directors for the purpose of the prohibition (section 330(5)).

A quasi-loan is a transaction under which the company pays or agrees to pay a sum of money to a third person, or reimburses or agrees to reimburse a third person, for expenditure incurred by the third person for the benefit of a director or a person connected with him, and the director or connected person has agreed to reimburse the company or is legally liable to do so (section 331(3)). A credit transaction is one by which the company supplies goods or services or sells, leases or hires land or goods to a director or a person connected with him in return for periodical payments or payment of a lump sum by instalments or at a deferred date (section 331(7)). Quasi-loans therefore include the payment of a directors' private debts by his company at his request, and credit transactions include a company entering into a hire-purchase agreement or a credit sale agreement with its director.

There are several exceptions to the general prohibition on companies making loans to their directors or entering into the other kinds of transactions mentioned above. Some of these exceptions depend on the purpose for which the financial accommodation is given, and many of them are conditional on the indebtedness of the director or connected person not exceeding a certain amount.

Curiously, contraventions of the statutory prohibitions on a company from making loans or providing financial accommodation for its directors or persons connected with them, are made criminal offences punishable by imprisonment or a fine or both only if the company is a public company or belongs to a group which includes a public company (section 342(1), (2) and (4)). The civil remedies available to a company which makes a prohibited loan or quasi-loan or enters into a prohibited credit transaction, on the other hand, are the same, whether the company is a public or private one, and the remedies are the same as those available to a company which has entered into a contract or arrangement with a director or a person connected with him for the acquisition or disposal of assets by the company when the contract or arrangement should have been approved by a general meeting of the company but has not been.

If the contract for the loan or financial accommodation is still executory and no advance has been made or credit given, the company may rescind the contract. If the contract has been carried out, the company may obtain restitution of its advance or any goods or property which it has supplied on credit, but it must then restore to the director or person connected with him any payment which he has made and cancel any security which he has given (section 341(1)). The company cannot rescind the transaction if restitution is not possible, or if the company has been indemnified against any loss it has suffered in consequence of the transaction, or if a third person has acquired rights under the transaction in good faith and for value without knowledge of the contravention (section 341(1)). Additionally, the company can recover from the director or connected person who has been financially accommodated, and also from any other director who authorised the transaction, the amount of any gain he has obtained directly or indirectly as a result of the transaction (e.g. the profit obtained on reselling property purchased by means of an illicit loan), or the amount of any loss or damage which the company has suffered in consequence of the transaction (section 341(2)).

The same observations apply about the alternative character of these remedies as were made above in connection with contracts or arrangements for the acquisition of assets from a company by a director, or by a company from a director, when the transaction has not been approved by a general meeting of the company. The damages recoverable by the company would, however, appear to be limited to the amount of the financial accommodation provided, plus interest and incidental expenses incurred by the company.

8.03 Compensation for loss of office

The remedy of restitution is also provided by the Companies Act 1985 when a director accepts compensation for loss of office from the company itself, or from a purchaser of the whole or part of its business undertaking, if the payment of the compensation has not been approved by a general meeting of shareholders by ordinary resolution (sections 312 and 313). The company's remedy is implicit in the statutory provision that the payment of compensation for loss of office in these circumstances is not lawful and, where the compensation is paid by a purchaser of the company's undertaking, there is a statutory provision that the director who receives the compensation holds it in trust for the company. The consequence of these provisions is that the company may recover the amount of compensation paid to the director in the same way as if a wrongful disposal of its own property had taken place.

8.04 Other statutory remedies

Restitution and claims for damages are the principal remedies given expressly by the Companies Act 1985, in the few situations where it does create remedies for breaches of directors' duties other than criminal prosecution. Other remedies have already been mentioned, such as the termination by reasonable notice given by a company of a director's service contract for more than 5 years when the duration of the contract has not been approved by a general meeting of shareholders (section 319(6)), and the power of a fraction of a company's shareholders who properly require directors to call an extraordinary general meeting to call it themselves on the directors' default (section 368(4)), and the power of the Secretary of State for Trade and Industry to call or direct the holding of an annual general meeting if the directors neglect to call it (section 367(1)).

REMEDIES IN THE ABSENCE OF STATUTORY PROVISION

It was observed at the beginning of Chapter 7 that most of the prescriptions of the Companies Act 1985, whether prohibitory or requiring action to be taken by a company or its directors, are sanctioned by the creation of criminal offences and the imposition of criminal sanctions. The few prescriptions in the Act which are not reinforced by penalties for nonconformity mostly take the form of conditions which must be fulfilled for the validity of certain acts or transactions which the company may wish to carry out or enter into, and the inherent sanction for the non-fulfilment of the prescription is the legal invalidity, ineffectiveness or unenforceability of the act or transaction.

The question remains, nevertheless, whether those prescriptions of the Companies Act 1985 which are backed by criminal sanctions also entitle the company or other interested parties acting on its behalf (in particular, shareholders) to obtain civil remedies against directors who do not comply. May the company recover damages to compensate it for any loss it has suffered because of the failure to comply and an injunction, or a mandatory injunction where positive acts are called for, to ensure compliance in the future? There is very little judicial authority on this question, and resort must therefore be had to general principles and deductions made from them.

8.05 Actions for damages and injunctions

The inclination of the courts in cases decided during the nineteenth century was to deny any civil remedy for breach of a statutory prescription when the statute imposed its own express criminal or other sanction. This was because the courts treated the statutory sanction as excluding all other possible remedies (*Patent Agents Institute* v. *Lockwood* (1894); *Pasmore* v. *Oswaldtwistle UDC* (1898)).

By the end of the century a more liberal view began to assert itself, however, and it was conceded in a succession of cases that if a statutory prescription is imposed for the protection of a definable class of persons, the presence of a statutory criminal sanction does not prevent any of those persons who has been particularly adversely affected from suing for damages for the loss he has suffered because of the defendant's failure to comply with the prescription (*Groves* v. *Lord Wimborne* (1898); *Black* v. *Fife Coal Co. Ltd* (1912); *Lonrho Ltd* v. *Shell Petroleum Co. Ltd (No. 2)* (1982) per Lord Diplock).

Nevertheless, it is a question of interpretation of the particular statute whether it was intended that persons who would benefit by its observance should be able to sue for damages if it was not complied with, and it did not always follow that they could (*Cutler* v. *Wandsworth Stadium Ltd* (1949)). As Lord Denning observed in *Ex parte Island Records Ltd* (1978), at pages 135–137 of the report, there has been no judicial consistency in deciding whether actions for damages should lie or not.

The courts have been somewhat more generous in awarding injunctions or mandatory injunctions to enforce statutory prescriptions which are accompanied by express statutory sanctions. An injunction will not be issued if the applicant's interest in the matter is simply that of a member of the public in having the law adhered to, but an injunction or a mandatory injunction will be issued to enforce compliance with a statutory prohibition or prescription if the applicant has a recognised legal right which will be safeguarded by compliance, or if he has an interest in the matter which may be adversely affected by continued non-compliance (*Gouriet* v. *Union of Post Office Workers* (1978); *Torquay Hotel Co. Ltd* v. *Cousins* (1969); *Ex parte Island Records Ltd* (1978)).

8.06 Application to the Companies Acts

There is no direct judicial authority on the question whether the different obligations and prohibitions imposed on directors by the Companies Act 1985 can be enforced by the company seeking injunctions (whether prohibitory or mandatory) against directors who are in default, or by the company suing them for damages to compensate it for any loss it has suffered in consequence of their default.

The absence of case law on this question is not surprising. The first and obvious reason for the lack of decided cases is that the directors themselves usually control the initiation of any litigation by the company, and it is not to be expected that they would bring proceedings in the company's name complaining of their own failure to comply with the Companies Acts. Secondly, there is a rule of law, usually known by the name of one of the earliest cases in which it was enunciated, the rule in *Foss* v. *Harbottle* (1843), which inhibits individual shareholders from litigating on their company's behalf to enforce rights or to protect interests vested in it and not in themselves personally. Most of the obligations and prohibitions imposed on directors by the Companies Act 1985, where there are no expressly enacted sanctions or only criminal sanctions, fall into this category. Nevertheless, as will be shown in Chapter 9 (where the limitations on litigation initiated by shareholders are dealt with) a general meeting of shareholders may always authorise the initiation or continuation of litigation in the company's name, even against the opposition of the board of directors (*Marshall's Valve Gear Co. Ltd* v. *Manning Wardle & Co. Ltd* (1909)). In practice, however, the power of a general meeting to authorise litigation is little used, and is of no use at all if the directors are themselves holders of a majority of the company's voting shares, or if the company's issued voting shares are fragmented among numerous shareholders, none of whom, and no cohesive group of whom, have voting control.

The only guidance as to the availability of civil proceedings to enforce the prescriptions of the Companies Act 1985, is to be found in three cases where shareholders, directors and auditors of companies sought unsuccessfully to enforce provisions of the Act against the board of directors and the company they served. In the earliest case, *Cuff* v. *London and County Land and Building Co. Ltd* (1912), the Court of Appeal held that an auditor cannot enforce against the company whose shareholders appointed him the provision in section 237(3) of the Companies Act 1985, that auditors shall at all times have access to the company's books, accounts and vouchers, and shall be entitled to call for such explanations as they think necessary from the company's officers. The court's reason for its conclusion was that if the court were to issue a mandatory injunction against the company or its officers, it would interfere with the conduct of the company's internal management, which it is precluded from doing by the rule in *Foss* v. *Harbottle*.

In the second case, *Conway* v. *Petronius Clothing Co. Ltd* (1978), Slade J held that a director of a company cannot obtain a mandatory injunction against the company to enforce the statutory provision in the Companies Act 1985 section 222(1) that its accounting records shall at all times be open to inspection by the company's officers. This provision was held to confer no statutory right on directors against the company, and the common law right of individual directors to inspect the company's records would only be enforced by the court issuing a mandatory injunction if there were no good reasons why the court should exercise its discretion not to do so. In other words, the director's so-called common law right to inspect was nothing more than an interest which the court has a discretion to protect or not.

Finally, in *Devlin* v. *Slough Estates Ltd* (1983), Dillon J held that a shareholder has no statutory right to have the annual accounts of a company properly prepared so as to give a true and fair view of the company's financial position in accordance with the Companies Act 1985 section 228(2). Moreover, in the absence of fraud on the part of the directors, the court will not allow a shareholder to enforce the company's right to have annual accounts giving a true and fair view prepared by its directors where the omission or other matter complained of was one which, in the exercise of their business judgment, the directors might consider immaterial.

All these cases illustrate the court's traditional reluctance to intervene in the internal management and conduct of a company's affairs, but it should be remembered that in each of these cases the company was not the plaintiff, but a defendant, and the litigation was initiated by a person who relied, not on a direct right, but only on an interest in having the company's affairs properly conducted. The court's attitude might be different if the company were the plaintiff. The only circumstances where the court may in practice be compelled to answer the question whether the prescriptions of the Companies Act 1985 generally confer corresponding rights of enforcement on the company would be where breaches of the Companies Act 1985 have been followed by the replacement of the responsible directors by a new board, which now sues in the company's name to recover damages to compensate it for the consequential loss it has suffered. This has not yet happened in circumstances where the company has not also had a parallel claim against the responsible directors for breaches of their fiduciary duties owed to it. In that situation it has always been the breach of the former directors' fiduciary duties which has been relied on.

8.07 Judicial evasion of the question whether breaches of statutory obligation are actionable

It may well be that the courts will avoid ever giving a direct answer to the question whether the company has a direct right against its directors to the fulfilment of their obligations under the Companies Act 1985, by the court imposing liability on them directly under the Act instead of giving a remedy for breach of the directors' appropriate fiduciary duties. If it adopts this strategy, the court will be able to order the appropriate remedy for breach of the fiduciary duty involved, whether the remedy is an injunction, an account or the payment of compensation or the rescission of a transaction.

The court has already treated breaches of statutory duty as amounting also to breaches of fiduciary duty in cases where the company or a shareholder suing on its behalf has sought to invalidate a transaction by which the company has given financial assistance for the acquisition of shares in itself or its parent company in contravention of the Companies Act 1948, section 54 (now the Companies Act 1985, section 151(1) and (2)). The ground on which the court has given a remedy in such cases, whether an injunction, rescission of a contract or an order for the payment of compensation to the company by the responsible directors, has been that the provision of financial assistance out of the company's assets was or would be a disposition of those assets in excess of the company's powers or an illegal disposition, and therefore a breach of the directors' first fiduciary duty (*Selangor United Rubber Estates Ltd* v. *Cradock (No. 3)* (1968); *Wallersteiner* v. *Moir* (1974); *Belmont Finance Corpn. Ltd* v. *Williams Furniture Ltd (No. 2)* (1980); *Armour Hick Northern Ltd* v. *Armour Trust Ltd* (1980)).

Similarly, the court has held directors liable to replace funds of a company which they have distributed as a dividend to its shareholders when the company had not earned equivalent profits. The court has imposed liability in such cases on the ground that the directors had disposed of the company's assets in excess of their powers, and they must therefore make restitution (*Re Kingston Cotton Mills Co. (No. 2)* (1896); *Dovey* v. *Cory* (1901)). Now that the prohibition on the payment of dividends otherwise than out of the surplus of the company's accumulated realised profits over its accumulated realised losses has been made statutory by the Companies Act 1985, section 263(1) and (3), a company may obtain an injunction to prevent the payment of an illicit dividend, or may recover the amount of a dividend improperly paid from its directors, by relying on the directors' fiduciary obligation not to dispose of the company's assets in excess of the company's powers or otherwise illegally.

Not all breaches by directors of the prescriptions of the Companies Act 1985 involve breaches of their fiduciary duty not to dispose of the company's assets improperly, of course. Those breaches of the Act which do not involve the company in any disposal of assets, but which may cause it loss, may nevertheless be treated either as being acts in excess of the company's powers or in excess of the directors' own powers conferred by the company's articles of association. Alternatively, they may be treated as acts or omissions involving the directors in breaches of their other fiduciary duty to conduct the company's affairs with proper care and skill. In either case, the directors will incur liability to the company for breach of the relevant fiduciary duty, and the company may obtain appropriate remedies against them. The court would then use the directors' disregard of the relevant prescription of the Companies Act 1985 as the basis for concluding that the directors had exceeded their powers or had acted negligently, and the resulting breach of their fiduciary duties would justify the award of appropriate remedies against them.

The only remaining question would then be whether the court would hold directors liable to the company absolutely if they had actively breached a prescription of the Companies Act 1985, or whether they would be liable only if they acted without exercising proper care and skill. The inclination of the courts is to impose absolute liability for breach of a statutory prescription only when the defendant has control over all the factors which are needed to ensure compliance (*Minister of Housing and Local Government* v. *Sharp* (1970), per Denning LJ). In other situations, the court requires the defendant merely to prove that all reasonable and practicable steps were taken to prevent a breach of the statutory prescription in order to escape liability (*Caswell* v. *Powell Duffryn Associated Collieries Ltd* (1940); *LPTB* v. *Lupson* (1949)).

Probably the court would adopt the second alternative in respect of most of the obligations imposed on directors by the Companies Act 1985. It would then impose absolute liability on directors for non-compliance only when the means of compliance were wholly at their disposal.

If the breach of fiduciary duty complained of were a total omission by directors to fulfil an obligation imposed by the Act, the only possible liability which could be imposed on them as fiduciaries would be for their failure to exercise proper care and skill. However, directors are expected to acquaint themselves with their statutory obligations, and so they are likely to escape liability for non-compliance only in situations where, despite the exercise of proper skill and care, they were unaware of the facts which gave rise to the duty to act.

8.08 Conclusions

The conclusions reached in this section of the present chapter are necessarily incomplete in view of the lack of decided cases. The uncertainty about the nature and extent of directors' liability for infringements of the Companies Act 1985 results from the refusal of English law to accept that failure to comply with a statutory prescription always results in the imposition of personal liability for consequential loss on the persons who are responsible for ensuring compliance. In this respect, French law is simpler, in that under it directors are liable to anyone who suffers loss as a result of their fault in not complying with the legislation which governs their company. The French law No. 66-537 of 24 July 1967 governing commercial companies provides, in article 244(1), that:

'... directors are liable jointly and separately... to the company and to third persons for infringements of the legislation and regulations applicable to companies, for violation of the instrument constituting the company [i.e. the equivalent of the memorandum and articles of association] and for faults in the conduct of the company's affairs.'

The corollary of the uncertainty in English law about the liability of directors to their companies for infringements of the Companies Act 1985, is that the courts have relied and inevitably will continue to rely on the fiduciary duties of the directors in order to give companies appropriate remedies when their directors fail to conform to the prescriptions of the Act. In one respect this secondary method of enforcing statutory obligations and prohibitions is, nevertheless, beneficial. The range of remedies available for breaches of directors' fiduciary duties are extensive and flexible, and are also well established by decisions of the equity courts over the last 200 years. As in so many other respects, the lack of system in this sector of English law does not result in companies having insufficient legal protection, but merely in the substantive law being more complex that it need be. Whether shareholders and creditors are also adequately protected by the law as it stands at present is a separate question, which will be examined in the following chapters.

Chapter 9

Directors' Duties and Liabilities to Shareholders

GENERAL IMMUNITY FROM LIABILITY

In general, directors owe no duties to shareholders of their company, or to its creditors or persons who enter into or negotiate transactions with it, merely because they act on behalf of the company in their capacity as directors, or because of their possession as directors of fuller information about the company's affairs than other persons have. This is so, even if by their acts directors cause the company to incur a legal liability, for example, if they cause the company to break a contract it has entered into, or if they induce the company to disregard or infringe the rights of a shareholder by refusing to allow him to vote at a general meeting, or by refusing to pay him a dividend which has been duly declared.

The fact that a director has personal interest in the matter in question does not of itself impose any obligation on him towards shareholders or creditors or other persons which he would not otherwise be under. A director is therefore under no duty to disclose relevant information in his possession as to the value of shares or debentures of a company when he negotiates a purchase of shares or debentures for himself from a shareholder or debenture holder, or when he negotiates a sale of his own shares or debentures to a shareholder or to anyone else. In this respect he is in exactly the same position as any other buyer or seller of shares or debentures.

9.01 Reason for directors' general immunity

The general immunity of directors from liability to shareholders and creditors of their company for their acts and omissions while acting as directors, and the absence of special duties imposed on directors toward shareholders and creditors because of their greater knowledge of the company's affairs and their power to influence the company's actions, is the result of the legal relationship which is created by a person becoming a director being one which exists exclusively between the director and the company as a separate legal entity apart from its shareholders and creditors. The company is incorporated and becomes a distinct legal person in its own right on its registration at the Companies Registry and the issue of its certificate of incorporation by the Registrar of Companies (Companies Act 1985, section 13(1) and (3)). It is, therefore, a separate legal person from the two or more persons who subscribe its memorandum and articles of association and become its first members, and from the other persons who later subscribe for shares in the company. The directors of a company owe duties to it both under the Companies Act 1985, and under the rules of common law and equity, as was shown in the preceding chapters. But the existence of these duties does not mean that directors are under parallel duties to the same effect owed to persons other than the company, even though those other persons, as shareholders and creditors of the company, will be the ones who suffer economically if the directors' duties to the company are disregarded.

It is not possible for shareholders or creditors to avoid the consequence of directors not owing duties to them individually by seeking to bring indirect actions to enforce directors' duties to the company or to recover reparation for the loss suffered by them as a result of breaches of those duties. Consequently, shareholders and creditors cannot recover damages for the fall in the market value of their shares, or for the company's assets being reduced to an amount insufficient to pay its debts, by suing directors for the wrong or tort of a conspiracy between themselves to act without justification in a way likely to cause loss to other persons, when the alleged conspiracy is simply the concurrence of the directors in acting in a way which is inconsistent with their duties to the company (*Prudential Assurance Co. Ltd* v. *Newman Industries Ltd (No. 2)* (1982)). Similarly, a person who has entered into a contract with a company which it has broken cannot bring an action against the company's directors for the wrong or tort of inducing another person, the company, to break a contract with the plaintiff (*Said* v. *Butt* (1920)).

Although the immunity of directors from liability to shareholders and creditors for acts and omissions by directors while acting as such can be legally justified by the existence of their duties to the company or by the company's sole responsibility for contracts it has entered into, the separate legal existence of the company logically provides no compelling reason for the courts refusing to impose duties on directors toward persons with whom they deal or with whom they assume a special, personal relationship. Nevertheless, this is what the courts have done in making the immunity of directors from liability to the company's shareholders and persons with whom they deal a consequence of the imposition on directors of duties to the company. However, there would be no logical inconsistency between the co-existence of directors' legal duties to their company and legal duties in the same or a modified form owed by directors to the shareholders with whom the directors deal directly. As will be shown later in this chapter, there has been a growing tendency in recent judicial decisions to recognise the existence of such duties toward shareholders. As yet, however, the courts have shown little inclination to impose parallel duties on directors in their dealings with creditors of the company or with persons with whom the company enters into ordinary business contracts. It is, of course, unusual for directors to deal with such persons otherwise than as representatives of the company, or for directors to have a personal interest in the fulfilment of the company's contractual obligations, except, possibly, as guarantors of the company's obligations under the transaction in question.

Before examining the exceptional cases where statute and judicial decisions have made exceptions to the general immunity conferred on directors from liability to shareholders of a company, it will be useful to examine a number of cases where the courts have held that such an immunity exists. These cases provide useful illustrations of the principle of immunity, and they also elaborate the reasons why the court is usually unwilling to depart from the principle.

9.02 Examples of directors' immunity as regards the company's shareholders

When directors act in their capacity as directors, exercising the powers and functions conferred on them by the company's memorandum and articles of association, they act as agents of the company. Like all other agents acting within the limits of their authority, they bring into existence legal relationships between the company and the persons with whom they deal on the company's behalf, but they do not also create legal relationships between those persons and themselves.

Consequently, when directors granted an option for a shareholder to subscribe for further shares in the company and so obliged the company to issue the further shares at the option holder's request, the court held that the directors were not personally liable to satisfy the option by transferring some of their own shares to the option holder when after granting the option they issued the whole of the company's unissued shares to other persons and so disabled it from issuing shares to the option holder (*Ferguson* v. *Wilson* (1866)).

Again, when directors exercise their powers, they owe fiduciary obligations to the company on whose behalf they act, but not to shareholders of the company, and this is so even where the director has a personal interest in the matter. A director of a subsidiary who negotiates the termination of his service contract with the subsidiary parent company is therefore under no duty to disclose to the parent company that he has committed breaches of his duties to the subsidiary which would entitle it to remove him from office instantaneously and without compensation. Consequently, a parent company which pays a director of its subsidiary a sum of money to obtain his resignation in such circumstances cannot recover it on later discovering that he could have been removed by the subsidiary without compensation (*Bell* v. *Lever Brothers Ltd* (1932), per Lord Atkin at page 223 of the report). Likewise, directors who negligently or wilfully allow money or assets of their company to be misapplied or disposed of disadvantageously are not liable to compensate the company's parent company for the consequent diminution in the value of the shares it holds in the company (*Lindgren* v. *L and P Estates Co. Ltd* (1968)).

In both these cases the parent company sued simply as the sole or majority shareholder of the subsidiary, but the court held that the fact that the parent company controlled the subsidiary imposed no additional duties toward it on the subsidiary's directors. The directors may therefore have been guilty of breaches of their fiduciary duties toward the subsidiary, but that did not entitle either majority or minority shareholders of the subsidiary to recover any loss which they suffered in consequence.

The same reasoning has been employed by the courts in cases where directors have bought shares in the company from other shareholders and then re-sold them at a profit, or have sold shares held by the directors to other shareholders for more than their current value. In the leading case, *Percival* v. *Wright* (1902), shareholders of a private company requested its directors to find purchasers for their shares, and the directors offered to purchase the shares themselves at a fair price, but without disclosing that they had already received an offer for all the shares of the company at a higher price from an outsider. The shareholders accepted the directors' offer and transferred their shares to them, and the directors then accepted the outsider's offer in respect of the whole of their holdings, including the shares they had just acquired.

On discovering this, the shareholders who had sold their shares to the directors sued them for the rescission of the sale so that they might accept the higher offer from the outsider. Alternatively, the shareholders sought an order that the directors should account to them for the profit which the directors had obtained by re-selling the shares to the outsider. There was no suggestion that the directors had misrepresented the company's financial condition or the value of the shares to the shareholders, or that they had exercised any undue influence over the shareholders to induce them to sell their shares. The shareholders' case rested entirely on the failure of the directors to disclose that they had received a higher offer for the company's shares than the price they offered to the shareholders. The court held that the directors owed no duty of disclosure to the selling shareholders, and consequently the sale of their shares to the directors could not be rescinded or the directors compelled to account for the profit they had made.

If the company had been a partnership and the directors and the selling shareholders had been partners, there would have been no doubt that the directors would have been under a fiduciary duty to disclose the outsider's offer (*Law* v. *Law* (1905)). A partnership, however, is an unincorporated association, and the fiduciary duties of partners are therefore owed to each other. A company, on the other hand, is incorporated, and so the fiduciary duties owed by its directors are owed to it alone, and not to its shareholders individually. Consequently, since the only duty which the directors could have possibly breached in the present case was their duty to make disclosure to the company and to account to it for the profit they made by re-selling the shares acquired by them, the court was compelled to hold that the directors were not liable at common law or in equity to account for the profit they made to the original holders of the shares, and that those shareholders could not rescind the sale of their shares.

It would, of course, have been otherwise if the directors had made positive misrepresentations to the shareholders, even without realising that they were false or misleading, or if the directors had exercised undue influence over the shareholders to induce them to sell their shares at the price paid (*Walsham* v. *Stainton* (1863)). In that case the misrepresentation or undue influence would itself have provided a ground for the rescission of the sale to the directors and the restitution of the shares to their original holders, and the status of the directors as purchasers of the shares at what was in fact a fair price would then have been irrelevant. But non-disclosure of material facts is a ground for rescinding a contract only in certain limited cases (e.g. a contract of insurance or guarantee), or when one party owes a fiduciary duty of

Directors' Duties and Liabilities to Shareholders

disclosure or a duty to account for unauthorised personal profits to the other party, and a contract for the sale by shareholders of their shares to directors of the company which issued them falls under none of these heads.

It has been suggested that *Percival* v. *Wright* would have been decided in favour of the selling shareholders if it had been the directors, and not the shareholders, who initiated negotiations for the sale of the shares to the directors. It is very doubtful whether this would have made any difference if there were no evidence of misrepresentation or undue influence on the part of the directors. The only breach of duty which could then be alleged against the directors would still be breach of a fiduciary duty, and the court held unequivocally in *Percival* v. *Wright* that no such duty exists between directors and shareholders.

DIRECTORS' LIABILITIES TO INDIVIDUAL SHAREHOLDERS AT COMMON LAW AND IN EQUITY

Both under the rules of common law and equity and by statute there are certain exceptions to the general immunity of directors from liability to shareholders and creditors of their company and to persons with whom their company has dealings. The exceptions derived from common law and equity do not form a system, but are merely the result of the application of rules relating to contract, wrongs or torts and fiduciary or similar relationships which are not confined to directors, but are general in application. The statutory impositions of liabilities are in most cases confined to directors, but not invariably so, and when directors are made statutorily liable to shareholders or creditors, their liability is always confined to particular circumstances or obligations.

The exceptional circumstances where personal duties and liabilities to shareholders are imposed on directors will be considered in this chapter, and the circumstances where duties and liabilities to creditors and other persons are imposed on them will be considered in Chapter 10.

9.03 Directors as agents of shareholders

A shareholder or shareholders may, of course, appoint one or more directors of the company in which they hold shares to act as their agents in respect of a particular transaction or series of transactions. If the directors accept the appointment, they owe the same fiduciary and other duties to the shareholders as all agents owe to their principals under the law of agency.

The appointment of directors as agents for shareholders usually occurs when the transaction to be negotiated and concluded involves the acquisition or disposal of shares by the shareholders. For example, shareholders of a private company for whose shares there is no readily available market, employ its directors to find purchasers for their shares at the best price obtainable, and they do this in the belief that the directors' bargaining power is stronger than their own. Alternatively, shareholders of a private or public company who collectively control the company authorise the directors to negotiate the price for the sale of the whole or a block of their shares to an outsider who is willing to pay a premium over the value of the individual shares in order to acquire control.

Instances of directors acting as agents for shareholders are not confined to such situations, however. Directors may also become agents for individual shareholders by being appointed to act as their proxies so as to represent them and vote on their behalf at general meetings of shareholders or at meetings of classes of shareholders. Usually proxy appointments are made for only one general or class meeting or adjournments of it, but it is possible for a proxy to be appointed to represent a shareholder at all meetings held during a specified period or until the shareholder revokes the proxy appointment. Normally a proxy appointment is made for the benefit of the holder of the shares in question, and in that case the proxy owes the duties of an agent to the shareholder. But if the appointment is made to protect the interests of the proxy himself and he gives value for it (for example, if the proxy lends money to the shareholder on the security of a mortgage of the shares), the proxy owes the shareholder no duties beyond the obligation to act in good faith and with reasonable care in realising any security he holds (*Cuckmere Brick Co. Ltd* v. *Mutual Finance Ltd* (1971)).

The duties of a director acting as an agent for a shareholder are to act within the limits of the authorisation given to him and to conform to the lawful instructions which the shareholder issues to him; to act in good faith and to promote the interests of the shareholder rather than other interests; not to obtain a profit or benefit from the transaction he is engaged to carry out without the shareholder's consent; and to exercise reasonable care. If he is engaged in a professional capacity, he must also exercise reasonable skill in carrying out the transaction. These fiduciary duties of an agent to his principal are basically the same as those of a director toward his company, but of course, their content in a given situation will be different because of the different roles the director or agent fulfils, and the different interests of the company or the principal which he is required to protect.

Directors negotiating sale of shareholders' shares

There are few decided cases where a director has been held to have acted as an agent for a shareholder. The leading case is *Allen* v. *Hyatt* (1914), where directors obtained options to purchase shares from shareholders so that the directors might negotiate the collective sale of those shares to an outsider at a price to be negotiated by the directors, which was not to be less than a stipulated price. The directors negotiated the sale of their own shares and the shares for which they held purchase options at a higher price than the stipulated minimum, but they then exercised the options to purchase the shareholders' shares at the stipulated minimum price and resold those shares to the outsider at the higher price which he was willing to pay.

The court held that the directors acted as agents for the individual shareholders in negotiating the sale of their shares to the outsider, and were consequently under a duty not to obtain a personal profit from the transaction and a duty to conclude a sale to the shareholders' best advantage. Because they had breached both these duties, the directors were accountable to the shareholders for the whole of the purchase price which the outsider agreed to pay for the shares comprised in the option.

Pre-emption provisions

It is an unresolved question whether directors act as agents for shareholders when they give effect to a pre-emption provision in the company's articles of association, under the terms of which a shareholder who wishes to sell his shares is required to offer them to the other shareholders at a certain price, and not to sell his shares to the purchaser he has found unless the other shareholders are unwilling to purchase them at that price. Usually pre-emption clauses provide machinery for giving effect to shareholders' pre-emption rights by requiring the selling shareholder to give notice to the directors or secretary of the company of his intention to sell his shares. The directors or secretary are then required to notify the other shareholders of their right to buy the shares at the price indicated in the articles within a certain period, to report the other shareholders' responses to the selling shareholder and to apportion the available shares among the other shareholders if they collectively seek to purchase more shares than are available for sale. If the selling shareholder is unwilling to transfer his shares to the other shareholders who have exercised their right to purchase them, the directors are usually empowered by the articles to execute instruments of transfer on behalf of the selling shareholder and to register the purchasing shareholders as holders of the shares. Sometimes the articles provide that the secretary or the directors shall be deemed to be appointed irrevocably as agents of the selling shareholder to give effect to the other shareholders' pre-emption rights, but often the articles are silent on the question of the capacity in which they act, that is, either as agents for the company, or as agents for the selling shareholder or for the other shareholders.

Where a pre-emption provision in articles of association provides a formula to ascertain the price at which the selling shareholder's shares must be offered to the other shareholders (for example, a certain multiple of the average of the company's profits attributable to those shares according to the company's annual profit and loss accounts for its last three complete financial years), or when the price is to be the value of the shares in the opinion of a designated person, such as the company's auditors, the functions of the directors or secretary in giving effect to the pre-emption provision are mechanical, and the capacity in which they act is rarely important. But if the directors are given a discretion, whether as regards the price at which the other shareholders may purchase the shares, or as to the apportionment of the shares between the other shareholders if the total of their acceptances exceeds the number of shares available for sale, or if the directors are given a discretionary power to absolve the selling shareholder from transferring his shares to other shareholders who wish to purchase them, it becomes important to determine on whose behalf the directors are acting.

As yet there is no judicial authority on this question, but it is tentatively suggested that in addition to their undoubted duty to the company to administer the pre-emption provision properly and fairly, directors owe the duties of an agent to the selling shareholder from the time he notifies them of his wish to sell his shares, and they also owe the duties of an agent to the other shareholders who notify their wishes to purchase the shares as from the time they do so. If this is correct, the directors will be liable to the selling or purchasing shareholders for any personal gain which the directors obtain from the transaction (apart from taking their quota of the shares available in their capacity as shareholders), and they will also be liable for any loss which they cause by exercising their powers in bad faith or negligently, or by failing to carry out the pre-emption procedure properly.

Shareholders' liability for directors' acts

In circumstances where directors act as agents for individual shareholders, they only incur the responsibilities of agents toward those shareholders. But they also expose the shareholders to vicarious or secondary liability to third persons if the directors exercise their authority wrongfully or improperly. Consequently, it was held by the House of Lords in *Briess* v. *Woolley* (1954), that when directors were authorised by shareholders to negotiate the sale of their shares collectively to whichever of certain bidders for the company's shares offered the best price, and the directors induced the plaintiff bidder to purchase the shares by making fraudulent misrepresentations about the company's financial conditions, the shareholders whose shares were purchased were liable in damages to the plaintiff for the difference between the price he agreed to pay and the lower real value of their shares. This was so even though the shareholders did not expressly authorise the directors to make the representations. Of course, the directors committed a breach of their duties as agents for the selling shareholders in making the fraudulent misrepresentations. The shareholders were therefore entitled to recover an indemnity from the directors for the damages which they had to pay to the plaintiff, but this, of course, did not exonerate the shareholders from liability to the purchasers.

9.04 Directors' duty to advise shareholders

The common law duty of care

During the last 25 years the courts have substantially extended the duties and liabilities of persons who give advice or information to others in the knowledge that those others will rely on it as the basis for taking action themselves and may suffer loss if the advice is not sound or the information accurate.

The first of these cases, *Hedley Byrne & Co. Ltd* v. *Heller and Partners Ltd* (1964), was decided by the House of Lords in 1963. In that case the House of Lords held that when a merchant bank gave a favourable credit reference to a firm of advertising agents whom a customer of the bank wished to engage to place television advertisements on the basis that the agent would incur personal liability for the advertisement fees payable to the television companies, the merchant bank owed a duty of care to the advertising agents to ensure that the information and advice it gave about the customer's creditworthiness was sound.

Later cases have emphasised that there must be a special relationship between the adviser and the persons advised for the duty to give information or advice carefully to arise, but there need be no contractual relationship between them, provided that the adviser is aware that the person advised intends to rely on the advice or information given and that if the adviser acts carelessly the person advised may suffer loss. Consequently, in a later case, *Arenson* v. *Casson Beckman Rutley & Co.* (1977), the House of Lords held that when chartered accountants prepared accounts and a report on the value of a private company's shares to assist the parties in arriving at an agreed price for the sale of a minority shareholder's holding to the controlling shareholder, the chartered accountants owed a duty to the minority shareholder to exercise proper skill and care and, although there was no contract between them, the accountants were liable for the loss which the minority shareholder suffered by selling his shares at the undervalue which the accountants negligently placed upon them.

Similarly, the Court of Appeal in *JEB Fasteners Ltd* v. *Mark Bloom Co.* (1983), held that when auditors of a private company's annual accounts gave an unqualified report on their accuracy, knowing that the company needed to raise capital and that anyone who was invited to invest in, or make a loan to, the company would be likely to rely on the audited accounts in deciding to do so, the auditors owed a duty to any such person to exercise proper skill and care to ensure that the accounts were accurate and complete. Consequently, the auditors would have been liable for the loss suffered by an investor who relied on the accounts if the auditors' unqualified report on them was unjustified. The auditors escaped liability in that case only because the court decided as a matter of fact that the plaintiff investor had not relied on the accounts or the auditors' report on them in making his investment decision.

In all these cases the plaintiff sued for the wrong or tort of negligence at common law. The novelty of the court's decisions lay in the extension of the general duty of care which all persons owe to others not to cause them harm by careless acts so as to impose a special duty of skill and care on those who give information and advice in circumstances where they know or must have realised that the recipient would rely on it.

Before the cases establishing such a duty of care in giving information or advice were decided, the courts had held that such a duty could exist only under a contract between the parties. In the absence of a contract a person who gave information or advice on which the recipient relied was held liable to the recipient for consequential loss only if that person acted fraudulently or deceitfully, that is, if he knew that the information he gave or the factual basis of his advice was false, or if he did not believe it to be true, or if he gave the information or advice recklessly, not caring whether it or the factual basis for it was true or false (*Derry* v. *Peek* (1889); *Candler* v. *Crane Cristmas & Co.* (1951)). The law established in the more recent cases raises the advisers' duty from one to abstain from fraud to a duty to act with due care, and if they are professionals, also with proper skill.

The fiduciary duty of care

Parallel to the common law cases in which the courts have established a non-contractual duty of care in giving information or advice, the courts have in recent years extended the equitable obligations of a person in whom another confides and on whose advice he shows he depends in deciding whether to enter into a contract or other transaction with the person who gives the advice or a third person whom he represents. If a relationship of dependency and confidence arises between two persons, the courts have held that the adviser owes a duty of fiduciary care to the person he advises. Consequently, if the adviser does not ensure that his advice is adequate and based on accurate information and that the person advised is warned fully of the consequences of entering into the transaction, the person advised may in equity rescind the transaction he enters into with the adviser or his principal (*Lloyds Bank Ltd* v. *Bundy* (1975), at pages 339–340 of the report per Denning MR and per Sachs LJ at pages 341–342); *National Westminster Bank Ltd* v. *Morgan* (1983), per Dunn LJ at pages 90–92).

In both these cases a close relative of a bank's customer had been induced to give a guarantee and a mortgage to secure bank loans made to the customer, and had done so as a result of advice given by bank officials without having the opportunity to obtain independent advice. The court held in both cases that, because the bank officials had not given full advice as to the possible consequences to the guarantor of the bank's customer defaulting, or as to the amount for which the guarantor might be liable, the guarantor was entitled to rescind the guarantee and the mortgage.

In both cases the court emphasised that the bank officials were subject to a conflict of duties, and also that the transactions were very substantial ones for the guarantor and that it was desirable that the guarantor should be given or, at least, advised to obtain independent advice before entering into the transaction. The interesting feature of the cases from the point of view of directors' duties to individual shareholders, however, lies in the fact that in both cases the court held that the adviser and his principal, the bank owed a duty of fiduciary care to the other party to the transaction. It would seem that a breach of this duty entitles the other party, not only to rescind the transaction he is induced to enter into, but also to seek the other equitable remedies of restitution, tracing assets he has parted with under the transaction, compensation for loss suffered and an account of any gains made by the fiduciary or his principal.

The application of the two duties

As yet the common law liability for loss caused by giving negligent advice and the equitable remedies available when a transaction is induced by the failure of a person who has established a confidential relationship to fulfil his fiduciary duties, have not been invoked in Great Britain in the context of communications between the directors of a company and its shareholders. In New Zealand, however, the Court of Appeal in *Coleman* v. *Myers* (1977), held that both at common law and in equity directors who give advice or make recommendations to shareholders about the exercise of their rights in respect of their shareholdings do owe duties to ensure that the advice is given carefully and is directed to promoting and protecting the shareholders' interests. Furthermore, it was held that the directors must ensure that all relevant information in their possession is disclosed to the shareholders. The sanctions for non-fulfilment of the directors' common law and equitable obligations were held to include the whole range of legal and equitable remedies, including claims for damages and rescission of any transaction which was induced by the directors' failure to comply with their obligations.

In *Coleman* v. *Myers*, the defendants were two directors of a private company, whose shares were held by members of one family and trustees of family trusts and whose principal assets were property held as an investment and a 50 per cent holding in another company which sold wine and spirits. The directors formed a third company which made a successful takeover bid for the whole of the share capital of the first company. The price offered reflected the current value of the first company's shares on the assumption that the company's assets would not be changed or put to a different use. The directors advised shareholders of the first company to accept the bid as a favourable one, but did not disclose their intention, as directors and sole shareholders of the third company, to sell the first company's property so as to realise its development value and to use the proceeds to expand the activities of the second company and to make distributions to the third company as sole shareholder of the first company. The proposed distribution would be sufficient to reimburse the third company for the cost of purchasing the shares of the other shareholders in the first company.

There was evidence of misrepresentations made by the two directors as to their intentions, but wholly apart from this, the Court of Appeal held that as directors of the first company, they owed a duty to the shareholders to whom their recommendation to accept the bid was addressed to disclose all material facts (including the directors' plans if they gained control of the first company), and to advise the shareholders where their personal interests lay, and also to tell them that the acceptance of the bid would result in their not obtaining the best possible price for their shares.

Woodhouse J, who gave the leading judgment, would have ordered the rescission of the transfers of the shares of the plaintiff shareholders to the third company under the takeover offer. However, the other two judges, Cooke and Casey JJ, considered that in the circumstances of the case after the takeover had been completed, rescission was inappropriate. The proper remedy, therefore, was an award of damages to the shareholders equal to the difference between the real value of their shares at the date when they accepted the takeover bid (taking the development value of the company's property into account) and the price paid to them under the bid.

With regard to the directors' fiduciary duty to the shareholders, Woodhouse J said (at page 324 of the report):

'In my opinion it is not the law that anybody holding the office of director of a limited liability company is for that reason alone to be released from what otherwise would be regarded as a fiduciary responsibility owed to those in the position of shareholders of the same company... the standard of conduct required from a director in relation to dealings with a shareholder will differ depending upon all the surrounding circumstances and the nature of the responsibility which in a real and practical sense the director has assumed towards the shareholder. In the one case there may be a need to provide an explicit warning and a great deal of information concerning the proposed transaction. In another there may be no need to speak at all. It is, however, an area where the courts can and should find some practical means of giving effect to sensible and fair principles of commercial morality in the cases which come before them; and while it may not be possible to lay down any general test as to when the fiduciary duty will arise for a company director or to prescribe the exact conduct which will always discharge it when it does, there are nevertheless some factors that will usually have an influence upon a decision one way or the other. They include, I think, dependence upon information and advice, the existence of a relationship of confidence, the significance of some particular transaction for the parties, and of course, the extent of any positive action taken by or on behalf of the directors to promote it...'

Woodhouse and Cooke JJ held on the facts that the directors in *Coleman* v. *Myers* had been guilty of breach of fiduciary duty, failure to fulfil their common law duty of care to the shareholders and deliberate misrepresentation or fraud. The third judge, Casey J, made no finding of breach of a duty of care, and he based his judgment on the directors' breach of fiduciary duty and fraud, but without ruling on the existence of a concurrent duty of care imposed on them. On the question whether the directors were also under a common law duty to exercise reasonable care in making their recommendation that shareholders should accept the bid made by the third company, Cooke J observed that the directors did not have an independent valuation made of the shares of the first company, taking account of the fact that its investment property could be sold at an enhanced price, and he commented (at page 352 of the report):

'The unqualified recommendation to accept the [third company's] takeover offer meant that after making [its] initial offer [it] was never called on to bargain. In the circumstances of this company it was not unreasonable of the directors to refrain from investigating the possibility of any *outside* takeover bid; but... directors who oppose a bid or seek a higher price from the offeror may well succeed in securing an improved offer. [Certain decided cases]... provide typical examples of that sort of bargaining by directors... no attempt in that direction was made by the directors here; indeed it would have been difficult because of the conflict of interest... One can be sure that, if faced with an outside bidder and if prepared to entertain at all the possibility of selling, they would certainly not have recommended acceptance of the first offer [made by the third company] without bargaining. In these circumstances I think that at the very least they should have refrained from a positive recommendation; and that the [selling shareholders] have made out their allegation that the [directors] knew or ought to have known that the price [offered by the third company] was not a fair one and should not have been recommended to the shareholders. Even assuming that they were under no fiduciary duty, I do not think that the recommendation to sell at the price [offered by the third company] was made with reasonable care for the interests of shareholders.'

Woodhouse J concurred with this finding of negligence on the part of the directors and in the consequent award of damages to the shareholders who accepted the takeover offer.

The two duties in future cases

When a case similar to *Coleman* v. *Myers* comes before an English court, there can be little doubt that the decision of the New Zealand Court of Appeal in that case will be followed. The two bases for the decision already exist in English law, namely the duty of care owed by a person who gives information or advice in the knowledge that the person to whom it is given will rely on it in ordering his own affairs, and the fiduciary duty of good faith and care owed by a person who gives advice to another person with whom he has established a confidential relationship and who is dependent on the former person for sound advice.

The application of the two rules of common law and equity by the English courts would not be confined to the particular professional or other relationships which have existed in the cases which have already come before the courts. Shareholders depend and rely on the information and advice given to them by the directors of their company in a whole range of situations, and their dependence and reliance on the directors' advice is inevitable in most situations where shareholders have to take decisions about their holdings. Directors are invariably better informed about the company's financial and commercial condition and its prospects and business opportunities than most shareholders, and shareholders expect them to provide a lead.

Probably shareholders are most dependent on the directors' advice in deciding whether to accept or reject a takeover bid, or which of two or more competing takeover bids to accept, but they are also dependent on such advice along with such independent professional advice as they choose to take when deciding whether to subscribe for further shares in the company; whether to sell or retain the whole or part of their holdings (particularly when the company has no Stock Exchange listing for its shares); whether to vote for or against a reorganisation of the company's share capital or an alteration of the rights attached to their own or any other class of the company's shares; and even whether to accept the directors' proposal that a dividend of a certain amount shall be distributed out of the company's profits and that the whole or part of the company's remaining profits and revenue reserves shall be capitalised and bonus shares issued to the shareholders. The degree of reliance on directors' advice by shareholders may vary in each of these situations, but in all of them shareholders rely to a substantial extent on that advice. Consequently, the directors must owe a duty of care, both in its common law and fiduciary forms, to each individual shareholder in all these situations, and it will simply be the standard or extent of that duty which will vary in different situations according to the importance of the matter to each shareholder, the relative levels of knowledge of the relevant facts already possessed by directors and shareholders, and the degree of sophistication required for each shareholder to make a sound decision on the course of action he should take.

If directors give information or advice to shareholders or intending shareholders who are invited to subscribe for shares in the company, it has already been accepted by three members of the House of Lords in *Hedley Byrne Co. Ltd* v. *Heller and Partners Ltd* (1964) per Lords Morris and Devlin at pages 500 and 518 of the report, and in the earlier case of *Nocton* v. *Lord Ashburton* (1914), per Lord Haldane at page 955 of the report, that the directors owe a duty of care to the intending subscribers to ensure that the information given is accurate and the advice sound.

The three members of the House of Lords who expressed this view also considered that the statutory liability of directors for misstatements of fact in prospectuses inviting the public to subscribe for shares does not overlap the common law and equitable duty of care imposed on them, and where it applies the statutory liability pre-empts and excludes the non-statutory duty. The statutory liability is now imposed by the Companies Act 1985, section 67, (which is dealt with in the next section of this chapter), but the liability applies only when the false statements complained of are contained in a prospectus. No statutory liability is incurred by directors for misstatements in invitations to subscribe for shares made to a restricted number of persons who do not constitute a section of the public, because the invitation does not then involve the issue of a prospectus (Companies Act 1985, section 59(1), section 60(1) and section 744).

It is in this situation of directors making invitations to subscribe for shares which are not addressed to the public or a section of it that the three members of the House of Lords considered that common law and equitable duties of care would be imposed on directors. The cases in which their lordships expressed this opinion were not concerned with invitations to subscribe for shares, and so their opinions do not amount to a binding precedent. On the other hand, since their opinion is wholly consistent with the courts' recent development of the non-statutory duty of care imposed on persons who give advice, their opinion is likely to be followed in future cases.

DIRECTORS' STATUTORY LIABILITIES TO SHAREHOLDERS

There are a number of provisions in the Companies Act 1985, which impose statutory liabilities on directors toward individual shareholders, and give shareholders or subscribers for shares who suffer loss, the right to recover damages or compensation from the directors who are in default or to pursue some other appropriate remedy.

9.05 Prospectuses containing untrue statements or omissions

Liability for untrue statements

The first of these statutory liabilities enables subscribers for shares or debentures under a prospectus to recover compensation from the directors who are responsible for issuing it for any financial loss which they suffer by reason of any untrue statement of fact contained in the prospectus (Companies Act 1985, section 67(1)). The directors incur this statutory liability whether the prospectus invites the public or a section of it to subscribe directly for the shares or debentures from the company itself, or whether the company has allotted or agreed to allot the shares or debentures to an intermediary, such as a merchant bank or other financial institution, and by the prospectus the intermediary offers the shares for sale to the public or a section of it (section 58(1) and (2)). The measure of compensation recoverable from the directors is the difference between the amount paid by the subscriber to the company or intermediary as the whole or part of the issue price of the shares or debentures for which he subscribed and the lower real value of the shares or debentures at the date they were allotted to him, taking into account the falsity of the statements which the prospectus contained (*Clark* v. *Urquhart* (1930)). The subscriber is entitled to recover compensation on proving the falsity of the statements in the prospectus of which he complains and the loss he has suffered in consequence, but a director who is sued can avoid liability by relying on one or more of six defences set out in the Companies Act 1985, and these defences reduce the director's liability to at most one for negligence.

These defences fall into two groups, the first of which comprise personal defences which do not require the defendant director to prove that he acted with proper care. A director may escape liability by showing either (a) that he withdrew his consent to act as a director of the company before the prospectus was issued (e.g. he renounced or resigned his directorship) and that he did not authorise the issue of the prospectus; or (b) that he did not consent to the issue of the prospectus (which may be proved by showing that he did not sign the copy of it which was delivered to the Companies Registry), and that on discovering that the prospectus had been issued, he gave reasonable public notice (e.g. in the newspapers in which the prospectus was published) that it had been issued without his consent; or (c) that he became aware of the falsity of one or more statements in the prospectus after it was issued, whereupon he withdrew his consent to it and gave reasonable public notice that he had done so before any shares were allotted under the prospectus (Companies Act 1985, section 68(1)).

Alternatively, a director who is sued for compensation can rely on one or more substantive defences to escape liability, namely (a) that the untrue statement complained of was contained in a statement or report by an expert who had consented in writing to its inclusion in the prospectus and had not withdrawn his consent before a copy of the prospectus was delivered to the Companies Registry, and that the defendant director honestly and reasonably believed that the expert was competent to make the statement or report; or (b) that the untrue statement was, and was expressed in the prospectus to be, a statement by a public official (e.g. a Minister or a member of the Government service of the UK or an overseas government) or a copy or extract from a public official document; or (c) that the director honestly and reasonably believed the statement complained of to be true up to the time when the plaintiff subscriber's shares or debentures were allotted to him (section 68(2) and (3)).

The last defence of honest and reasonable belief will be relied on by a director only if he cannot avoid liability on any other ground, because to establish the defence he must satisfy the court both that his belief in the truth of the statement was genuine and that he was not guilty of negligence in allowing the prospectus to include the statement. This does not mean that the director must verify each statement in the prospectus personally. He may rely on assurances by professionals engaged by the company that information which they have checked is correct (e.g. a reporting accountant's assurance that the profit and dividend record of the company is truly stated), and he may also rely on the affirmative assurances of officers or employees of the company, such as its secretary or departmental managers, if they have no incentive or interest to conceal the truth (*Stevens* v. *Hoare* (1904); *Adams* v. *Thrift* (1915)).

Omissions from prospectuses

The statutory liability of directors for loss resulting from false statements in prospectuses does not extend to the omission from a prospectus issued generally (that is, to a wider section of the public than the company's existing shareholders and debenture holders) of information about the company which is required to be included in it by the Companies Act 1985 (section 56(1) and Schedule 3). The omission of information required to be included in a prospectus is not equated with the inclusion in it of untrue information, even though the omission of material information can be as misleading as the inclusion of false information.

Consequently, if directors are to be held liable to subscribers for the omission of statutory information from a prospectus, they must be sued for breach of the statutory duty imposed on them to include it, and the damages recoverable will be calculated under the ordinary common law rule that all directly consequential loss must be compensated. It has been said in two cases that a subscriber may sue the directors for breach of statutory duty, but in neither case was the remedy of damages sought, and so the court's opinion does not create a binding precedent.

There is also uncertainty whether an action for damages or a statutory claim for compensation can be brought against directors by subscribers or purchasers of shares under a prospectus which takes the form of listing particulars published in connection with an application to the Stock Exchange for the shares to be listed. The relevant legislation, the Stock Exchange (Listing) Regulations 1984, excludes the application to listing particulars approved by the Stock Exchange of the provisions of the Companies Act 1985, 'with respect to prospectuses and their contents, or with the consequences attending... the inclusion of any statement in, or the omission of anything from, a prospectus' (Regulations, para 7(1)(*b*)). It was pointed out earlier that this provision is equivocal, and it is uncertain whether the statutory liability of directors in respect of untrue statements in listing particulars which serve the purpose of prospectuses is eliminated or preserved by this provision. On the other hand, if the statutory liability under the Companies Act 1985, is excluded, it is possible that a subscriber for, or a purchaser of, shares listed on the Stock Exchange, who relies on the contents of the listing particulars may be able to sue the directors of the company for damages as persons responsible for the particulars by relying on a breach of their statutory duty to ensure that all the information required by the Stock Exchange (Listing) Regulations 1984 is included in the listing particulars and that all the information given in the particulars is true.

It is a sad comment on the lack of precision in the legislation governing the marketing of a company's shares that the only questions about liability for defective prospectuses which can be answered with confidence are questions as to the liability of directors for false statements (but not omissions) in prospectuses inviting subscriptions for shares which will be admitted to dealings on the Unlisted Securities Market, the 'over the counter market' or no market at all.

9.06 Incomplete share subscriptions and Stock Exchange listing undertakings

Minimum subscriptions

Directors may incur statutory liabilities to shareholders under various other provisions of the Companies Act 1985 relating to the issue of shares. Directors are prohibited from allotting shares offered under a prospectus unless all the shares comprised in the offer are subscribed, or unless the prospectus states that the number of shares applied for will be allotted in any event or if specified conditions are fulfilled, and those conditions are fulfilled (e.g. if a minimum number of shares specified in the prospectus are applied for) (Companies Act 1985, section 84(1)).

Additionally, if the prospectus is the first one published by the company under which it allots shares, the directors are prohibited from allotting any shares unless the total amount payable as the issue price for the shares subscribed at least equals the amount which the directors specify in the prospectus as the minimum amount which the company requires to meet the purchase price of any property or business which it is acquiring, the preliminary expenses of incorporating the company and raising its initial share and loan capital (including commissions), the cost of repaying temporary loans raised to meet such a purchase price and preliminary expenses, and the amount of working capital needed by the company (section 83(1) and (7)).

If the number of shares which must be subscribed under these two provisions before any allotments are made is not subscribed within

40 days after the prospectus is first issued, all money received from applicants for shares must be returned to them, and if any such money is not returned within 48 days after the first issue of the prospectus, the directors of the company are personally liable to repay it with interest at 5 per cent per annum from that day. A director may escape this liability, however, by proving that the failure of the company to repay was not due to his own negligence or misconduct (section 83(4) and (5) and section 84(2) and (3)).

If any shares are allotted in contravention of the prohibitions, the allottee may rescind the allotment to him within one month after it is made, and may recover from the company the amount he has paid for the shares. If the allottee does not rescind within the one month period, he may still sue the directors of the company who knowingly contravened the prohibition on allotment within 2 years after the allotment is made, and he may recover from them the amount he cannot recover from the company. If the allottee does rescind the allotment within the one month period, the company can within 2 years after the allotment sue its directors who knowingly contravened the prohibition on allotment to recover compensation for the loss the company suffers by having to return the money paid by the allottee for the shares (section 85(1) and (3)).

The personal liability of directors under these statutory provisions to refund amounts paid on applications for shares offered by a prospectus is in practice rarely of practical importance. If the company has underwritten the whole of the shares offered for subscription, or has agreed to allot them to a financial institution so that it may offer them for sale to the public, all the shares offered by the prospectus are bound to be taken up, if not by members of the public as subscribers, then by the underwriters or the sponsoring financial institution. It is only where a company makes a public offering of shares direct to the public without underwriting the shares that the statutory provisions can have an impact.

Listing applications

Directors may also incur personal liability to refund amounts paid to subscribers for shares or debentures under a prospectus which states that an application has been or will be made to a stock exchange for the shares or debentures to be listed on it and admitted to dealings, and either the application for a listing is not made before the third day following the first issue of the prospectus, or a listing is refused by the stock exchange within three weeks (which may be extended to six weeks by the exchange) after subscriptions for the shares or debentures close. In either of those events, any allotment of shares or debentures under the prospectus becomes void, and all money received from applicants for shares or debentures must be returned to them immediately after the three days for applying for a listing expire without the application being made, or immediately upon the listing being refused. If the money is not returned within eight days, the directors of the company become personally liable to repay it with interest at 5 per cent per annum from the eighth day, and they can escape liability only by proving that the company's failure to repay is not due to any misconduct or negligence on their part (section 86(1), (2), (4) and (5)).

This provision in fact applies to applications for a listing of shares on the Stock Exchange of the United Kingdom and Ireland only if the application is refused within three to six weeks after it is made. All applications for a Stock Exchange listing must be accompanied by or precede the submission of a draft of the listing particulars which will be published in connection with the application, and so the possibility of the listing particulars being published first and an application for a listing being made later is excluded. The statutory provision does not apply to applications for shares to be admitted to dealings on the Unlisted Securities Market of the Stock Exchange, because such shares are not listed, nor does it apply to applications for shares to be dealt in by dealers on the 'over the counter market', because the market is not a stock exchange. Nevertheless, the statutory provision will apply in full when an application is made or intended to be made for the shares to be listed on an overseas stock exchange if the prospectus published in connection with the application does not require the prior approval of the stock exchange authorities.

9.07 Preferential subscription rights

The preferential subscription rights of existing equity shareholders of a company when further equity securities are offered for subscription have already been dealt with above in connection with directors' duties to their companies when share or loan capital is issued [7.06]. The statutory liability of directors to equity shareholders for loss caused by failing to offer equity securities to them in accordance with their preferential subscription rights was also mentioned there (section 92(1)). Proceedings to recover compensation must be brought by the equity shareholder whose preferential rights have been disregarded within two years after the company delivers a return of the allotments made of the equity securities to the Registrar of Companies (section

Directors' Duties and Liabilities to Shareholders

92(2)). Presumably the compensation which the equity shareholder may recover from the directors will be the value of his preferential subscription rights, namely, the difference between the market value of the equity securities at the time they were allotted inconsistently with the plaintiff's subscription rights and the lower price at which the securities were issued by the company.

9.08 Compensation for loss of office

The final statutory liability which directors may incur to individual shareholders arises when compensation for loss of office is paid to directors by a person who makes a general offer to acquire shares of a company and the shareholders affected do not consent to the compensation being paid. The liability can attach only if the offer is made to all the shareholders of the company to acquire the whole or a proportion of their holdings; or if the offer is made by another company to acquire so many shares that if the offer is accepted in full the company will become a subsidiary of the other company or a subsidiary of its parent company; or if the offer is made by an individual and a full acceptance of the offer will result in his controlling at least a third of the votes exercisable at a general meeting of the company; or if the offer is conditional on its acceptance by the holders of a minimum fraction of the shares sought to be acquired (section 314(1)).

If the offeror proposes to pay compensation to the company's directors for loss of office or in consideration of their retirement from office, the proposed payment must be notified to the shareholders to whom the offer is made. Unless those shareholders approve the payment by passing an ordinary resolution at a meeting of all those shareholders and all other shareholders of the same class or classes to whom the offer does not extend (if any) the compensation payment may not be made (section 314(2) and section 315(1)). The meeting called to approve the payment will comprise all the classses of shareholders whose shares are the subject of the offer, and so if a single offer is made for two or more classes of shares, a joint meeting of all those classes must be held. The meeting will not necessarily be a general meeting of the company, however; it will be a general meeting only if the offer relates to all or some of the company's shares which carry voting rights at general meetings and is confined to those shares.

If compensation for loss of office or a payment in consideration of retirement is paid by the offeror to directors of the offeree company without the approval of a meeting of shareholders of the class or classes concerned, the recipient directors hold the amounts they respectively receive in trust for those shareholders who sell their shares as a result of the offer. Presumably such shareholders can each recover from the recipient directors a fraction of the amount which each of the directors has illegitimately received proportionate to the nominal value of the shares which each shareholder sells to the offeror (section 315(1)).

The Companies Act 1985 provides that the shareholders who become the beneficiaries of the statutory trust are those who sell, not those who transfer, their shares. This presumably means that if the offer made is to exchange the offeree shareholders' shares for new shares or debentures of the offeror company, offeree shareholders who accept the offer will not be entitled to recover the payment received by the directors of the offeree company, because the offeree shareholders would not have sold their shares to the offeror for a cash consideration, which is essential for the transaction to be a sale (*Re Westminster Property Group plc* (1985)). It may nevertheless be possible for the courts to compel the directors to account in this situation by imposing an equitable obligation on them to do so parallel to the statutory obligation.

The provision for directors' accountability to selling shareholders for compensation for loss of office which directors receive from the offeror under a bid for the company's shares is part of a group of provisions in the Companies Act 1985, imposing liabilities on directors for illegitimate gains. These provisions also make directors liable to the company itself, and not to its shareholders, if they receive compensation for loss of office or a payment in consideration of retirement from office when the payment is made by the company itself or by a purchaser of the company's business undertaking or property (sections 312 and 313). For the purpose of all these provisions, including that relating to a bid for the company's shares, compensation for loss of office does not include damages paid to a director in good faith for any breach of his service contract, nor to a pension paid to him in respect of his past service (section 316(3)). It has also been held by the Judicial Committee of the Privy Council under New Zealand legislation in identical terms, that compensation for loss of office does not include a payment which the company is contractually bound to make to a director on the premature termination of his service contract (*Taupa Totara Timber Co. Ltd* v. *Rowe* (1978)). It would not seem possible, however, for any of these exceptions to apply to a payment made to a director of a company by a person who makes a successful bid for shares of that company if the director retires or is removed from office in consequence of the bid.

Chapter 10

Directors' Duties and Liabilities to a Company's Creditors

GENERAL IMMUNITY FROM LIABILITY AND EXCEPTIONS TO IT

10.01 Immunity of directors as regards the company's creditors and contractors

Directors are in general not personally liable for the company's debts or other obligations to its creditors or persons with whom they deal on its behalf, nor do they owe duties themselves to such persons.

The reason for this general immunity from liability to the company's creditors, to persons with whom the company contracts and to third persons generally for wrongs or torts committed by the company, is the same reason that underlies the directors' immunity from liability to the company's shareholders. Directors act as agents of the company, which is a distinct legal person from themselves, in incurring debts or making contracts on the company's behalf and in running its business undertaking, and the fact that the company incurs liability as a result of its agents' acts does not mean that its directors, as such agents, incur liability as well.

Because of this immunity, directors have been held not to be liable at common law or in equity for debts which they incur on the company's behalf at a time when they know that it is already insolvent, and is therefore incapable of paying the new debts they incur (*Wilson* v. *Lord Bury* (1880); *Multinational Gas and Petrochemical Co.* v. *Multinational Gas and Petrochemical Services Ltd* (1983), per Dillon LJ at page 487 of the report). Nor are directors liable at common law or in equity to the company's creditors or persons with whom it has contracted, if they manage the company's affairs negligently and so disable it from paying its debts and fulfilling its contracts (same cases).

If a company creates a general or floating charge over the whole of its assets and undertaking to secure a loan, so that the sufficiency of the lender's security depends on the proper management of the company's affairs, its directors are not liable to the lender for the insufficiency of the assets of the company to repay the loan which is caused by the directors' negligent mismanagement (*Clark* v. *Urquhart* (1930), per Lord Sumner at page 53 of the report).

The fact that directors disregard their fiduciary duties to the company and in consequence creditors of the company suffer loss, does not make the directors liable to the creditors. Consequently, in a case where directors paid up the whole of the capital unpaid on their shares before it became due in order to enable the company to discharge a debt which they had guaranteed, it was held that in the subsequent winding up of the company its creditors could not rely on the fact that the directors may have acted in breach of their fiduciary duties to the company in paying up the capital on their shares and using it to pay a selected debt of the company so as to relieve themselves from liability on the guarantee they had given. The liquidator therefore could not compel the directors to pay the unpaid capital on their shares a second time in order to augment its assets available to pay all its creditors (*Re Wincham Shipbuilding, Boiler and Salt Co., Poole, Jackson and Whyte's Case* (1878)).

Directors are not liable for wrongs or torts committed by their company or by persons acting on its behalf, even though the tort is one of commission rather than omission, and even though the act done was sufficiently important for a decision of the board of directors to have been taken authorising it, or at least authorising transactions or activities in the course of which the wrong was committed.

Consequently, the House of Lords held that directors were not personally liable for damage resulting from an explosion and fire at the company's premises where it stored explosive and inflammable goods in proximity to neighbouring premises, although the storage must have been known to the directors (*Rainham Chemical Works Ltd* v. *Belvedere Fish Guano Co. Ltd* (1921), per Lord Buckmaster). Similarly, the court held that directors were not liable in tort when their company marketed products which infringed the plaintiff's patent, or put on a theatrical performance which infringed the plaintiff's copyright (*British Thomson-Houston Co.* v. *Sterling Accessories Ltd* (1924); *Performing Rights Society* v. *Ciryl Theatrical Syndicate Ltd* (1924)).

If a director is to be made personally liable for a wrong or tort for which his company is responsible, it must be proved that the director personally participated in the commission of the tort, or that he personally authorised its commission by another person, and it is not sufficient to prove that he authorised an activity or action which was not itself wrongful, but in the course of which the tort in question was committed (*C. Evans and Sons Ltd* v. *Spritebrand Ltd* (1985)).

On the other hand, where the evidence shows that the director did the act complained of or expressly authorised its commission, the fact that the company is concurrently liable for the wrongful act does not absolve the director from personal liability. Members of the board of directors of a company who issue a prospectus inviting subscriptions for its debentures or loan stock knowing that the prospectus contains material false statement of fact, commit the tort of deceit, and are therefore personally liable to subscribers who suffer loss in consequence of their subscriptions (*Edgington* v. *Fitzmaurice* (1885)). The fact that the subscribers could also or alternatively sue the company for damages does not absolve the directors from personal liability.

Notwithstanding the general immunity of directors, in a number of situations directors who negotiate contracts believing that they are acting only as agents on behalf of their company, so that only the company will incur legal responsibility for fulfilment of the promises made by the directors, in fact incur liability either alone or concurrently with their company to persons with whom they contract on its behalf or to whom they incur liabilities. Additionally, statute may exceptionally impose personal liability on directors in the liquidation of a company in respect of a company's debts and liabilities. In these different ways the immunity which directors normally enjoy from liability for their companies' debts and legal obligations is taken away, and they are exposed to liability themselves. If the company is primarily liable in respect of the debt or obligation in question, however, directors who are additionally or collaterally liable are in general entitled to be indemnified by the company (*Brooks Wharf and Bull Wharf Ltd* v. *Goodman Brothers* (1937)).

SITUATIONS WHERE DIRECTORS ARE LIABLE BUT THE COMPANY IS NOT

10.02 Exclusive personal liability of directors

Directors may incur personal liability in respect of a contract which they negotiate without the company incurring any liability at all if the directors do not contract in the company's name or on its behalf, and are therefore taken as contracting personally, or if they contract in its name or on its behalf but in excess of their authority to represent the company.

10.03 Contracts by directors personally

When negotiating a contract for his company, a director or other agent should make it clear to the other party that the contract will be entered into by the company, and not by the director personally. If he does not do this, and the other party believes that he is contracting with the director or agent and not the company, the contract they conclude will be a personal one made with the director, and he will be personally liable for fulfilment of the promises which he believed he was making on the company's behalf.

This was held by the court to be the situation when a director of a company which owned a ship placed an order for its repair with ship repairers without indicating that he was doing so on the company's behalf. The contract was held to be a personal one with the director even though the repairers knew that the company was the owner of the ship (*Bridges and Salmon Ltd* v. *The Swan (Owner)* (1968)). The same conclusion was reached by the court in another case where a director of a land development company instructed an architect to prepare drawings for the erection of houses and flats on land which he and other persons had purchased with a view to transferring it to the company, but the director did not inform the architect that he was giving the instructions on behalf of the company (*Abt* v. *Fraiman* (1974) (unreported)).

In these cases the contract was made orally by the director, and was an isolated transaction. If a supplier of goods or services to the company fulfils repeated orders and is paid by the company, or if the supplier has a standing arrangement with a company to supply goods or services to it on call, and in either case a further order is given by a director or agent to the supplier without mentioning that it is given on behalf of the company, it would, of course, be implied that the further order is given by the company just as the preceding orders have been, and the director or agent would then not contract personally.

In several cases, directors or agents have been held personally liable to make payments under negotiable or other instruments which they have signed with the intention of binding the company and not themselves, but they have not made this intention clear. For example, in cases where directors have signed bills of exchange or cheques with their personal signatures and added words describing themselves as directors or agents of the company, they have been held personally liable as drawers to make payment to the payees (*Landes* v. *Marcus and Davids* (1909); *Kettle* v. *Dunster and Wakefield* (1927)). Similarly, where directors gave a creditor of the company a promissory note by which they 'as directors of the company [naming it] promise to pay' the amount of the company's debt to the creditor, it was held that the directors were personally liable to the creditor as payee of the note (*Dutton* v. *Marsh* (1871); *Penkivil* v. *Connell* (1850)).

On the other hand, where directors of a company accepted and so engaged to pay a bill of exchange drawn on the company by writing an acceptance across the face of the bill in the form of their personal signatures with a description of themselves as directors of the company, it was held that the directors were not personally liable to pay the amount of the bill. This was because a bill of exchange can only be accepted by the person on whom it is drawn – here the company – and so if the directors' signature had not been treated as being an acceptance on behalf of the company, the signatures would have been ineffective to bind either the company or themselves (*Elliott* v. *Bax-Ironside* (1925)). Again, in a recent case it was held that if a cheque form has the name of the company printed at the top beneath that of the bank at which the company has an account, the personal signature of such a cheque by a director of the company in the place where the drawer's signature normally appears, whether with or without the addition of a description of the signatory as a director, does not make the cheque one drawn by the director personally, and the payee's only redress if the cheque is unpaid is to recover its amount from the company (*Bondina Ltd* v. *Rollaway Shower Blinds Ltd* (1986)).

10.04 Breach of warranty of authority

In the situations dealt with in the preceding paragraphs, directors have been held liable on contracts by which they intended to bind the company and not themselves, and the reason for the directors' personal liability has been that on the facts they were held to have contracted personally. The other situation where a director or other agent may be held liable to the other party to a contract is where, although he expressly contracts in the company's name or on its behalf, he does not have authority from the company to enter into the contract as its agent. In this case the director or other agent is not liable as a party to the contract, but for breach of a promise or warranty which he gives impliedly when the contract is concluded that he has authority from his principal, the company, to bind it by the contract. The other party can sue the director or agent for damages for breach of this implied warranty of authority, but he cannot sue the director or agent for breach of the contract he negotiated or seek to compel him to perform it specifically, because the contract was not made with the director or agent personally.

The measure of damages recoverable in an action for breach of warranty of authority is the value which the contract would have had if it had been binding on the company. This will, of course, be less than the value of performance of the promises made in the company's name if the company is insolvent or would for any other reason be unable to carry out the promises in full if it had been bound by them (*Firbank's Executors* v. *Humphreys* (1886)). It would appear also that the director may reduce the damages recoverable from him in an action for breach of warranty of authority by tendering or offering performance of the promises he made in the company's name by carrying them out himself or by a third person, except where the other contracting party relied on the promises being performed by the company itself (which is rarely so in the case of commercial contracts).

Liability for breach of warranty of authority is incurred by a director or other agent who concludes the contract, or by the members of the board of directors if it authorises the contract, if the contract is unrelated to the business which the company is authorised to carry on by the objects clause of its memorandum of association, and the company is not expressly empowered by its memorandum to enter into contracts of that kind. In that case the contract is beyond the powers of the company or *ultra vires*, and the implied warranty of authority given to the other party by the director or agent or by the members of the board of directors collectively embodies a promise that the contract is within the company's lawful powers (*Weeks* v. *Propert* (1873); *West London Commercial Bank Ltd* v. *Kitson* (1883)).

Liability for breach of warranty of authority may also be incurred by a director or agent, or by the members of the board of directors collectively, when the contract is made in the company's name and is within the company's lawful powers, but it is beyond the powers of its directors to enter into the contract (e.g. because the company's memorandum of association reserves the power in question to its shareholders in general meeting). Liability for breach of warranty of authority may similarly be incurred because the director or agent who concludes the contract has not been given delegated authority by the board of directors to act on its behalf (*Cherry and McDougall* v. *Colonial Bank of Australasia* (1869)).

If a contract is beyond the powers of the company, or beyond the powers given to its board of directors by its memorandum or articles of association, the other contracting party may enforce the contract against the company if he entered into it in good faith and was unaware of the deficiency in the powers of the company or the board (Companies Act 1985, section 35(1)). Furthermore, if the articles of association of a company empower its board to enter into certain transactions only if specified conditions are fulfilled, or if a specified procedure is followed, a third person who enters into such a transaction with the board, or with a director or other agent to whom the board has delegated authority to conclude it, is not concerned to ensure that the conditions have been fulfilled or the procedure followed, and he can enforce the transaction against the company, unless he knows or suspects that they have not (*Royal British Bank* v. *Turquand* (1855)).

However, these rules merely enable the other party to the transaction to treat it as valid and binding on the company if he wishes. The rules do not validate the transaction for all purposes, and they do not enable the company to treat the transaction as binding on the other party. Consequently, if the other party chooses to repudiate the contract he has entered into with the board or with a director or other agent of the company, and the other party abandons any claim he may have to enforce the contract against the company, he may still pursue a claim for damages against the director or agent or the members of the board collectively (as the case may be) for breach of warranty of authority (*Cherry and McDougall* v. *Bank of Australasia*). In deciding whether to enforce the contract against the company or to sue for damages for breaches of warranty of authority, the other party to the contract will no doubt be guided by the relative solvency of the company and the person or persons who negotiated or authorised the contract.

The only doubtful situation in respect of contracts negotiated by a director is where the board has no express power by the company's articles of association to delegate authority to conclude the contract on the company's behalf. If the company's articles contain such a power of delegation and the board leads the other party to the contract to believe that the director has been given the necessary authority, or if the board acquiesces in the director's exercising such an authority, or if the board ratifies and approves the contract after it has been made, the contract is or becomes binding on the company, and there can then be no question of the director who concluded it being liable for breach of warranty of authority (*Biggerstaff* v. *Rowatt's Wharf Ltd* (1896); *Hely-Hutchinson* v. *Brayhead Ltd* (1968)).

But if there is no power for the board to delegate its powers in the company's articles, and the board has merely acquiesced in one of its directors making contracts of the kind in question in the past, it is uncertain whether the company may be treated as bound by the contract which the director has concluded. In the one case where the Court of Appeal has dealt with this situation, *Freeman and Lockyer* v. *Buckhurst Park Property (Mangal) Ltd* (1964), Diplock LJ, held that the one director acting alone has lawful authority to bind the company, and so such a director cannot possibly be liable for breach of warranty of authority. The other two members of the Court of Appeal were content to hold that the company could be held liable on the contract in that case because the company's articles of association in fact contained a power for the board to delegate its powers to any of the directors. By its acquiescence in similar contracts made by the director, the board had represented to the other party that the director who made the contract had the necessary delegated power to do so. If Diplock LJ was wrong in supposing a wider rule, it could be that in the absence of a power of delegation in the articles of the company, a director who concludes a contract in its name cannot bind the company despite the board's acquiescence, and unless the board subsequently ratifies the contract, he will be liable to the other party for breach of warranty of authority.

SITUATIONS WHERE DIRECTORS ARE CONCURRENTLY LIABLE

10.05

The first and most obvious situation where a director may be concurrently liable with his company for fulfilment of a contract it has entered into, or for payment of a debt which it has incurred, is where the director has agreed to guarantee performance of the company's obligations. However, there are additionally four other situations where statute may make a director concurrently liable for a debt or contractual obligation of his company. In two of these situations, persons other than directors may also incur a concurrent personal liability, though directors are in practice the persons most likely to do so.

10.06 Guarantees by directors

A guarantee is a contract entered into by a person, known as a guarantor or surety, by which he undertakes that a debt owed by another person will be duly paid to the creditor, or that contractual obligation of another person will be duly performed. A guarantee presupposes the existence of a primary contractual obligation owed by the promisor or debtor, and the guarantee is a secondary or collateral contractual undertaking by the surety to the creditor or the beneficiary of the primary obligation that the debt will be paid or the obligation fulfilled.

Guarantees of a company's debts and contractual obligations can, of course, be given by anyone, but they are mostly given in practice by directors and principal shareholders of the company. If the company fails to pay the guaranteed debt or to perform the guaranteed contract, the creditor or the other party to the contract may resort to the company or the surety, or both of them, to recover the debt or damages for breach of the company's obligations under the contract.

Unless the guarantee expressly limits a surety's liability he is liable to the full extent of his personal fortune to pay the debt or satisfy the claim for damages. The creditor or beneficiary cannot, of course, recover in total from the company and the surety more than the amount of his debt or his loss. A surety who satisfies the whole or part of the guaranteed liability is entitled to be indemnified by the promisor or principal debtor. Moreover, if there are two or more sureties, any surety who satisfies the whole or part of the promisor's liability is entitled to contributions from the other sureties. If they have all given guarantees for the full amount of the company's liability and have not agreed between themselves to contribute in different proportions, the contributions recoverable by a surety who has satisfied the company's obligations will result in all the sureties bearing equal shares of the cost of doing so (*Duncan Fox & Co.* v. *North and South Wales Bank Ltd* (1880)).

The creditor or beneficiary of a company's contractual undertaking may sue a director or other person who guarantees it without first suing the company or giving notice of the company's default to the surety, unless the terms of the guarantee expressly require these things to be done (*Wright* v. *Simpson* (1802) per Lord Eldon; *Walton* v. *Mascall* (1844)). On the other hand, the surety can require the creditor or beneficiary to exercise whatever remedies he has against the company for the surety's benefit if the surety indemnifies him against the cost of doing so (*Rouse* v. *Bradford Banking Co. Ltd* (1894)). When a surety has discharged the company's obligations or has paid damages to the creditor or beneficiary for the company's failure to do so, the surety is entitled to have transferred to himself all rights and securities vested in the creditor relating to the guaranteed obligation (*Lake* v. *Brutton* (1856); *Forbes* v. *Jackson* (1882)).

A surety may be discharged from liability on the guarantee he has given in a variety of ways, the most important of which are: (a) by the creditor or beneficiary agreeing with the company to alter the terms of the company's obligations in a way which would make the surety's position more burdensome (e.g. by the creditor agreeing with the company to extend the date for payment of the guaranteed debt) (*Clarke* v. *Henty* (1838); *Holme* v. *Brunskill* (1878)); (b) by the creditor or beneficiary breaking a term of his contract with the company which is of significance to the surety (e.g. making advances to the company covered by the guarantee before the dates on which the creditor promised to make them by the terms of the loan contract) (*General Steam Navigation Co.* v. *Rolt* (1858)); (c) by the creditor or beneficiary impairing a security held by him for performance of the company's obligation (e.g. releasing a mortgage given to the creditor by the company, or acquiring all the company's rights and title to the mortgaged property and so extinguishing the mortgage) (*Pledge* v. *Buss* (1860)); or (d) by the creditor or beneficiary failing to take proper steps to preserve the surety's right to take over in an unimpaired condition any security or remedies which the creditor or beneficiary has to ensure fulfilment of the company's obligation (e.g. by the creditor failing to give notice of dishonour of a bill accepted by the company when the payment of the bill is guaranteed by the surety) (*Philips* v. *Astling* (1809)).

On the other hand, the termination by the creditor or beneficiary of a contract with the company on the ground that the company has broken an essential term of the contract, does not release a surety who has guaranteed the fulfilment of the contract, and the surety remains liable for breaches of contract committed by the company before the contract was terminated (*Moschi* v. *Lep Air Services Ltd* (1973); *Hyundai Heavy Industries Co.* v. *Papadopoulos* (1980)).

Because of the obligation imposed on a creditor or a beneficiary of a contract entered into by a company toward a surety for the company's obligation, the relationship between the creditor or beneficiary and the surety bears some of the marks of a fiduciary relationship. This is only in respect of the creditor's or beneficiary's obligation to protect and preserve the rights and securities which the surety is entitled to take over on satisfying the company's obligations, however. A true fiduciary relationship only arises between the creditor or beneficiary and the surety if the surety is or becomes dependent on the advice of the creditor or beneficiary when negotiating the terms of the guarantee (*Lloyds Bank Ltd* v. *Bundy* (1975); *National Westminster Bank Ltd* v. *Morgan* (1983)). Consequently it is only where there is such a relationship of confidence in the creditor and dependence on his advice by the surety that the creditor is required in equity to exercise special care to advise the intending surety fully, and to ensure that he is given all the information in the creditor's possession which relates to the risk to which he will expose himself by giving the guarantee.

10.07 Inadequacy of a public company's initial capital

If a company is incorporated as a public company, it must obtain a certificate from the Registrar of Companies that it is entitled to commence business (its 'trading certificate') before it may lawfully enter into any contract or borrow money. To obtain this certificate it must deliver to the Registrar a statutory declaration signed by a director or the secretary of the company showing that the company's issued share capital is not less than £50,000; that there has been paid up on the company's issued shares a specified amount, which must equal at least 25 per cent of the nominal value of those shares plus the whole or any additional share premium payable by the subscribers under the terms on which the shares were issued; that the amount or estimated amount of the preliminary expenses of incorporating the company and issuing its first issue of shares and debentures is or will be a specified amount, which has been or will be paid by the company or another named person or persons; and that benefits of a stated amount, or no benefits at all, will be given to the promoters of the company, and where applicable, there must also be stated the consideration given for such benefits (e.g. promotion services) (Companies Act 1985, section 101(1), section 117(1) to (3) and section 118(1)). If the Registrar's certificate is not obtained before the company enters into a contract or borrows money, the company and its directors or officers who are in default commit a criminal offence punishable by a fine, but the contract which the company enters into, or the loan which it contracts, is valid and enforceable by the other party and by the company (section 117(7) and (8)).

Because of the risk that the company may be undercapitalised if it has not issued shares with a total nominal value of at least £50,000, the Companies Act 1985 provides that if the company has not obtained its trading certificate before it enters into a contract or borrows, the other party may call on it to do so within 21 days after he makes his demand, and if it does not, the directors of the company will be jointly and separately liable to indemnify the other party for any loss or damage he suffers by reason of the company failing to comply with his demand (section 117(8)).

The extent of the director's liability is not co-extensive with the loss which the other party suffers because the company fails to fulfil its contract or to repay the loan, however, but is limited to the loss he suffers as a result of the company not issuing sufficient shares (i.e.

£50,000 in total nominal value) and receiving on application for those shares the minimum payable by law (i.e. £12,500, or if the company has issued shares at a premium, £12,500 plus the total amount of the issue premium) less the amount of paid-up capital and share premiums which the company has in fact received. If the company has issued shares with a total nominal value of £50,000 or more and has received the minimum amount payable in respect of them on application, but has not obtained a trading certificate, the directors will incur no liability in respect of contracts which the company has made or in respect of loans which it has obtained, because the amount of capital available to the company to meet its obligations will then be equal to or greater than the amount of capital it needs to raise to obtain a trading certificate, and so the other contracting party will have suffered no loss in consequence of its failure to do so.

It is uncertain whether, if the company has entered into several contracts or contracted several loans without obtaining its trading certificate, its directors are liable to each of the other contracting parties for damages not exceeding the amount of paid-up capital and issue premium it should have received, or whether that amount is the global maximum which is amount recoverable by all such contractors or lenders together, in which case the amount recovered from the directors would have to be distributed to the claimants rateably in proportion to their respective claims. Whatever the total amount recoverable may be, however, a director who is compelled to pay it may recover contributions from his fellow directors so that the burden is shared by all the directors in the proportions considered just and equitable by the court (Civil Liability (Contribution) Act 1978, section 1(1) and section 2(1)).

It is unlikely that directors' liability in respect of contracts entered into, or loans obtained, by a public company at its inception will be incurred frequently, because trading certificates are required only by public companies which are initially registered as such, and not by public companies which were incorporated as private companies and later re-registered as public companies. The latter is in practice the usual way in which public companies are established. A director of a private company incurs no statutory liability in connection with its initial contracts and borrowings, whether it is later converted into a public company or not.

10.08 Sole member of a company

If a company carries on business with only one member for more than six months, the sole member is liable jointly with the company and also separately for all debts contracted by the company after the six months have expired and during the time that he remains the sole member of the company and is aware of that fact (section 24). The purpose of this provision is to ensure that companies always have a minimum membership of two. The reduction of its membership to one does not bring about the dissolution of the company, but it does provide a ground on which the court can order that the company shall be wound up (section 517(1)(e)).

The situation of the company having only one member (i.e. one shareholder whose name is entered into the company's register of members (section 22(2)) for more than an unbroken period of six months will, however, result in any person who remains the sole member of the company after that time becoming liable for debts contracted by the company while he remains the sole member. It is, of course, unnecessary that the sole member should be a director of the company, although it is most likely that he will be, unless the sole member is itself a company, in which case it will be a parent company and the original company will be its subsidiary (section 736(1)).

The debts of the company for which the sole member becomes liable after the expiration of the six months period are those 'contracted' by the company, that is debts which result from contracts which the company enters into. This means that the company's debts which arise by operation of law or as the result of statute (such as judgment debts, taxes, local rates and liability for fees or other imposts created by legislation) do not also become the liability of the sole member. Moreover, it would appear that the debts contracted by the company for which the sole member becomes liable are confined to its liabilities which become debts during the continuance of his sole membership, but it is not necessary that they should become due during that time. Contractual obligations to make money payments only become debts when they are certain in amount or become susceptible of exact calculation (e.g. a price of £x per ton supplied only becomes a debt when the amount supplied is known). When an obligation gives rise only to a claim for unliquidated damages if it is not fulfilled, the claim does not become a debt when it arises, but only when the amount payable in satisfaction of the claim is agreed upon by the parties or ascertained by the court. Because of this, a sole member of a company cannot be made liable for unliquidated damages payable by a company for breach of contract or for wrongs committed by it.

10.09 Liability of signatories of negotiable instruments

The Companies Act 1985 provides that if an officer of a company (such as a director) or a person acting on its behalf signs or authorises the signature of a bill of exchange, promissory note, cheque or order for money or goods in which the company's name is not set out in full, he commits an offence punishable by fine, and he is also personally liable to the holder of the bill of exchange, promissory note, cheque or order for money or goods for its amount unless it is paid by the company (section 349(4)).

The purpose of this provision is to ensure that the company's acceptance of liability under any of the instruments mentioned is made clear by the full and accurate statement of its name, but the misstatement of its name does not absolve the company from liability if there is no uncertainty as to the company intended to be bound (*Croydon Hospital* v. *Farley* (1816)). The sanction for the complete and exact statement of the company's name in the instrument is the imposition by statute of a concurrent liability under it on the signatory and any person who authorises the signature of the instrument on the company's behalf.

A company's name is not stated in full in an instrument if part of the name is contracted or represented by an 'etc.' (*Atkins* v. *Wardle* (1889); *Durham Fancy Goods Ltd* v. *Michael Jackson (Fancy Goods) Ltd* (1968)). Also the omission of the last word 'limited' from the statement of a company's name results in it not being fully stated (*Penrose* v. *Martyr* (1858); *British Airways Board* v. *Parish* (1979)). On the other hand, the representation of the final words of a company's name, 'limited' or 'public limited company', by the contractions 'ltd' or 'p.l.c.' is treated as equivalent to the full expression of those words (Companies Act 1985, section 27(1) and (4)), and the contraction of the word 'company' to 'co' is also accepted as sufficient (*Banque de l'Indochine et de Suez S.A.* v. *Euroseas Group Finance Co. Ltd* (1981)). If these contractions are used and the company's name is otherwise fully stated, the signatory incurs no liability.

Personal liability on a bill of exchange etc. is incurred not only by the signatory, but also by the person who authorised the signatory to sign the instrument in which the company's name is not fully stated, but the person who authorised the signatory is not liable unless he knew or must have realised that the instrument which the signatory signed either omitted the company's name completely or did not state it correctly (*John Wilkes (Footwear) Ltd* v. *Lee International (Footwear) Ltd* (1985)). However, if the instrument is prepared by the person who sues on it (e.g. the payee of a bill of exchange), and he misstates the company's name in it, he cannot sue the officer or agent who signs the instrument on the company's behalf, because the claimant must bear the consequences of his own act (*Durham Fancy Goods Ltd* v. *Michael Jackson (Fancy Goods) Ltd*). On the other hand, if the fact that the company's name is misstated in the instrument is known at the time it is signed to the person who seeks to enforce the company's obligation under it against the signatory, the plaintiff's knowledge affords the signatory no defence. Consequently, where a director signed a cheque on behalf of his company, and inserted the business name in which it carried on its undertaking in the cheque instead of its corporate name, the director was held liable to the payee, even though the payee knew that the name given was not the company's name (*Maxform S.p.A.* v. *Mariani and Goodville Ltd* (1981)).

The liability of the person who signs or authorises the signature of a bill of exchange etc. without the company's name being set out in full is a concurrent obligation with that of the company to the holder of the instrument (that is, in the case of a bill of exchange or cheque, the payee or the most recent indorsee), and the content of the signatory's obligation is the same as the company's. If the instrument is an order for the supply of money or goods which is not a negotiable instrument, the concurrent liability is to the person to whom the order is addressed, because such an order cannot be transferred by indorsement like a negotiable instrument, and an assignee of the right to payment under it (e.g. the price of the goods ordered and supplied) cannot sue the signatory. Although the concurrent liability of the signatory of a bill of exchange etc. resembles that of a surety under a contract of guarantee, he is not in fact a surety, and so if the contract to which the instrument relates is subsequently varied by agreement between the company and the other party, the signatory is not released from liability, as a surety would be (*British Airways Board* v. *Parish*).

10.10 Persons prohibited from being or acting as directors

Under the provisions of the Company Directors Disqualification Act 1986, the court may disqualify persons who are found unfit to act as directors in various circumstances (including conviction of criminal offences in relation to companies, responsibility for wrongful or fraudulent trading in the insolvent liquidation of a company, and on repeated defaults in filing or documents with, or reporting matters to, the Registrar of Companies), from being appointed, or acting as a director of any company, or acting in several other capacities in relation to a company, or being concerned in the promotion or management of a company, for a period fixed by the court, which may be as long as 15 years (sections 2 to 6, 8 and 10). If such an order is made the disqualified person may not then be appointed or act as director of any company during the periods of disqualification without leave of the court (section 1). Additionally, a person who is an undischarged bankrupt may not act as a director of any company until he obtains his discharge in bankruptcy, unless the court gives him leave to do so (section 11(1)).

If a person who is disqualified from acting as a director of any company under the foregoing provisions acts as a director, or is involved in the management, of any company without leave of the court, or if anyone who is not personally disqualified knowingly acts in the management of a company on the instructions of such a disqualified person and the court has not given leave to him to do so, the disqualified person and the person who acts on his instructions are made personally liable for all the debts and liabilities incurred by the company during the time he was involved in its management while disqualified, or during the time he accepted instructions from a disqualified person (as the case may be), and anyone who acts on the instructions of a disqualified person is deemed to continue to do so until he proves that he has ceased to accept instructions from him (section 15).

The liabilities imposed on a disqualified person or anyone who accepts the instructions of a disqualified person are concurrent with the corresponding liabilities of the company, and the disqualified person and anyone who acts on his instructions are liable jointly and separately with the company to creditors and others who have claims against it. The liabilities which may be enforced against a disqualified person or anyone who acts on his instructions are all debts and other liabilities incurred by the company during the period he is involved in the management of the company or accepts instructions from the disqualified person (as the case may be). It would appear that all debts, whether contracted by the company, or otherwise incurred by it (e.g. judgment debts, taxes etc.), and all liabilities of the company, whether for breach of contract or for torts or wrongs committed by it or by persons for whom it is responsible, may be recovered from, or enforced against, the disqualified person or anyone who acts on his instructions.

It is doubtful whether a person who is compelled to pay debts or to satisfy liabilities of the company under these provisions has a right to be indemnified by the company as someone who is only secondarily liable for its obligations. This is because it is a criminal offence for a disqualified person to act in the management of a company, or for any person to act on the instructions of a disqualified person in doing so (section 13), and the illegality of his conduct would seem to preclude him from claiming an indemnity. Nevertheless, the court may order contributions to be paid toward satisfying the debts or liabilities of the company by all or any of the persons who are liable for them (including the company itself). Consequently, a disqualified person who is compelled to pay debts or satisfy liabilities of the company may recover from the company and from other such disqualified persons (e.g. other disqualified persons who have also acted in the management of the company) such fractions of the amount he has paid as the court considers just and equitable, and a contribution ordered against any of the other persons who are liable may amount to a complete indemnity (Civil Liability (Contribution) Act 1978, section 1(1) and section 2(1) and (2)).

Apart from ordering a contribution, however, it seems that the court has no power to exonerate a disqualified person or anyone who acts on his instructions from personal liability for debts and liabilities of the company incurred while he was active in its management, and that the general power of the court to exonerate a director or officer of a company from liability under the Companies Act 1985 section 727(1), if he acted honestly and reasonably and ought fairly to be excused, does not apply to personal liability incurred under the present statutory provision (*Customs and Excise Commissioners* v. *Hedon Alpha Ltd* (1981)).

DIRECTORS' LIABILITIES IN THE LIQUIDATION OF A COMPANY

10.11 Directors' liability to contribute

The liabilities of directors to creditors and other persons under the common law and statutory rules previously considered in this chapter have all been cases of liability to individual creditors, contracting parties or claimants. Each such person is able to enforce his claim directly against the responsible director by an individual action and to recover a debt or damage from him without regard to similar claims which may be made against him by other persons.

These claims may be pursued against directors individually, whether the company is a going concern or in liquidation, but there are additionally three further statutory liabilities which can only be enforced against directors if the company is being wound up, whether by order of the court or voluntarily. The enforcement of such liabilities is entrusted to the liquidator, who adds any amount he recovers from the responsible directors to the general assets of the company, which the liquidator employs to pay all debts and liabilities of the company which are provable in its winding up. These statutory liquidation liabilities of directors are therefore nominally liabilities to the company, and not to individual creditors and claimants. They are, however, enforced by the liquidator for the collective benefit of all the creditors of the company, who share rateably in the amounts the liquidator recovers, in the same way as they share rateably in the proceeds of realising all the other assets of the company in the liquidation.

10.12 Directors who are personally liable by the company's memorandum

The Companies Act 1985, section 306(1), enables the memorandum of association of a limited company to provide that the liability of each director, manager or managing director of the company shall be unlimited. When the company is wound up its liquidator may then call on the persons who hold any of those offices at the commencement of the liquidation, or who have held any such offices within a year beforehand, to contribute the amount required to augment the company's assets sufficiently so that its debts and liabilities and the costs of the liquidation may be paid in full, and the present and past directors, managers and managing directors are then personally liable to contribute that amount (section 503(1)). However, directors, managing directors and managers who are personally liable may be called on to make contributions only if it appears that the company's assets and the amount of capital unpaid on the company's issued shares which the liquidator can recover will not be sufficient to discharge its liabilities and the cost of the winding up in full. Furthermore, a person who is no longer a director, manager or managing director but held office within a year before the liquidation began, can only be compelled to contribute toward debts and liabilities of the company incurred before he ceased to hold office (section 503(1) and (2)).

Provisions in limited companies' memoranda making directors liable to contribute to discharging the company's liabilities when it is wound up are rarely met with in practice. To be effective for this purpose, the personal liability must be expressly imposed on directors by the company's memorandum. It does not suffice that the memorandum provides that the company and the conduct of its affairs shall be subject to the rules of a trade or professional association to which it belongs, and that those rules make the directors of companies which are members of the association personally liable for debts incurred by them in connection with transactions regulated by the association (*Mitton, Butler and Priest Co. Ltd* v. *Ross* (1976)). Where directors are made personally liable to contribute toward the company's debts and liabilities by its memorandum, their legal position is similar to that of the one or more personally liable shareholders or managers of a French *société en commandite par actions* or a German *Kommanditgesellschaft auf Aktien*, both of which are rare forms of companies nowadays.

10.13 Directors' liabilities for fraudulent and wrongful trading

If in the course of the winding up of a company, whether by order of the court or voluntarily, it appears to the court that the company's business has been carried on with intent to defraud its creditors or the creditors of any other person, or for any fraudulent purpose, the court may declare that any persons who were knowingly parties to carrying on the company's business in that way shall make such contribution to the assets of the company as the court thinks proper without any limitation of liability (Insolvency Act 1986, section 213).

To obtain an order making individuals personally liable under this provision, it must be proved that they took an active part in the management of the company during the period while debts or other liabilities were incurred fraudulently, and it is not sufficient that they advised the directors of the company in a professional or other capacity, or were in possession of information showing that the company was incurring indebtedness which it could not meet and, as employees or officers of the company, they were under a duty to communicate that information to the directors (*Re Maidstone Building Provisions Ltd* (1971)). Furthermore, it must be proved that the director or other person whom it is sought to make liable was guilty of fraud, and not merely of negligent mismanagement. Nevertheless, fraud can be proved, showing that the director or other person incurred indebtedness on behalf of the company despite his awareness that it was already insolvent and unable to pay its existing debts as they fell due, or that he incurred an obligation for the company to make a payment which he knew the company would be unable to meet by the time it fell due (*Re William C. Leitch Brothers Ltd* (1932); *R v. Grantham* (1984)). Moreover, personal liability can be imposed on a director even if he has incurred an obligation fraudulently on behalf of the company in connection with only one transaction, and the fraud may consist of a dishonest intention not to fulfil the company's obligations under that transaction when it is entered into, or knowledge by the director that the company will be unable to fulfil the obligation when it falls due for performance (*Re Gerald Cooper Chemicals Ltd* (1978)).

Fraudulent trading is a criminal offence and may be committed whether the company is subsequently wound up or not (Companies

Act 1985, section 458). Because of this, the same high standard of proof of fraud on the part of directors or those in control of management is required to obtain an order imposing personal liability on them as is required for a criminal conviction. Shadow directors in accordance with whose directions or instructions the directors of a company act in carrying on its business fraudulently may be included in orders imposing personal liability on directors, because to be shadow directors they must have been parties to carrying on the company's business by giving the directors instructions which they have carried out. However, to impose personal liability, the same proof of fraud on the part of shadow directors must be given as in the case of directors. A controlling shareholder or controlling shareholders who act together (including a parent company of a group) may be made personally liable only if they have controlled the management of the company so as to qualify as shadow directors and have also acted fraudulently (section 741(2)). Controlling shareholders and parent companies cannot have orders made against them for payment of any part of their controlled or subsidiary companies' liabilities merely because of their position as controlling shareholders or parent companies.

The Insolvency Act 1985 widened the powers of the court to order directors, former directors and shadow directors of insolvent companies to contribute to their assets when they are wound up so as to extend to cases of wrongful trading as well as fraudulent trading. Such an order may now be made under the Insolvency Act 1986, whether the company is wound up by the court or voluntarily, if the assets of the company at the commencement of its liquidation were insufficient to satisfy its debts and other liabilities and the costs of the liquidation in full (Insolvency Act 1986, section 214(1), (6) and (7)). However, an order may be made against a director, former director, or shadow director only if it is shown that at some time before the winding up commenced while he was a director or shadow director of the company, he knew or ought to have realised that there was no reasonable prospect that the company would avoid going into liquidation in an insolvent condition (section 214(2)). A director, former director or shadow director may escape having an order made against him, however, if he proves that after he discovered, or should have realised, that the company would go into an insolvent liquidation, he took every step with a view to minimising the loss to the company's creditors which he ought to have taken (section 214(3)).

Once it is shown that a director ought to have realised that the company could not avoid going into an insolvent liquidation, the burden of proof imposed on the director is a heavy one if he is to escape liability. It does not suffice that he took reasonable steps to avoid an insolvent liquidation of the company. He must take *every* step which he should take (e.g. by seeking to raise further capital or loans, reducing the operating costs of the company, selling its assets which can safely be disposed of without impairing the company's main business (such as trade investments), and proposing moratoria or other appropriate arrangements to the company's creditors). If a director does not take all such steps as are available in the circumstances, it would seem that he cannot establish the statutory defence and avoid liability, but the court would undoubtedly take his efforts into account in deciding on the amount of the contribution to the company's assets which he is ordered to make.

The director's defence does not fail because his efforts to avoid loss to the company's creditors prove unavailing, however, and in deciding whether the director has taken all the steps he should have taken, it is to be assumed that, at the time he made efforts to minimise loss to the company's creditors it was known to the directors that the company would eventually be wound up in an insolvent condition. The director's acts or failure to act are not therefore to be judged by asking whether he did what was reasonable to avoid the company being wound up at all, but whether he did everything which was reasonable and practicable to reduce to a minimum the loss which is suffered by the company's creditors because of the insufficiency of the company's assets.

In deciding whether a director or former director knew or ought to have realised the inevitability of the company's insolvent liquidation, and whether he took every reasonable and practicable step to minimise the creditors' loss, the facts which the director ought to have known or ascertained, the conclusions which he ought to have reached and the steps which he ought to have taken are those which would be known, ascertained, reached or taken by a reasonably diligent person with the general knowledge, skill and experience to be expected of a director who carried out the functions in the company which the director carried out or which were entrusted to him, and also the general knowledge, skill and experience which the director or former director in fact possessed (section 214(4) and (5)). In other words, the director's conduct is to be judged by an objective standard, namely the conduct to be expected of a reasonably competent director of a company of the nature and size of the company in liquidation, but if the director's ability is greater than that of the average reasonably competent director, he is to be judged by the standard that he personally should have attained.

Liability may be imposed by an order of the court under these provisions of the Insolvency Act 1986, for the negligent management of a company's affairs by its directors resulting in its insolvency. Bearing in mind that the burden of disproving negligence rests on the directors once it is shown that they should have realised the inevitability of the company being wound up in an insolvent condition, the potential personal liability of the directors is much wider than their exposure to an order being made against them because of fraudulent trading.

Applications for orders imposing personal liability on directors or on persons who participated in the management of companies which go into liquidation can be made only by the liquidator (section 213(2) and section 214(1)). Formerly an application for an order imposing personal liability on directors who were guilty of fraudulent trading could be made by a creditor or shareholder of the company, as well as by its liquidator, and if the application was made by a creditor who had been defrauded, the court could order the delinquent director or directors to pay the whole or part of his claim directly to the creditor, so that if the director were solvent and the company insolvent, the creditor would gain an advantage over its other creditors (*Re Gerald Cooper Chemicals Ltd* (1978)). This is no longer possible, because all applications for orders imposing personal liability on directors must now be made by the liquidator, and the amount recovered from a person against whom such an order is made will be held by the liquidator as part of the general assets of the company which are distributable rateably amongst all its creditors. The court cannot now order that any part of that amount shall be segregated for the benefit of a particular creditor or creditors (*Re William C. Leitch Brothers Ltd (No. 2)* (1933)).

On the other hand, where the court makes an order imposing personal liability on a director or other person who is himself a creditor of the company, the court may order that in the liquidation, the whole or part of any debt owed to him by the company shall only be paid out of its assets after all other debts of the company have been paid in full (section 215(4)).

The amount which the court may order a director or other person to pay under an order requiring him to make a contribution to the company's assets is 'such contribution (if any) to the company's assets as the court thinks proper'. Under the original terms of the Companies Act 1985, in respect of orders imposing personal liability for fraudulent trading, the court could make an order for payment equal to 'all or any of the debts or liabilities of the company', and it was held that under this provision the court would not order payment of any amount exceeding the debts and liabilities of the company incurred during the period of fraudulent trading (*Re William Leitch Brothers Ltd* (1932); *Re Patrick and Lyon Ltd* (1933)). Nevertheless, Denning MR expressed the view that the court could quantify the amount of the order by reference to the maximum amount of the company's debts and liabilities outstanding at any time during the period of fraudulent trading, including debts and liabilities incurred beforehand (*Re Cyona Distributions Ltd* (1967)). Under the present legislation the court may order directors or other persons against whom an order is made to contribute to the company's assets whatever amount the court thinks appropriate, and presumably the court will calculate the contribution to be made by reference to the diminution in the company's assets or the increase in the company's liabilities resulting from the director's fraud or misconduct, whichever is greater.

Chapter 11

Litigation Concerning Directors' Duties

Directors' duties may be enforced by the court in three ways, whether the duties are owed to the company, or to any of its shareholders or creditors, or to persons who have entered into transactions with it.

11.01 Modes of enforcement by litigation

The first way is by the court compelling directors who are in default to carry out the duty in question specifically according to its terms and to do the very act which the law requires of them. Except in cases where the act to be done is the payment of money or where the duty is to abstain from doing something or pursuing a certain course of action, the law rarely facilitates the specific enforcement of directors' duties by the courts, whether the duties are statutory under the Companies Act 1985, or arise at common law or in equity. The appropriate means of judicial enforcement in such exceptional cases is for the court to issue a mandatory injunction, which commands the directors to remedy the default complained of. If a special remedy is provided by the Companies Act 1985, the court instead makes an order giving that statutory remedy (such as an order rectifying the company's register of shareholders, or requiring directors to issue a new share certificate to a transferee of shares (section 185(1), (6) and (7) and section 359(1) and (2)).

More usually, however, the remedy available for a breach of directors' duties is a compensatory or restitutive one. Such remedies comprise the award of damages or compensation to be paid by the directors in default to the company or to a shareholder or creditor whose rights have been infringed, and an order that directors shall restore to the company assets which they have misappropriated or misapplied, or that they shall account to it for the proceeds of such assets or for personal profits which they have improperly obtained.

Thirdly, in addition to specific remedies and compensatory and restitutive remedies, the court can make declaratory orders annulling transactions which are invalid or defective because directors have contravened a statutory rule or a rule of common law or equity (for example, a court order declaring a contract or transaction to be void because outside the company's objects as defined by its memorandum of association). Alternatively, the court may make an order declaring the rights of the parties (for example, a declaration that certain shares of the company carry voting rights in the circumstances of the case, or that debentures charged on the company's assets rank in a certain order of priority).

The remedies mentioned in the preceding paragraphs are all judicial (that is, are remedies given by the court on an application made to it), and they are directed to redressing a certain irregular situation by giving relief in a standardised form, such as an award of damages, an injunction or an order that the situation shall be regularised. The court also has jurisdiction under the Companies Act 1985 to give relief in whatever form it thinks fit according to the circumstances of the case on the application of a shareholder of the company who alleges that its affairs are being, or have been, conducted in a manner which is unfairly prejudicial to some part of its shareholders (including himself). Although the Act specifies certain remedies which may be given on such an application, the court has a general discretion to devise whatever remedies it thinks appropriate in order to give effective relief to the applicant in the particular circumstances (section 459(1) and section 46(1) and (2)).

11.02 Other modes of enforcement

In addition to remedies by litigation, certain remedies may be pursued under the Companies Act 1985 which do not involve litigation at all. For example, the Secretary of State for Trade and Industry may in certain circumstances appoint inspectors to investigate a company's affairs and to report on any irregularities they find. The Secretary of State may also in any circumstances where he thinks fit require a company's books, papers and records to be produced for inspection to a person nominated by him (sections 431, 432 and 447). If irregularities are discovered as a result of such an investigation or an examination of the company's records ordered by the Secretary of State, he may bring proceedings in the company's name or otherwise so that the court may give the appropriate judicial remedies (section 438(1), section 440 and section 460(1)).

Other remedial powers may be exercised by the Secretary of State with immediate effect, and they do not depend on the making of a court order for them to become operative (e.g. the power of the Secretary of State to order that shares of a company shall not be transferred and that dividends may not be paid in respect of them when an investigation or enquiry ordered by the Secretary of State into the beneficial ownership of shares is impeded (sections 442, 444, 445 and 454)). Such self-executing orders or directions made by the Secretary of State, however, do not affect directors as such directly. They are mostly addressed to the company and require it to take action, but if the directors fail to comply on the company's behalf, they as well as the company may be prosecuted and fined for their default.

Orders under the Companies Act 1985 which directly affect directors as such can invariably be made only by the court. The most dramatic example of this is the court's power to order that a person shall not for a period of up to fifteen years be or act as a director of any company without leave of the court, if he is convicted of certain criminal offences, or if he is found guilty of fraudulent trading in the liquidation of a company, or if he is found unfit to be a director of any company by reason of his conduct as a director of a company which goes into an insolvent liquidation, or if he is ordered by the court to make a contribution to the assets of such a company because he has been guilty of wrongful trading (Company Directors Disqualification Act 1986, sections 1 to 6, 8 and 10).

11.03 Arrangement of subject matter

In this chapter and Chapter 12 an account will first be given of the way in which directors' obligations and liabilities to their companies and to individual shareholders and creditors of their companies may respectively be enforced by litigation, both while the company is a going concern and when it is being wound up. There will then be examined the extent to which shareholders of a company may initiate proceedings against directors and others for breaches of duties owed by directors to the company and not to shareholders individually. In Chapter 12, consideration will be given to the special statutory proceedings by which shareholders may seek relief from the conduct of a company's affairs in a way which is unfairly prejudicial to them. Finally, at the conclusion of that chapter, an assessment will be made of the adequacy and appropriateness of the judicial remedies available as means for protecting the interests of companies and their shareholders.

LITIGATION BY A COMPANY TO ENFORCE DIRECTORS' LIABILITIES

11.04 Litigation in the company's name

If the duties of directors to their company are broken or not fulfilled, the company can sue them for damages, compensation, an injunction or a mandatory injunction, an account or any form of statutory remedy which is appropriate. The company sues in this situation to enforce a right or a cause of action which is vested in it, and the company is the plaintiff or applicant to the court. In general, the form of the litigation initiated by the company is an action commenced by writ, and if the directors are alleged to have breached any of their fiduciary or contractual duties to the company and it is not in liquidation, an action commenced by writ is universally the proper form of proceeding.

Nature of relief sought

The relief sought by the company will depend on the nature of the directors' duties which they are alleged to have broken. Directors' fiduciary duties are equitable in character, having been created or recognised by the Court of Chancery and its successor, the Chancery Division of the High Court of Justice. Consequently, the relief which should be sought for breaches of directors' fiduciary duties will be equitable remedies, and will be adapted to the circumstances of the case. Those remedies are injunctions, mandatory injunctions, an order that the defendant shall account to the company for money or assets which belong to it or which he holds on its behalf, and the award of compensation for loss suffered by the company in consequence of the defendants' breaches of fiduciary duties.

Compensation for material loss appears to be identical with the award of damages at common law and its amount is assessed by the same standards. Nominally, a claim for damages does not lie for breach of purely equitable obligations, although the court has a statutory power to award damages in addition to, or instead of, issuing an injunction in any situation where an injunction would be an appropriate remedy (Supreme Court Act 1981, section 50). In fact, the court has always had power in equity to award pecuniary compensation for loss suffered as a result of breaches of equitable obligations, and it has done so frequently in recent years when directors have breached their fiduciary duties by engaging the company in illegal transactions or disposing of its assets illegally

(*Selangor United Rubber Estates Ltd* v. *Cradock* (1968); *Wallersteiner* v. *Moir* (1974); *Belmont Finance Corpn Ltd* v. *Williams Furniture Ltd (No. 2)* (1980); *Armour Hick Northern Ltd* v. *Armour Trust Ltd* (1980)).

If directors breach their contractual duties to the plaintiff company, that is, if they fail to fulfil their express or implied obligations to it under their service contracts, the company may claim damages for the loss it has suffered in consequence. If the contractual obligations are negative in substance, the company may also seek an injunction to prevent a repetition of the breaches of contract. Often the express obligations imposed on directors by their service contracts overlap or duplicate their fiduciary duties, and in that case the company may both claim damages for past breaches of contract and seek equitable remedies which are appropriate to the circumstances.

Positive contractual duties of directors to their company (for example, a duty to devote their whole time and attention to the company's affairs) can rarely be enforced by a mandatory injunction, because the court will not generally enforce contracts for personal services specifically, nor will it enforce specifically obligations of a continuing character which would call for prolonged supervision by the court (*Whitwood Chemical Co.* v. *Hardman* (1891)). Moreover, if a positive contractual obligation is buttressed by negative terms (for example, an obligation imposed on a full-time director not to act as a director or employee of any other company), the negative obligation will not be enforced by an ordinary injunction if the practical result would be to compel the director to fulfil his positive contractual obligation (*Rely-a-Bell Burglar and Fire Alarm Co. Ltd* v. *Eisler* (1926)).

Directors' breaches of statutory duty

When the Companies Act 1985, or other legislation, imposes an obligation on directors toward their company, or subjects them to a liability to it, but does not provide a procedure for enforcing the obligation or liability, the company may enforce it by bringing an action commenced by writ against the directors who are in default. If the legislation does not specify what remedies shall be available to the company, the company may claim damages for past defaults and an injunction or mandatory injunction (if appropriate in the circumstances) to compel compliance with the obligation in the future.

It is assumed for the present purpose that the provision of the Companies Act 1985, or other legislation, does in fact impose an obligation or liability on the directors toward the company, and that the court does not interpret the legislation as imposing liability to prosecution for a criminal offence on the company or its directors as the only sanction for non-compliance. The question whether disregard of provisions of the Companies Act 1985 gives rise either to a liability of directors to pay damages to their company or, alternatively, to an indirect liability to compensate their company for breach of fiduciary duty, was discussed in Chapter 8. If all contraventions by directors of prescriptions in the Companies Act 1985 were held by the court to involve breaches of fiduciary duty, the company would be able to sue its directors for compensation or an injunction or mandatory injunction for any failure by them to comply with the Act, but it is not certain that this is so.

As was shown in Chapter 8, there are many cases of contraventions of the Act where it is certain, or fairly certain, that the company does have a right to sue its directors for damages or compensation for the loss it suffers in consequence, and also to obtain injunctive relief to prevent future contraventions. Moreover, an injunction may be obtained to restrain future contraventions in all situations where the company has an interest in securing compliance with statutory provisions, even though it has no statutory right to their fulfilment. It may well be, therefore, that the company may obtain an injunction to compel its directors to fulfil all or, at least, most of their statutory obligations, and to conform to all the prohibitions and restrictions imposed on them by the Companies Act 1985, even though the company may not be able to recover damages or compensation for the failure of its directors to comply in the past with certain of those obligations, prohibitions or restrictions.

Award of damages for breach of statutory duty

Examples of provisions of the Companies Act 1985, where no specific remedies are prescribed (apart from liability to criminal prosecution) but where the company may undoubtedly claim damages or compensation from its directors, have been given in Chapter 8. Additional examples where the court would, or probably would, award damages to the company against its directors include contraventions of the prohibition on public companies allotting shares which are credited as paid up by the company accepting undertakings to do work or perform services (section 99(2)), or undertakings of any other kind which will not be fully performed within five years after the shares are allotted (section 102(1)); the prohibition against public companies allotting shares credited as paid up by a consideration other than cash, unless the consideration is first independently valued by a person qualified to be appointed to be the company's auditor who reports on the value of the consideration within six months before the shares are allotted (section 103(1)); and the prohibition on a public company agreeing that the company shall acquire or dispose of assets worth more than 10 per cent of its issued share capital for any consideration whatsoever without the assets first being independently valued by a person qualified to be the company's auditor before the agreement is entered into, but this prohibition applies only if the other party to the agreement is a subscriber of the company's memorandum of association and the agreement is made within two years after the company becomes entitled to commence business, or if the other party to the agreement is a member of the company at the time of its conversion from a private to a public company and the agreement is entered into within two years after the conversion (section 104(4) and (5)).

Further examples of statutory obligations of directors which are undoubtedly remediable by an award of damages to the company are the obligations imposed on directors not to allot unissued shares of their company, whether public or private, unless an authorisation given by its articles of association or an ordinary resolution of a general meeting of its shareholders is currently in force (section 80(1)); the obligation imposed on directors of public and private companies not to have the comany acquire an interest in its own shares, except in those cases where the Companies Act 1985 expressly permits this to be done (section 143(1) and (3)); and the obligations on directors not to give financial assistance out of the company's assets to enable anyone to acquire shares in the company or its parent company, except where the Act expressly permits this to be done (section 151(1)). Furthermore, the Companies Act 1985 explicitly enables public companies to recover compensation from their directors if they allot shares of the company under its first prospectus, when the minimum amount specified therein as required to enable the company to purchase the business it is to acquire and to provide the company with working capital is not fully subscribed, or when the directors allot shares under any offer they make if the whole of the shares offered or such fraction of them as is specified in the offer is not subscribed (section 83(1), section 84(1) and section 85(2)). Equally explicit are the provisions of the Act which enable any company to recover from a director the amount of compensation paid to him for the loss of any office held by him under the company or for retirement from office, if the compensation has been paid by the company or a purchaser of the company's business undertaking and the payment has not been approved by an ordinary resolution passed by a general meeting of the company's shareholders (sections 312 and 313).

11.05 Power to sue in the company's name

A matter which has been considered more systematically by the courts than the appropriate redress which a company may seek (apart from prosecution) if its directors breach their obligations to it or incur liabilities to it, is the question whether one particular organ of the company or another is the appropriate one to decide that litigation shall be initiated in the company's name.

Litigation authorised by the board or a general meeting

Usually the articles of association of a company confer power on its board of directors to manage the company's business and to exercise all the powers of the company, (including the power to litigate), except those powers which are expressly reserved to the shareholders in general meeting by the Companies Act 1985, or by the company's memorandum or articles of association. If the articles do so provide, the decision whether or not to sue in the company's name must be taken by the board of directors, and unless the articles expressly reserve the power to the shareholders in general meeting to give directions or instructions to the directors as to the exercise of their powers, the shareholders in general meeting cannot by passing an ordinary resolution require the directors to abandon litigation which they initiate in the company's name (*John Shaw & Sons (Salford) Ltd v. Shaw* (1935)).

On the other hand, whether the company's articles reserve power to the shareholders in general meeting to give directions or instructions to the board or not, the shareholders can by passing an ordinary resolution at a general meeting override a decision by the board of directors not to bring proceedings in the company's name to enforce an obligation or liability to the company, whether the obligation or liability is that of directors or other persons (*Marshall's Valve Gear Co. Ltd v. Manning Wardle and Co. Ltd* (1909)). If a general meeting resolves that the company shall sue notwithstanding the opposition of the board of directors, the general meeting may designate one or more of the shareholders, or it would seem, any other person to initiate and conduct the proceedings in the company's name (*Danish Mercantile Co. Ltd v. Beaumont* (1951)).

Individual shareholders or a group of shareholders may not without the sanction of an ordinary resolution passed by a general meeting initiate litigation in the company's name, and if they do, the defendant may apply to the court to strike out the proceedings as not brought with the company's authority (*Silber Light Co. Ltd v. Silber* (1879);

Airways Ltd v. *Bowen* (1985)). However, instead of striking out the proceedings, the court may direct that a general meeting of shareholders shall be held so that they may decide whether the proceedings shall continue, and if the meeting so resolves, the proceedings will not be struck out (*Pender* v. *Lushington* (1877); *Lawson* v. *Financial News Ltd* (1917)). Furthermore, proceedings improperly brought by a shareholder in the company's name may be adopted and ratified by the board of directors, or if the company goes into liquidation, by its liquidator. The proceedings are then treated retrospectively as though they had been properly authorised from the start and may consequently be continued (*Danish Mercantile Co. Ltd* v. *Beaumont* (above); *Alexander Ward & Co. Ltd* v. *Samyang Navigation Co. Ltd* (1975)).

Costs

A shareholder who is authorised by a general meeting or by the board of a company to institute or continue litigation in its name acts on the company's behalf and for its benefit, and is therefore entitled to be indemnified out of the company's assets for the costs he properly incurs, (*Williams* v. *Lister* (1913); *Simpson and Miller* v. *British Industries Trust Ltd* (1923)). The court can order that the company shall pay amounts to the shareholder on account of costs at any time after he has issued a writ in the company's name, and will be inclined to do so if the shareholder establishes a *prima facie* case and the application is unopposed (*Wallersteiner* v. *Moir (No. 2)* (1975)). Before making an order for the payment of the costs of the action, however, the court will hear the submissions of the directors and any shareholders of the company who support or oppose the making of an order. If a substantial number of shareholders argue against costs being made payable out of the company's assets in any event, the court will only order a payment on account of the litigating shareholder's costs if the action brought by him in the company's name is reasonably likely to succeed (*Smith* v. *Croft* (1986)).

Compromises and settlement of actions

When proceedings in the company's name have been instituted by the board of directors or by a shareholder or group of shareholders with the approval or ratification of a general meeting, the board or the shareholder or group of shareholders is in exclusive control of the litigation, and can therefore agree to a compromise or settlement of the proceedings with the defendants. The agreement to compromise or settle the action is binding on the company, and can be set aside by the court only if fraud was practised on the company or if it made a fundamental mistake in assenting to it (*Re South American and Mexican Co., ex p. Bank of England* (1895); *Re Roberts* (1905)). This is so even if the compromise or settlement is made after judgment has been given in favour of the company, but in that situation any other interested parties (such as other shareholders of the company) may be authorised by the court to enforce the judgement according to its terms, since they are not personally bound by a compromise entered into after judgment has been entered (*Re Alpha Co. Ltd* (1913)).

Company in liquidation or receivership

An action commenced by writ may be brought against directors for breaches of duty after the company has gone into liquidation, or after a receiver of its assets has been appointed by or on behalf of its debenture holders or by the court on their application. If the company is in liquidation, the action should be brought in the company's name by or with the consent of its liquidator, but if the liquidation is one ordered by the court, the liquidator must obtain the approval of the court or the liquidation committee representing creditors and shareholders which is appointed to supervise his acts (Insolvency Act 1986, section 165(3) and section 167(1) and Schedule 4, para 4).

If a receiver is appointed by or on behalf of the holders of debentures secured by a floating charge over the whole or substantially the whole of the company's assets, the receiver may bring actions against directors for breaches of duty (Insolvency Act 1986, section 42(1) and Schedule 1, para 5). A receiver appointed by the court to enforce any security over the whole or substantially the whole of a company's assets for the benefit of debenture holders may bring actions against directors in the company's name if expressly empowered to do so by the court (*Viola* v. *Anglo-American Cold Storage Co.* (1912)).

The directors and shareholders in general meeting of a company may not institute or authorise the institution of litigation in its name against its directors after the company goes into liquidation or if a receiver of the whole or substantially the whole of its assets is appointed by the court, but they may do so if a receiver has been appointed out of court by or on behalf of debenture holders and the bringing of the action will not impede the receiver in carrying out his functions (*Newhart Developments Ltd* v. *Co-operative Commercial Bank Ltd* (1978)).

11.06 Proceedings against directors in a company's liquidation

If a company is in liquidation, whether as a result of the court making a winding up order or a general meeting of shareholders resolving that the company shall be wound up voluntarily, the court may on a summary application made by the official receiver or any creditor, or with leave of the court, any contributory of the company, make a remedial order against any present or past director or officer of the company or any person who has been concerned or taken part in its management. The court's order may require such a person to repay or restore to the company or to account to it for any money or property which he has misapplied or retained or for which he is accountable, or to contribute to the company's assets such amount as the court thinks just as compensation for any misfeasance or breach of fiduciary or other duty to the company of which he has been guilty (Insolvency Act 1986, section 212(1), (3) and (5)).

This provision re-enacts in a slightly amended form section 63 of the Companies Act 1985, which itself re-enacted provisions of the earlier Companies Acts going back to 1862. The purpose of the provision is not to define or enlarge directors' duties to their companies, but to provide a speedy, summary and cheap means of enforcing directors' liability to compensate a company in liquidation for any diminution in its assets which has been caused by breaches of duty committed by them.

The summary procedure is initiated by a summons which gives a date for the hearing of the application instead of by a writ commencing an action, and instead of lengthy pleadings and a hearing where oral evidence is given, the arguments for and against an order being made are set out in affidavits filed by the parties which set out the facts and the supporting evidence, and oral testimony is given on the hearing only so far as is necessary to supplement the affidavits or to facilitate cross-examination. The only order which the court can make on the hearing of the summons is for the payment of money or compensation or the transfer or delivery of property to the company; no remedy may be given by way of an injunction or other specific relief, whether prohibitory or mandatory. Furthermore, although the order which the court most commonly makes is for the payment of money compensation to the company, the respondent director cannot set off any debt or monetary liability which the company is under to him against the amount he is ordered to contribute to the company's assets (*Re Anglo-French Co-operative Society, Pelly's Case* (1882). The company therefore recovers the compensation in full if the respondent is solvent.

The court may, under the Insolvency Act 1986, order a director or former director to pay compensation to the liquidator in respect of 'any misfeasance or breach of any fiduciary or other duty in relation to the company', whereas under the former legislation such an order could be made only against a director who had been 'guilty of any misfeasance or breach of trust in relation to' the company. The word 'misfeasance' means simply 'wrongdoing', but it was held under the former legislation that in the context, which included a reference to breach of trust, it meant deliberate wrongdoing and did not include negligence (*Re B. Johnson & Co. (Builders) Ltd* (1955)). This was surprising, because it had been held in earlier cases that compensation could be awarded against liquidators and auditors of a company for negligence in summary proceedings in a company's liquidation (*Re Windsor Steam Coal Co. (1901) Ltd* (1929); *Re London and General Bank Ltd* (1895)). Loss can be caused to a company as much by the negligent mismanagement of its affairs by its directors as by their deliberate wrongdoing. Moreover, the purpose of the summary procedure is to augment the company's assets available to pay its creditors' claims by recovering compensation for loss caused to those assets by its officers. It is therefore difficult to understand why the court held that compensation for loss caused by the negligence of a director could not be recovered summarily. However, it would seem that the altered wording of the present legislation enables all claims for breach of any duties owed by directors or other officers of a company to be enforced against them summarily in a liquidation, and this includes claims for compensation for negligence and for breach of contractual obligations as well as breaches of fiduciary duties.

11.07 Defendants, contribution and indemnity

A company may take proceedings by writ or by misfeasance summons in its liquidation against all or any of its directors or former directors who have been guilty of breaches of duty to it, and each director is liable to compensate it for the whole of the loss it has suffered (*Re Carriage Co-operative Supply Association* (1884)). If a director obtains a personal profit or gain from a breach of his duties, he alone is accountable to the company for it, but since the gain is treated as property of the company, the other directors who actively concurred in their fellow director obtaining the gain are also personally liable to compensate the company for its amount (*Parker* v. *McKenna* (1874); *Gluckstein* v. *Barnes* (1900)). Where judgment is given against several directors to pay compensation to the company for a breach of duty in which they have all participated, the company may recover the compensation by levying execution on the property and possessions of any of them for the whole amount of the compensation. Nevertheless, the court may also make such order as it thinks fit for the payment of contributions toward meeting the judgment by the directors as between themselves. In deciding on the amount of their contributions, the court will principally have regard to the personal benefits (if any) which the directors have respectively obtained as a result of their breaches of duty and their respective degrees of responsibility for the breaches, and the court may award a complete indemnity of any one director by the others, (Civil Liability (Contribution) Act 1978, section 1(1) and section 2(1) and (2); *Ramskill* v. *Edwards* (1885); *Gluckstein* v. *Barnes*).

Any person other than a director who knowingly collaborates in a breach of fiduciary duty by directors can be sued by the company for compensation in an action commenced by writ, but not by way of misfeasance proceedings in the company's liquidation (*Belmont Finance Corpn Ltd* v. *Williams Furniture Ltd* (1979)). Furthermore, if as a result of a breach of duty by directors, assets of the company or the proceeds of such assets come into the hands of a person who knows or suspects that the assets have been disposed of by directors improperly, the company may recover such assets, proceeds or their value from that person as well as from its directors (*Selangor United Rubber Estates Ltd* v. *Cradock (No. 3)* (1968)). Persons who may be sued as concurrently liable for directors' breaches of duty in such cases are not necessarily shadow directors of the company, that is, persons in accordance with whose directions or instructions the directors of the company are accustomed to act (Companies Act 1985, section 741(2)). Nor are shadow directors, as such, liable concurrently with the directors of a company for their breaches of duty, unless the shadow directors have actively participated in the breaches of duty complained of. Where persons are concurrently liable with directors for collaborating in breaches of their duties, the court can make contribution or indemnity orders in favour of or against such persons, and they may be joined as parties to the procedure for that purpose (Civil Liability (Contribution) Act 1978, section 1(1) and 2(1) and (2)).

LITIGATION BY SHAREHOLDERS AND CREDITORS TO ENFORCE PERSONAL CLAIMS

11.08 Form of litigation

If a director owes a duty or incurs a liability to a shareholder or a creditor of his company or to any other person (e.g. the victim of a tort or wrong committed or authorised by the director), the complainant may initiate litigation to obtain the appropriate remedy by bringing an action against the director commenced by writ. There are no special forms of proceeding established by the Companies Act 1985 in such cases, and the extent of the director's liability is governed by the general law, except so far as the Companies Act 1985 makes special provision (e.g. in respect of the liability of directors of a public company who enter into contracts on its behalf before obtaining a certificate of entitlement to commence business from the Registrar of Companies).

Consequently, actions by subscribers for shares to recover compensation for false statements in the prospectuses which induced them to subscribe, by creditors of a company to recover debts from a director who is a sole shareholder of the company or from a director who has been disqualified by an order of the court from being or acting as a director of any company, are all commenced by the issue of a writ naming the shareholder or creditor as plaintiff and the responsible directors as defendants, and the actions follow the normal procedure. If a shareholder or creditor of a company or any other person wishes to enforce a liability of any of its directors when the company is in liquidation, he does not need to obtain leave of the court before issuing a writ, as he does if he wishes to sue a company which has been ordered to be wound up by the court (Insolvency Act 1986, section 130(2)). Moreover, whether the liquidation is by order of the court or voluntary, the court cannot order that an action brought against a director of the company shall be stayed or shall not be continued as it can in respect of actions brought against the company itself (section 112(1) and section 126(1)).

The summary procedure described in the preceding section of this chapter by which the court may order a director or former director of a company in liquidation to restore any money or property to it or to pay compensation to it for breaches of duty by him, cannot be used by a shareholder or creditor of the company to pursue a personal claim against a director or former director. This is because the only orders which the court can make in such summary proceedings are for the transfer or delivery of property or the payment of money or compensation to the company, and not to anyone else.

Similarly, the enforcement of the liabilities imposed by the Companies Act 1985 on directors or former directors who are made personally responsible for the company's debts by its memorandum of association, or who have orders made against them that they shall contribute sums to the assets of the company because they have carried on its business with intent to defraud its creditors, or because they have traded wrongfully in the knowledge that the company could not avoid going into insolvent liquidation, cannot be used by individual creditors of the company or by persons with claims against it to obtain orders for payment of their claims directly to themselves by the delinquent directors. This is because such liabilities of directors and former directors can only be enforced on an application made to the court by the liquidator, and because the only payments which the court may order the directors to make are payments to the liquidator and not to individual creditors. Consequently, the benefit of such orders is enjoyed by the company's creditors collectively, and cannot be employed to benefit particular individual creditors.

LITIGATION BY SHAREHOLDERS TO ENFORCE LIABILITIES TO THE COMPANY

11.09 Enforceability by shareholders

In principle, a company, which is a separate legal person from its shareholders and creditors, should alone be entitled to enforce obligations of its directors and former directors to itself. English law does not recognise a right for a third person to enforce obligations or liabilities incurred by a defendant to someone other than himself, even though he is interested in the obligation or liability being fulfilled, because, for example, he is a creditor of the person to whom the obligation is owed or to whom the liability was incurred.

There are, it is true, a few situations when one person is by law subrogated or substituted to the rights of another – that is, enabled by law to enforce such rights against a defendant so as to give effect to rights which he himself has against the original person in whom the rights are vested. For example, a guarantor or surety who has paid the debt of another person which he has guaranteed is entitled to recover an indemnity from the principal debtor by enforcing the rights and remedies which the creditor had against that debtor, and realising any securities vested in him. These situations are exceptional, however, and they do not extend to that of a shareholder who suffers loss by a fall in value of his shares in the company as a result of the non-payment of debts which third persons owe to the company, or as a result of wrongs done to that company by its directors or other persons causing a diminution in the value of its assets.

The basic rule of English law is that a wrong done to a company is not necessarily a wrong done to its individual shareholders, and the right of a company to enforce an obligation or liability to it by suing for damages or an injunction cannot be enforced by a shareholder

Litigation Concerning Directors' Duties

individually or as a representative of the company (*Foss* v. *Harbottle* (1843)). The rule is buttressed by the courts' reluctance to interfere in the internal management of a company if the matter complained of may be rectified by the board of directors or by a general meeting passing an ordinary resolution. For this reason the court has held that it will not issue an injunction to prevent directors who continue to act after their terms of office have expired from exercising the powers of the board (*Mozley* v. *Alston* (1847); *Lord* v. *Copper Miners Co.* (1848)), or to prevent a director whose election was probably defective from acting as a director (*Harben* v. *Phillips* (1883)). But the basic principle is wider than this reason justifying it, and in situations where a company has a right to sue its directors or former directors for breach of duty, it is generally true that an action can be brought only in the name of the company as plaintiff. Also, the action can be initiated, as indicated earlier in this chapter, only if the board of directors or a general meeting of shareholders by ordinary resolution so decide.

11.10 The derivative action

Origins and character

For over 200 years the Court of Chancery and the High Court of Justice as its successor, have in certain limited circumstances permitted one or a few shareholders to initiate litigation in their own name, suing on behalf of themselves and all other shareholders of the company (except the defendants), in order to enforce obligations owed by the defendants to the company in which they hold shares and to recover damages or obtain other remedies for the benefit of the company. The form of the action resulted from the need in Chancery suits involving many persons that numerous plaintiffs or defendants with common interests should be represented by one or a few of their number, so that the court could give a judgment binding on and for the benefit of them all without process having to be served on each of them individually.

The commonest use of this representative procedure was in connection with wrongs done by promoters and directors of unincorporated joint stock companies formed under a contract or deed of settlement. Such a contract or deed was entered into by all the members of the company, and was expressed to be binding on them and their successors in whom their shares were vested from time to time, whether as a result of transfers or transmission by law. These companies were unincorporated, and wrongs done to one of them were therefore in fact wrongs done to its members or shareholders collectively. Therefore, if the shareholders were numerous a representative action was an appropriate procedure for enforcing their collective rights and claims.

However, the courts also permitted representative actions to be brought by the shareholders of incorporated companies, such as companies incorporated by special Act of Parliament (as all the railway companies were) or by royal charter (such as the East India Company and many of the British overseas trading companies). The obligation which it was sought to enforce, or the wrong which it was sought to remedy, in such cases was an obligation owed to the company as an incorporated legal person or a wrong done to it as such. It was not an obligation owed to the company's shareholders collectively or a wrong done to them all, but this was disregarded by the courts and representative actions were allowed.

The representative action was a useful procedural device to obtain a judicial ruling on a matter in which several persons had a common interest, and in this respect there was no difference between the shareholders of an unincorporated joint stock company and a company which was incorporated. It was thus an easy extension of current practice to make the representative action available to shareholders of companies incorporated by registration under the earliest Companies Acts of 1844, 1856 and 1862. The problem which now occupied the courts was not to justify the availability of representative actions, but to define the circumstances in which they could be brought.

The recognition was slow to come that there is a difference between, on the one hand, a representative action brought to enforce rights belonging to the class of persons whom the plaintiffs represent and on whose behalf they sue (such as actions brought to enforce the rights and securities of a class of debenture holders) and, on the other hand, a representative action brought by certain shareholders of a company on behalf of all its shareholders to enforce the rights of the company and not the rights of the shareholders. The latter kind of representative actions are brought to enforce the company's rights, and the right to sue is derived from it, and is not vested in the plaintiff shareholders and their fellows personally. Consequently, to distinguish this kind of representative action from one where the action is brought to enforce the individual rights of the persons represented, a representative action to enforce the company's rights is now known as a derivative action, and has its own special rules.

Derivative actions lie only where the company could sue

A derivative action can only be brought if the company could have brought an action in its own name, and so it cannot be brought if the company has been dissolved and so no longer exists (*Coxon* v. *Gorst* (1891); *Clarkson* v. *Davies* (1923)). But if the company is being wound up, it continues to exist until it is dissolved at the end of the liquidation, and so a derivative action may still be brought against its directors and others, and in a winding up by the court it may give leave for this to be done (*Re London, Bombay and Mediterranean Bank Ltd* (1866); *Hagell* v. *Currie* (1867)).

A shareholder may bring a derivative action in respect of wrongs done to the company or in respect of liabilities incurred to it before he became a shareholder (*Seaton* v. *Grant* (1867)), but he may not continue the action if he ceases to be a shareholder, and in that event the court may order that another shareholder shall be substituted as plaintiff so that the action shall not be dismissed for want of prosecution (*Ffooks* v. *South Western Rly Co.* (1853)).

The company must be joined as a nominal defendant in a derivative action together with the real defendants against whom relief is sought. The reason for this is that if the action is successful, judgment will be given in favour of the company, and it needs to be a party so that it may enforce an award of damages or an injunction or an order for the restitution of property or money to it. Also, the company must be a party so that if the action is unsuccessful, the company will be bound by the judgment, and will not be able to bring a second action on the same facts in its own name (*Spokes* v. *Grosvenor Hotel Co.* (1897)).

Costs

Because a derivative action is brought for the company's benefit, the court can in its discretion order the company to indemnify the plaintiff shareholder against the whole or any part of the costs he incurs. An order to that effect, extending to the whole or part of the costs, may be made at any time after the action has been brought, even after judgment has been given, and the court may order a complete or partial indemnity whether the action is successful or not (*Wallersteiner* v. *Moir (No. 2)* (1975)). On the other hand, in the early stages of an action the court will not order payments on account of costs to be made to the plaintiff shareholder out of the company's assets, unless he satisfies the court that his action stands a reasonable chance of success, and before deciding whether it does, the court will consider submissions made by the company and by its directors and shareholders who support or oppose the action proceeding (*Smith* v. *Croft* (1986)).

Independence of the plaintiff shareholder

Although a derivative action is brought for the company's benefit, the plaintiff does not act as an agent for it or the shareholders on whose behalf he is expressed to sue. Consequently, the plaintiff shareholder can compromise or abandon the action at any time before judgment without obtaining the consent of the company or of his fellow shareholders, but if his action is successful and an award of damages or any other remedy is made in favour of the company, the plaintiff cannot effectively agree with the defendants to forgo the benefit of the judgment so as to prevent the company or any other shareholder from enforcing it (*Re Alpha Co. Ltd* (1903)). Furthermore, if the plaintiff shareholder does not conduct the action properly or if he proposes to abandon it, the court may in its discretion substitute another shareholder as plaintiff (*Re Services Club Estate Syndicate Ltd* (1930)). Apart from this, the other shareholders on whose behalf the derivative action is nominally brought have no control over the conduct of the action, and if the plaintiff shareholder is unsuccessful they are not personally liable to pay or contribute toward the defendants' costs (*Price* v. *Rhondda UDC* (1923)).

11.11 Situations where derivative actions lie

Although the courts have been liberal in giving the plaintiff shareholders in a derivative action almost complete control over its conduct, they have been restrictive in defining the circumstances in which such an action may be brought, and this is particularly so in the case of actions brought to enforce directors' liabilities to their company.

Nevertheless, in early cases the court showed an inclination to allow a derivative action to be brought in most situations where the company could not sue in its own name (e.g. because the prospective defendants were its own directors who constituted a majority of the board), or where the company did not choose to sue in its own name (e.g. because the board of directors and a general meeting had resolved not to sue). This was particularly so when the derivative action was brought against promoters or directors alleging breaches of their fiduciary duties to the company. The court permitted such actions to proceed if it was shown that the promoters or directors were supported by so many other shareholders that the plaintiff shareholders would be unable to persuade a general meeting to pass an ordinary resolution that the company should sue them in its name (*Apperly* v. *Page* (1847); *Davidson* v. *Tulloch* (1860); *Attwool* v. *Merryweather* (1867)).

In *Russell* v. *Wakefield Waterworks Co.* (1875), at page 482, Sir George Jessel MR approved these early cases, and summed up their results by holding that a derivative action lies:

'... if it can be shown either that the wrongdoer has command of the majority of the votes, so that it would be absurd to call [a general] meeting; or if it can be shown that there has been a general meeting substantially approving of what has been done, or if it can be shown from the acts of the corporation as a corporation, distinguished from the mere acts of the directors of it, that they have approved of what has been done, and have allowed a long time to elapse without interfering, so that they do not intend and are not willing to sue.'

In the last quarter of the nineteenth century, however, a judicial reaction set in which, with a few notable exceptions, continues still. The result of this reaction has been that the courts have categorised, seemingly exhaustively, the kinds of wrongs done and liabilities incurred to a company which are susceptible to redress by derivative actions, with the corollary that wrongs and liabilities which do not fall into the established categories can be made the subject of actions brought by the company, but not of derivative actions brought by its shareholders.

The most extreme expression of this restrictive view of the scope of derivative actions is found in the opinion of the Judicial Committee of the Privy Council in *Burland* v. *Earle* (1902), where Lord Davey (at page 93) said:

'But an exception is made to the ... rule [that an action to redress a wrong done to a company must be brought by the company itself] where the persons against whom the relief is sought themselves hold and control the majority of the shares in the company, and will not permit an action to be brought in the name of the company. In that case the courts allow the shareholders complaining to bring an action in their own names, [but] the cases in which the minority can maintain such an action are ... confined to those in which the acts complained of are of a fraudulent character or beyond the powers of the company.'

Later cases have shown that it must now be accepted that the categories of wrongs and liabilities which may be redressed by derivative actions are limited, and (as the Court of Appeal has recently affirmed in *Prudential Assurance Co. Ltd* v. *Newman Industries Ltd (No. 2)* (1982)) the court cannot allow a derivative action to be brought merely because the justice of the case so requires. Nevertheless, they also show that the categories of cases where directors may be sued in derivative actions for derelictions of their duties are not confined to situations where they have been guilty of fraud or of applying the company's assets for purposes unconnected with carrying on the business activities which it is authorised to engage in by its memorandum of association. Moreover, derivative actions can be brought for certain purposes which do not concern breaches of duty by directors (e.g. to prevent anticipated breaches of the company's memorandum or articles of association, and to invalidate resolutions which have been passed by general meetings which have not been properly convened). However, since this book is concerned only with directors' duties and liabilities and not with derivative actions generally, the only exceptional situations where derivative actions may be brought which will be examined here will be those which concern directors' breaches of duty. These situations may be considered under the heads of (a) acts by directors which are unrelated to the pursuit of the company's objects (*ultra vires* acts) or which are illegal or otherwise in breach of the company's memorandum or articles of association; (b) fraud or oppression of minority shareholders; and (c) breaches of fiduciary duties by directors.

11.12 *Ultra vires* acts, breaches of the company's constitution and illegal acts

Injunctive relief

Any shareholder, however small his shareholding, may bring a personal action against the company and its directors for an injunction to prevent them from doing an act, or entering into or carrying out a transaction, which is unrelated to the proper pursuit of the company's objects set out in its memorandum of association, or which is otherwise illegal (*Simpson* v. *Westminster Palace Hotel Co.* (1860); *Hoole* v. *Great Western Rly Co.* (1867)). The shareholder's individual and personal right to sue is conferred on him by the company's constitution or by the notional contract which binds both members of a company and the company itself to conform to the terms of its memorandum and articles of association (Companies Act 1985, section 14(1)). The interest which the shareholder is entitled to protect in bringing the action is in ensuring that his investment in the company is not used by it to carry on activities which are not authorised by its constitution or which are otherwise unlawful.

As an alternative to bringing a personal action to restrain the company and its directors from exceeding its objects or doing an illegal act, a shareholder may bring a derivative action against its directors for an injunction to prevent them from doing so (*Preston* v. *Grand Collier Dock Co.* (1840); *Hare* v. *London and Northwestern Rly*

Co. (1861); *Simpson* v. *Westminster Palace Hotel Co.* (1860); *Wallersteiner* v. *Moir* (1974)). The real defendants in the action are then the directors, and the company is joined as a co-defendant simply so that it may enforce any injunction which is issued against its own directors. The advantage to the plaintiff shareholder of bringing a derivative instead of a personal action is that in a derivative action he can apply to the court for an order that his costs shall be advanced or met out of the company's funds. If he obtains such an order he will not be dependent on an order for costs being made against the directors on the successful conclusion of his action in order to obtain reimbursement for his personal outlay.

If a derivative action is brought for an injunction, it is not necessary for the plaintiff shareholder to show that shareholders holding a majority of the voting rights at general meetings of the company were opposed to the company suing its directors in its own name. Even if those shareholders procured the passing of a resolution by a general meeting approving the proposed *ultra vires* action by the directors, the resolution would be invalid, and the company could itself or through any of its members still seek to prevent the action from being carried out (*Burland* v. *Earle* (1902); *Ashbury Rly Carriage and Iron Co.* v. *Riche* (1875) per Lord Cairns LC).

A shareholder may by bringing a personal or a derivative action also seek an injunction to prevent any breach of provisions of the memorandum or articles of association of the company, other than acts in excess of or in conflict with its objects. The reasons for the availability of the alternative forms of proceeding are the same as those which make legitimate the bringing of personal or derivative actions to prevent the commission of *ultra vires* acts.

A personal action may be brought by a shareholder either because he seeks to enforce his interest in the observance of the company's constitution, or because he sues to compel the company to fulfil its notional contractual obligation, under the Companies Act 1985, to conform to its memorandum or articles (*Hoole* v. *Great Western Rly Co.*). On the other hand, a derivative action may be brought against the directors of the company to restrain them from acting in breach of its memorandum or articles of association, and the company must then be joined as a co-defendant in the action so that it may enforce any injunctions made against its directors (*Salmon* v. *Quin and Axtens Ltd* (1909), affirmed by the House of Lords, (1909); *Mosely* v. *Koffyfontein Mines Ltd* (1911)).

The institution or continuation of such a derivative action cannot be prevented by a general meeting of the company resolving that the proposed infringing act of the directors shall be approved, or by a general meeting passing a special or other appropriate resolution altering the company's memorandum or articles. Such an alteration could only operate for the future, and would not validate a decision already made by the directors which conflicted with the company's memorandum or articles at the time it was made (*Imperial Hydropathic Hotel Co. Blackpool Ltd* v. *Hampson* (1882)).

Damages, compensation and restitution

An individual shareholder is well equipped to take legal proceedings to prevent prospective *ultra vires* or illegal acts or prospective breaches of the company's memorandum or articles by the company or by its directors. He is less well equipped to obtain reparation when an *ultra vires* or illegal act has already been committed, or a breach of the company's memorandum or articles has already occurred. He is not totally remediless, however.

Any shareholder may bring a derivative action against directors to compel them to pay damages or compensation to the company for any loss they have caused it by an *ultra vires* or illegal act or transaction which they have authorised or for which they are responsible (*Hare* v. *London and Northwestern Rly Co.* (1861) per Page Wood VC; *Simpson* v. *Westminster Palace Hotel Co.* (1860); *Spokes* v. *Grosvenor Hotel Co.* (1897); *Wallersteiner* v. *Moir* (1974)). To initiate such an action the plaintiff shareholder need not first seek to call a general meeting to discover whether a majority of shareholders wish to bring an action in the company's name, and he need not show as part of his case that the persons who, as majority shareholders, control the voting in general meetings are opposed to an action being brought in the company's name. Furthermore, by bringing a derivative action a shareholder may seek an order that any of the company's assets which have been misapplied under an *ultra vires* or illegal transaction shall be restored to it, either by its directors or by third persons who have collaborated with them in the transaction (*Salomons* v. *Laing* (1850)).

On the other hand, the fact that the company has suffered loss as a result of a breach of some provision of its memorandum or articles other than the clause defining its objects, so that the act or transaction is not *ultra vires* and therefore absolutely void, does not entitle a shareholder or number of shareholders to bring a derivative action to recover compensation for the company or the restitution to it of any of its assets which have been improperly or irregularly disposed of or misapplied (*Hare* v. *London and Northwestern Rly Co.* (1861) per Page Wood VC; *Russell* v. *Wakefield Waterworks Co.* (1875) per Jessel MR).

The reason for this distinction is that irregular acts and transactions, for example, transactions which are within the objects of the company but beyond the powers conferred on its directors by its articles, are not void like *ultra vires* and illegal transactions. They can be approved and validated by an ordinary resolution which may be passed later by a general meeting (*Grant* v. *United Kingdom Switchback Rlys Co.* (1888); *Regal (Hastings) Ltd* v. *Gulliver* (1967) per Lord Russell of Killowen; *Bamford* v. *Bamford* (1970)). To allow a minority shareholder to bring a derivative action for restitution or the payment of compensation to the company in these circumstances would therefore deprive the shareholders in general meeting of their power of approval and ratification.

Nevertheless, if the irregularity complained of also involves fraud, a derivative action may be brought by a minority shareholder under the second head dealt with below.

11.13 Fraud or oppression of minority shareholders

The courts of equity have always given relief against fraud and oppression, even in circumstances where the acts complained of are not themselves illegal, but merely an abuse of lawful power. In the context of the relationship between minority shareholders and those who control the company, equity has therefore permitted shareholders who cannot sue in the company's name to obtain redress for wrongs done to the company by the persons who control it through their majority voting power at general meetings, but only if the acts of the defendants are fraudulent or oppressive. The adjective 'fraudulent' in this connection has a wider meaning than its common law signification of deceitful or misleading, and it comprises all acts which are inconsistent with decent, conscientious standards, or which are deliberately unfair.

Most of the successful derivative actions brought under this second head have been concerned with the restitution to the company of undisclosed profits made by promoters or directors selling to the company at an inflated price properties or businesses which they had acquired cheaply themselves (*Atwool* v. *Merryweather* (1867); *Spokes* v. *Grosvenor Hotel Co.* (1897)), or have been actions for the recovery of compensation for the deliberate misapplication of the company's assets by promoters or directors (*Mason* v. *Harris* (1879)), or for the specific restitution of the company's assets which have been misappropriated by directors or controlling shareholders (*Menier* v. *Hoopers Telegraph Works Ltd* (1874)).

Control of the company by the defendants

In all such cases it has been a necessary condition for the court to intervene that the defendant promoters, directors or controlling shareholders should by reason of their controlling voting power at general meetings be able to prevent the company from suing them itself. Consequently, derivative actions brought on the ground of fraud or oppression are inevitably minority shareholders' actions. It is not necessary, however, that a majority in voting power of all the minority shareholders (that is, the shareholders other than the defendants) should support the bringing of a derivative action (*Atwool* v. *Merryweather*). Any minority shareholder can institute a derivative action despite the opposition of his fellow minority shareholders. This is because the action is brought to remedy a wrong done to the company, and the fraudulent or oppressive character of the defendants' acts coupled with their control over general meetings are merely preconditions for the plaintiff minority shareholder to sue, and not the wrong which he seeks to remedy. Moreover, the control which the wrongdoers are able to exercise over general meetings so as to prevent the company from suing may be derived from the voting power inherent in shares held by themselves or their nominees, or from that power combined with voting power inherent in other shares where the exercise of that power is controlled by the wrongdoers as a result of voting agreements, proxy appointments or the other shares being held by another company which the wrongdoers control (*Pierce* v. *S. Mills and Co. Ltd* (1920); *Pavlides* v. *Jensen* (1956); *Bamford* v. *Bamford* (1970)).

Infringement of shareholders' personal rights

It is possible for minority shareholders who have been treated fraudulently or oppressively by the persons who control a company (whether directors or not) to obtain equitable relief for infringements of their personal rights as shareholders, and in such cases the question whether a wrong has been done to the company is irrelevant. Consequently, although a minority shareholder who is the victim of oppression may bring a representative action on behalf of himself and all other shareholders who are similarly victims, the action is not a derivative one if the shareholders' personal rights have been infringed.

An example of such a situation is where one company induces shareholders who collectively possess controlling voting power at another company's general meetings to vote at a general meeting of that company in favour of investing its resources in the first company or merging their company with the first one, when the inducement to vote is spiced with the offer of advantages (e.g. payment or facilities for acquiring shares in the first company) which are not made equally and proportionately available to all shareholders of the other company (*Kerry* v. *Maori Dream Gold Mines Ltd* (1898)). Another example is a scheme by controlling shareholders to deprive shareholders who are temporarily disfranchised under the company's articles from ever acquiring voting rights by making it impossible for them to fulfil the conditions set out in the company's articles which they must fulfil to acquire voting rights (*Estmanco (Kilner House) Ltd* v. *Greater London Council* (1982)).

Such cases do not involve breaches of duty by directors as such, however, even if the controlling shareholders are also directors of the company concerned. In determining whether a representative action is also a derivative one brought to redress a breach of duty by controlling directors, therefore, the crucial question is whether the wrong complained of is one done to the company.

11.14 Breaches of fiduciary duties by directors

During the last 80 years the courts have developed and refined the second head under which derivative actions may be brought for wrongs done to a company by controlling shareholders, so as to generate a new and distinctive head for the bringing of derivative actions against directors and persons who assume the functions of directors. Such persons owe fiduciary duties to the company, as explained in Chapters 3 and 4, and breaches of those duties, which are equitable in origin, have been treated by the courts as involving constructive fraud, so that if the directors in default control the voting power at general meetings of the company, it is legitimate to allow derivative actions to be brought against them. The significance of this extension of the second head under which derivative actions may be brought lies in the fact that only directors or perons who act as directors owe fiduciary duties to the company. Consequently, when derivative actions are brought against directors or persons who act as directors, it is not necessary for the plaintiff to show that they have acted fraudulently or oppressively toward minority shareholders. It is necessary, nevertheless, to show that they control the voting power at general meetings of the company and so can prevent the company from suing them in its own name.

Fiduciary duty and negligence

Under this third head, derivative actions have been permitted against directors to obtain the restitution of the company's assets applied in contravention of the Companies Acts (*Wallersteiner* v. *Moir* (1974)); for an account of profits made by the directors exploiting for their own personal gain a business opportunity which had been offered to the company (*Cook* v. *Deeks* (1916)); and to have the court invalidate an allotment of shares made by directors to themselves and their nominees in order to maintain the directors' voting control in general meetings (*Piercy* v. *S. Mills & Co. Ltd* (1920)) or in order to defeat a takeover bid (*Hogg* v. *Cramphorn Ltd* (1967)), or in order to favour one of two competing takeover bidders (*Howard Smith Ltd* v. *Ampol Petroleum Ltd* (1974)).

On the other hand, it has been held that a derivative action cannot be brought against directors for failure to exercise their powers without proper skill and care (e.g. where directors negligently sell the company's assets at an undervalue), even though historically it would appear that directors' duties of skill and care are fiduciary in origin (*Pavlides* v. *Jensen* (1956)). This reservation is undoubtedly the result of the present head under which derivative actions may be brought being an extension of the second head. Under that second head the plaintiff minority shareholder must prove fraud or oppression on the part of the defendants, and the law draws an antithesis between deliberate breaches of fiduciary duties, which constitute constructive or equitable fraud, and negligence, which involves the unintended causing of harm and is therefore not even constructively fraudulent.

The court's rejection of negligence as a ground for derivative actions was implicitly confirmed by the Court of Appeal's decision in *Prudential Assurance Co. Ltd* v. *Newman Industries Ltd (No. 2)* (1982), although the principal reason for the court's refusal to entertain a derivative action in that case was that the defendant directors did not control the voting power at general meetings, and it was therefore possible for an independent majority of shareholders to resolve that the company should not sue them. In one situation, however, the court has held that a derivative action for negligence may be brought against controlling directors, namely where they profit personally at the company's expense from their own ineptitude, for example, by negligently selling assets of the company to themselves at an undervalue (*Daniels* v. *Daniels* (1978)). The probable explanation of this exception is that because it is a breach of directors' fiduciary duty not to obtain a profit from the exercise of their functions, it is also a breach of their fiduciary duty for them to retain a profit which they have made as the result of the negligent exercise of their powers. If this is so, it means that the company's cause of action against the directors is not their negligence but the retention by them of the windfall profit resulting from their negligence.

Necessity of director control

A derivative action can be brought by a shareholder against directors for a breach of their fiduciary duties only if they control a majority of the votes which can be cast at a general meeting of the company, and so can block an ordinary resolution that the company shall sue them in its own name (*Prudential Assurance Co. Ltd* v. *Newman Industries Ltd (No. 2)* (1982)). The reason for this limitation on derivative actions against directors is the same as the corresponding limitation on the power to sue of a shareholder who relies on fraud or oppression on the part of the persons who control general meetings of the company. In both situations, no derivative action may be brought if an action in the company's name is at all possible.

The rule is mechanical in its operation, and means that the plaintiff shareholder must show that the defendant directors could defeat a resolution at a general meeting that the company shall sue them by casting against such a resolution the aggregate of the votes which the directors control. These comprise the votes which can be cast in respect of the directors' own shares and also in respect of shares which are held by their nominees, shares for which the directors or their nominees hold proxies and shares belonging to other companies of which they are directors or controlling shareholders (*Piercy* v. *S. Mills & Co. Ltd* (1920); *Pavlides* v. *Jensen* (1956); *Bamford* v. *Bamford* (1970)). No regard is paid to the number of shares in respect of which votes are likely to be cast at the hypothetical general meeting, nor to the percentage of abstentions from voting at general meetings in the past. Moreover, no regard may be paid to the way independent shareholders are likely to vote, so that a minority of votes controlled by directors cannot be treated as a majority by adding the votes of shareholders who have declared or made clear their intention to approve what the directors have done (*Prudential Assurance Co. Ltd* v. *Newman Industries Ltd (No. 2)* (1982)). Furthermore, the fact that the directors control an absolute majority of the votes which can be cast at a general meeting must not only be proved, but the fact that they have such control and the way in which they can exercise it must be stated in the plaintiff shareholders' statement of claim if the derivative action is to be allowed to proceed (*Birch* v. *Sullivan* (1958)).

Effect of the limiting factors

The two limiting factors on derivative actions brought against directors for breaches of fiduciary duties, namely, the rule that such actions can be brought only for deliberate breaches of duty, and not for negligence, and the rule that the defendant directors must be shown to control more than half of the total votes which can be cast at a general meeting, obviously make derivative actions against directors a far less effective means of securing redress for their defaults than it would otherwise be. A company may be as seriously harmed by a director's negligence as by his breach of any other of his fiduciary duties, and there is no logical or practical reason why the derivative action should not be possible to enforce the very qualified duty of skill and care which is imposed on directors by the present law. The availability of derivative actions would not of itself involve making the standards of skill and care required of directors more exacting, but it is certainly true that if those standards were made stricter by judicial decision, the case for enabling minority shareholders to bring derivative actions for directors' negligence would be even stronger.

The other limiting factor, the requirement that the defendant directors should control general meetings of the company, can be explained by the origin of derivative actions for breaches of directors' fiduciary duties as an extension of derivative actions for wrongs done to a company in circumstances where minority shareholders are the victims of fraud or oppression, but this does not commend the limitation as either logical or necessary. When the limitation is applied mechanically, as it has been for the last 100 years, it serves merely to give defaulting directors who control 49.9 per cent of the votes which can be (not are) cast at a general meeting on a resolution that the company shall sue them an immunity which directors who control 50.1 per cent of the votes do not have.

11.15 The American solution

The courts of the United States adopted in the early years of the nineteenth century a rule restricting the power of individual or minority shareholders to enforce claims of their companies against directors for breaches of duty which was identical with the contemporary British rule. The rule was that such claims should be enforced by the company suing in its own name, and derivative actions brought by shareholders should be permitted only if the company could not sue (e.g. because it was controlled by the defaulting directors) or if the company had declined to sue or had resolved not to do so. The idea of the derivative action as a last resort to be used only if redress was not possible or practicable in any other way was common to both systems of law. It is over the last 100 years that the law of the two countries has developed in different directions, with the result that in American law derivative actions may now be brought in many circumstances where they cannot be brought under English law.

The rule requiring preliminary demands

The basic rule of American law is that a shareholder may initiate a derivative action against directors for any breach of their duties if the company cannot or will not sue them itself. To prove the unwillingness of the company to sue, the prospective plaintiff shareholder must make successive demands on its board of directors and at a general meeting of its shareholders, and his demand must be rejected by both of them (*Hawes* v. *Oakland* (1882)). A demand on the board of directors need not be made, however, if the directors have already clearly stated their intention not to sue the defaulting directors in the company's name (*Smith* v. *Sparling* (1957)), or if a majority of the directors currently holding office are accused of breaches of duty to the company and so are unlikely to vote for a board resolution that the company shall sue (*Untermeyer* v. *Fidelity Daily Income Trust Inc* (1978)).

If the demand made on the board is unavailing, a demand must be made on a general meeting of shareholders that it shall resolve to bring an action in the company's name. This is so whether the board of directors reject the initial demand made on them, or whether such a demand need not be made (*Claman* v. *Robertson* (1955)). However, if the prospective plaintiff and his supporters are not entitled to call or require the directors to call a general meeting themselves under the relevant statutory provisions or under the company's articles of incorporation, it suffices that the prospective plaintiff should call on the board of directors to convene a general meeting to resolve on the bringing of an action by the company and that the directors refuse to call such a meeting (*Pollitz* v. *Wabash Railroad Co.* (1912)).

Notwithstanding the basic rule, a demand need not be addressed to a general meeting that the company shall sue if a shareholder or shareholders controlling a majority of the votes which could be cast at such a meeting have expressly refused to bring an action in the company's name or have stated their intention to vote against a resolution that the company shall sue (*Halprin* v. *Babbitt* (1962)). Nor need a demand be made at a general meeting if the directors accused of a breach of duty themselves control a majority of the votes which can be cast at a general meeting, or a majority of the votes which are likely to be cast, bearing in mind the number of votes which, because of abstentions, are not expected to be cast either for or against a resolution to sue in the company's name (*Meltzer* v. *Atlantic Research Corpn* (1964)).

The business judgment and non-ratifiability exceptions

The American rule to determine when derivative actions may be brought against directors is basically a procedural one, and is not concerned with the nature of the breach of duty which is alleged. Nevertheless, the basic rule is subject to two modifications which do make the nature and the seriousness of the alleged breach of duty relevant.

The first is that if a general meeting of the board of directors or, preferably, an independent committee of the board not comprising any of the prospective defendants, decides in good faith that for sound business reasons the company should not sue them in its own name, a derivative action may not be brought by a minority shareholder as an alternative (*United Copper Securities Co.* v. *Amalgamated Copper Co.* (1917); *Gall* v. *Exxon Corpn* (1976); *Gaines* v. *Haughton* (1981)). The board or the committee or the general meeting must have investigated the circumstances of the alleged breach of duty impartially before deciding not to sue in the company's name, and if the decision is made by the board, it must be the decision of a majority of the directors who are not implicated in the alleged breach of duty (*Groel* v. *United Electric Co. of New Jersey* (1905)).

The second modification of the basic rule is that no demand for the company to sue need be made on either the board of directors or a general meeting if the alleged act or transaction by the directors is one which a general meeting of shareholders cannot confirm or ratify. Such non-ratifiable acts and transactions comprise those which are tainted by fraud on the part of the prospective defendants, those which involved breaches of the directors' fiduciary duties (including their duty to act with skill and care when exercising their powers) and those which involved *ultra vires* or illegal acts (*Continental Securities Co.* v. *Belmont* (1912); *Smith* v. *Brown Borhek Co.* (1964); *Michelson* v. *Duncan* (1979)). The list of non-ratifiable acts and transactions has, in fact, become so extensive as a result of successive judicial decisions that the only situations where it is still essential for a shareholder to address a demand that the company shall sue to its board of directors and a general meeting before launching a derivative action now appear to be where the complaint against the directors is that they failed to exercise their powers in circumstances when they should have done (*Smith* v. *Brown Borhek Co.*), or that they were guilty of a procedural irregularity or failed to obtain an authorisation from the board which was necessary to enable them to represent the company in carrying out an act or transaction (*Mayer* v. *Adams* (1958)).

The consequence of the judicial extension of non-ratifiable acts and transactions is that the principal control over the availability of derivative actions in the United States is now the power of a general meeting or the board or a disinterested committee of the board to decide that an action shall not be brought in the company's name for sound business reasons. Such a decision prevents a derivative action from being brought, whatever the wrong which the directors are alleged to have committed. But since the court must be satisfied that the decision not to sue was reached after proper investigation and deliberation and that the decision was made in good faith and on reasonable grounds, the court still has a flexible but substantial discretion to permit derivative actions to be brought for serious breaches of duty by directors. The court will in practice be strongly inclined to permit derivative actions to be brought unless both the board and a general meeting have resolved not to sue and have done so for sound reasons and in good faith.

Contrast with British law

The differences between the British and American rules governing the availability of derivative actions for breaches of duty by directors are fundamental. The British rule marks out certain breaches of duty as not remediable by derivative actions, and in most cases where breaches are so remediable, British law imposes the further mechanical requirement that the wrongdoers should be in control of general meetings of the company. In contrast, the American rule pays no regard to the nature of the breaches of duty alleged, beyond considering their seriousness in deciding whether the company had a sound business reason for not suing itself. In those situations where ratification of the directors' acts by a general meeting is possible, American law also has regard to the likelihood that the directors will dominate the general meeting in fact. The American rule is more flexible than the British one and is also fairer, and despite the litigious propensities of Americans, the American rule does not appear to have overloaded the courts with the burden of trying derivative actions which turn out to be baseless.

Chapter 12

Shareholders' Remedies for Unfair Treatment and Conclusions

STATUTORY RELIEF FOR SHAREHOLDERS

12.01 Statutory jurisdiction of courts

The Companies Act 1948 established, for the first time, a statutory jurisdiction for the court to give relief to members of a company who complained that its affairs 'were being conducted in a manner oppressive to some part of its members including themselves', and the court was empowered to 'make such order as it thinks fit... with a view to bringing to an end the matters complained of' – in particular, to regulate the conduct of the company's affairs in the future, to alter the company's memorandum or articles of association and to require any shares held by members of the company to be sold to other members or to the company itself (section 210(1) to (3)).

This enactment was historically derived from the exercise by the courts of their statutory power to order the winding up of a company because it was just and equitable to do so in view of the subjection of minority shareholders to extended or persistent oppressive treatment by the persons who controlled the company (section 222(f), re-enacting earlier Companies Acts back to the Companies Act 1862, section 79(5)). The typical situations where winding up orders had been made were where the directors who held a majority of the company's issued shares had failed to hold annual general meetings, or to lay accounts and directors' reports before the shareholders for several years, with a view to coercing the minority shareholders into selling their shares to the directors for a price substantially less than their real value (*Loch* v. *John Blackwood Ltd* (1924)), and where controlling directors had for a long time excluded a director who was a minority shareholder from board meetings and the exercise of his functions as a director, and had refused him access to the company's accounts and records (*Thomas* v. *Drysdale* (1925)). The purpose of the new provision in the Companies Act 1948 was to enlarge the minority shareholder's remedies for the oppression to which he had been subjected, and instead of winding the company up, to empower the court to devise a remedy appropriate to the circumstances of the case so as to enable the company to continue carrying on its business, but subject to restrictions and requirements which would protect the minority shareholders' interests.

12.02 The present legislation

The statutory provision for the relief of minority shareholders from oppression was re-enacted with substantial changes in the Companies Act 1980 section 75, and the re-enactment was embodied in the Companies Act 1985, sections 459 and 461. The statutory provisions now enable any member of a company to apply to the court for relief 'on the ground that the company's affairs are being, or have been, conducted in a manner which is unfairly prejudicial to the interests of some part of its members (including at least himself), or that any actual or proposed act of the company... is or would be so prejudicial' (section 459(1)). If the court is satisfied that the grounds for relief have been established, it 'may make such order as it thinks fit for giving relief in respect of the matters complained of' (section 461(1)). This enables the court to fashion the relief ordered according to the circumstances of the case and to terminate the unfair treatment of the petitioner effectively.

A number of specific powers are expressly conferred on the court, namely, a power to regulate the conduct of the company's affairs in the future, to enjoin the company from doing acts complained of by the petitioner or to require it to do acts which it has omitted to do, to authorise the bringing of civil proceedings in the company's name, and to order the purchase of any members' shares by other members or by the company itself (section 461(2)). These specific powers are not intended to be exhaustive, and the court's jurisdiction to give appropriate relief is unlimited, and therefore equitable in character. In this respect the court's power is unique, because in all other instances where the Companies Act 1985 empowers the court to make remedial orders, the nature and scope of the remedy which may be given are defined in detail by the statutory provision. There are no such limitations on the court's power to devise remedies for the unfairly prejudicial conduct of a company's business which adversely affects the interests of minority shareholders.

The statutory provision enabling the court to order relief for shareholders who have been unfairly treated is not primarily designed to enable them to obtain remedies for breaches of directors' duties to the company or to the shareholders themselves. Nevertheless, situations where directors are in breach of their duties often involve the unfair treatment of minority shareholders, and by granting relief for that unfair treatment, the court may also indirectly give remedies for breach of directors' duties. This does not mean to say that directors' fiduciary duties can be added to by the inventiveness of the court in relieving minority shareholders from unfair treatment. Whether conduct by directors against which the court gives a minority shareholder relief also involves a breach of duty for which the company may seek a remedy itself depends on whether the directors' conduct also involves breaches of their fiduciary or other duties dealt with in Chapters 3 and 4. However, it is of practical importance for directors and shareholders to be aware of the kinds of conduct by directors for which relief will be given on a minority shareholder's application, even though the conduct may not involve any breach of duty to the company for which an action in its name, or a derivative action or misfeasance proceedings in the company's liquidation, could be brought.

The examination of the statutory provisions for judicial relief against the unfair treatment of minority shareholders which follows will therefore be confined to situations where the conduct of the company's directors was material. In most of the cases so far decided under the statutory provisions, the company has been a small or medium-sized concern without a Stock Exchange listing or admission to dealings on the Unlisted Securities Market, and the oppression or unfairness complained of has been made possible by the controlling voting power in general meetings of the persons responsible for the oppression or unfairness. Nevertheless, it is possible to isolate the conduct of directors in many of these cases, whether they were also controlling shareholders or not, and to deduce the kind of behaviour by directors which is likely to induce the court to give relief. It is also important to identify the interests of minority shareholders which the court will protect by giving relief, in the same way as it is important to identify such interests when considering the availability of derivative actions to minority shareholders. Finally, the conduct of shareholders who seek relief which will induce the court to refuse it must be considered.

12.03 Conduct by directors meriting relief

The criterion for relief under the present statutory provision, that 'the company's affairs are being or have been conducted in a manner which is unfairly prejudicial to the interests of some part of its members', would appear to cover the same ground as the former criterion that 'the affairs of the company are being conducted in a manner oppressive to some part of its members' (Companies Act 1985 section 459(1); Companies Act 1948 section 210(1)). The word 'oppressive' is somewhat more subjective than the substituted expression 'unfairly prejudicial', which envisages conduct which harms the interests of minority shareholders, whether intended to do so or not by the perpetrators. However, it was held under the former statutory provision that conduct was oppressive whether harm was intended or not, and to obtain relief a minority shareholder had only to show that the conduct complained of was unconscionable or unfair and that it either seriously impaired his rights or prevented his legitimate expectations from being fulfilled (*Scottish Co-operative Society Ltd* v. *Meyer* (1959); *Re H.R. Harmer Ltd* (1958)). This would appear to be an accurate paraphrase or exposition of the new criterion 'unfairly prejudicial', and the only important difference between the old and new provisions seems to be that the court can now not only give relief against both current and past unfairly prejudicial conduct under the new provision, but also that it can now also give relief against 'any actual or proposed act or omission of the company' which is or would be unfairly prejudicial. Cases decided under the former statutory provision therefore remain relevant in construing the present one.

Examples of unfairly predudicial conduct

The acts of the management of a company in respect of which relief has been given in cases decided by the court comprise: (a) persistent disregard by a managing director of the provisions of the company's articles of association as to the powers and functions of the board and the arrogation of the board's powers by him to the exclusion of the other directors (*Re H.R. Harmer Ltd*); (b) the removal of a director from office or the exclusion of a director from his functions when the removal or exclusion was effected in breach of the articles and was part of a campaign to exclude the director from membership of the company as well (*Re Westbourne Galleries Ltd* (1970), later reversed on other grounds (1971)); (c) the diversion of a major business opportunity from the company to another company controlled by a director who was a majority shareholder of the first company (*Re London School of Electronics Ltd* (1985)); (d) the award of excessive remuneration to managing directors by a board of directors controlled by them, and the issue of further shares to such directors by the board so as to enable them to control the voting at general meetings (*Re*

Jermyn Street Turkish Baths Ltd (1971)); and (e) the deliberate failure by the majority of the directors at the instance of the shareholder who had majority voting power at general meetings, to obtain stocks of materials which the company required to carry on its business so that the value of the minority shareholders' shares would fall and the controlling shareholder could buy them cheaply (*Scottish Co-operative Wholesale Society Ltd* v. *Meyer*). From this last decision it is possible to deduce that relief will be given to minority shareholders in general if the board of directors conduct the company's business otherwise than in the interests of its shareholders taken as a whole.

Conduct which is not unfairly prejudicial

On the other hand, the court will not involve itself in questions of business policy or the wisdom of business decisions on hearing applications for relief under the statutory provision, even though the policy which the board of directors has pursued or the decisions which it has taken have resulted in a fall in the value of minority shareholders' holdings. Consequently, the failure of the board to recommend the declaration of dividends commensurate with the company's profits will not be treated as unfairly prejudicial to minority shareholders, unless it is part of a plan to coerce them into selling their shares for unrealistically low prices (*Re Jermyn Street Turkish Baths Ltd*). Likewise, the court will not give relief to a shareholder who wishes to dispose of his shares and who complains that the company has refused to acquire them from him under the powers to do so conferred by the Companies Acts, despite the fact that the company has ample undistributed profits available to effect the purchase (*Re A Company* (1983)).

Moreover, although the court will give relief against deliberate mismanagement of a company's affairs, it will not give remedies to minority shareholders who complain that the incumbent directors or managing director have carried on the company's business negligently, unskillfully or ineptly, or to minority shareholders who allege that the company's affairs have been deliberately mismanaged but prove only that they have been poorly managed (*Re Five Minute Car Wash Service Ltd* (1966)). On the other hand, it may be that if the board of directors refuse to bring an action in the company's name against a managing director who has caused the company substantial loss by negligent mismanagement, a minority shareholder could complain that the board's decision not to sue is unfairly prejudicial to shareholders' interests if there is no good business reason for it and the action would be likely to succeed. The unfairly prejudicial act complained of would then be the board's groundless refusal not to sue in the company's name, and not the managing director's negligence, and the court could give relief by exercising its power to direct that an action shall be brought against the managing director in the company's name.

12.04 The interests of a shareholder seeking relief

Interests as a member

It was held by the court under the former statutory provision, which required a shareholder seeking relief to show that 'the affairs of the company [were] being conducted in a manner oppressive to some part of its members', that the petitioning shareholder must prove oppression of himself alone, or of himself and other shareholders, in his or their capacity as shareholders. Consequently, the court dismissed an application for relief by a director who was also a shareholder of a company when its board of directors or shareholders in general meeting had removed him from office in exercise of their powers conferred by law on the company's articles, but in circumstances which made his removal harsh and unfair (*Elder* v. *Elder and Watson Ltd* (1952)).

Under the new statutory provision the petitioning shareholder must prove that the company's affairs are or have been carried on 'in a manner which is unfairly prejudicial to the interests of some part of its members (including at least himself)', but the result remains the same, namely, that the interests which are shown to be prejudicial must be those of minority shareholders as such. Consequently, a second reason which the court gave for rejecting an application for relief by a minority shareholder who complained that the directors had refused to exercise the company's statutory power to purchase his shares was that the interest he sought to protect was that of a prospective seller of shares in the company, and not his interests as a person who would continue to be a member of it (*Re A Company* (1983)).

Nevertheless, as was shown above, if a minority shareholder proves that his unfair treatment in a capacity other than that of a member of the company is part of a plan to deprive him of his membership, or to coerce him into selling his shares at a depressed price, or otherwise impairing his rights as a member or shareholder, the court may give relief. Furthermore, one of the rights which a member of a company has as a member is to have the company's affairs conducted in conformity with the provisions of the Companies Act 1985, and its memorandum and articles of association, and if the board of directors infringe those provisions, a minority shareholder may seek relief against future infringements and reparation for past ones (*Re H.R. Harmer Ltd*).

It is noteworthy that in all the cases where the court has given relief against oppression or the unfairly prejudicial conduct of a company's business, it has emphasised that it did so to protect or safeguard the interests of the petitioning member of the company and, in appropriate cases, the similar interests of other members who were affected in the same way as himself. Relief was not given simply to uphold the personal rights of the petitioner, or to redress wrongs done to him or to the company by a controlling shareholder or shareholders, or to enforce the duties of directors to the company or to individual shareholders. The statutory provisions enabling the court to give relief were not, and are not, concerned with the definition and enforcement of the rights and duties of directors or controlling shareholders, but with the giving of relief of an equitable character in situations where minority shareholders have in fact been unfairly treated.

The conclusions of the court as to where and when relief should be given do not therefore extend or modify in any way the duties and liabilities imposed on directors by law which can be enforced by the company or its members as matters of right. The House of Lords recognised that this was so in the first case to be decided by it under the provisions of the Companies Act 1948. Both Lord Keith and Lord Denning in that case held that the conduct of the controlling shareholder and the directors of the company may not have amounted to legal wrongs done to the company or the minority shareholders which were remediable by actions for damages, compensation or an injunction, but that did not prevent their conduct being oppressive to minority shareholders and so remediable under the statutory provision (*Scottish Co-operative Wholesale Society Ltd* v. *Meyer* (1959)).

Petitioner need not be a minority shareholder

Although in all the cases so far brought before the courts, the shareholder seeking relief under the statutory provision has been a minority shareholder, and in most of the cases the persons of whose conduct he has complained have been controlling shareholders, the existence of these features is not essential in law for an application for relief to succeed. Both the original and the present statutory provisions merely require the petitioner to be a member of the company, and neither provision makes any mention of the capacity in which the persons responsible for the unfair treatment of the petitioner have acted, or required that they should be in control of the company. Consequently, it has been held under similar enactments in South Africa and Australia that it is not necessary for the petitioning shareholder to show that his interests are or have been unfairly prejudiced as the result of the acts of directors who are supported by controlling shareholders or by the acts of controlling shareholders themselves (*Benjamin* v. *Elysium Investments (Pty) Ltd* (1960); *Re Associated Tool Industries Ltd* (1963)). The law is no doubt the same under the British statutory provisions.

The reason why the petitioners in the cases where British courts have given relief have always been minority shareholders is that the companies concerned have been small or medium-sized private companies in which the shareholders have been divided into two factions with unequal voting power. Alternatively, there has been a single controlling shareholder or a cohesive group of shareholders who together have exercised control, and the petitioning shareholders have been unable to obtain redress within the company (e.g. by appointing or removing directors, bringing actions in the company's name or altering the memorandum or articles of association). When cases come before the courts involving larger public companies where the directors or a group of shareholders have effective control over general meetings, even though they do not hold more than half of the votes which may be cast at a general meeting, minority shareholders may nevertheless seek and obtain relief against unfair treatment because the inaction of the other shareholders in opposing the controlling group prevents the minority from obtaining redress within the company.

Capacity in which the wrongdoers act

The capacity in which the persons responsible for the unfairly prejudicial conduct of the company's affairs act in managing or controlling them is immaterial. If the conduct complained of is that of the board of directors who are supported by controlling shareholders, it is no defence to a petition for relief to show that the immediate responsibility for the unfair conduct rests with the directors who hold no shares in the company, or to show that the controlling shareholders were merely exercising their rights as shareholders in supporting the board and that they were not personally guilty of misconduct themselves (*Scottish Co-operative Wholesale Society Ltd* v. *Meyer* (1959)). In the same way it is no defence to a petition for a director or controlling shareholder who was responsible for the unfair conduct of the company's affairs to show that at the date the petition was presented he had ceased to be a director or shareholder of the company (*Re A Company (No. 005287 of 1985)* (1986)).

12.05 The conduct of the petitioning shareholder

Because the power of the court to give relief against the unfairly prejudicial conduct of a company's business is discretionary and equitable in character, the court may take the conduct of the petitioning shareholder into account in deciding whether to give relief at all, even if he makes out a case for it, and in determining the form of any relief which is given.

Consequently, if the petitioning shareholder's motive is not to obtain relief as a shareholder, but to put pressure on the company to induce it to pay a debt it owes him, the petition will be dismissed (*Re Bellador Silk Ltd* (1965)). Similarly, if the evidence shows that the petitioner has acquiesced in the conduct of which he complains, for example, by accepting his unjustified exclusion from board meetings and from participation in management without objection despite the fact that he remained a director of the company, the petitioner will be precluded from relief by his own conduct (*Re R.A. Noble and Sons (Clothing) Ltd* (1983)).

Delay in presenting a petition for relief may also induce the court to refuse it, particularly if the delay indicates that the petitioner has acquiesced in the improper conduct of the company's affairs and has waited to make his complaint until the company's business proves successful (*Re Jermyn Street Turkish Baths Ltd* (1971)). On the other hand, the fact that the petitioner has taken retaliatory action of the same kind as that of which he complains on the part of his fellow directors who control the company (e.g. diverting business opportunities which would otherwise be open to the company) will not prevent the court from giving relief. Such conduct, however, may be taken into account when the court devises the relief to be awarded, and may induce the court to order that the petitioners' shares shall be acquired by the controlling shareholder at a fair price instead of giving him injunctive relief (*Re London School of Electronics Ltd* (1985)).

CONCLUSIONS

A critique of the litigation process as a means of enforcing directors' duties and liabilities and of protecting shareholders' and creditors' interests in the proper management of a company's assets and undertaking must address itself to three basic questions, namely: (a) whether there are more effective and efficient ways of achieving these objectives than litigation; (b) whether the conditions to be fulfilled before litigation can be initiated under the present law are appropriate, fair and practicable; (c) whether the litigation procedures at present available are as efficient as they can be made and reduce, as far as possible, the twin evils of all litigation, delay in doing justice and incurring avoidable expense.

12.06 Supervision of directors

Any alternative to litigation for the enforcement of directors' obligations must involve either the concurrent supervision of directors' activities and performance, or investigations after the event into alleged failures by directors to measure up to their responsibilities. Effective supervision of directors' current performance under the present structure of companies has to take the form of frequent periodic reporting by directors to shareholders or creditors, coupled with the requirement that major decisions by directors shall be subject to approval by shareholders in general meeting.

At present, the law requires accounts and reports to be presented to shareholders only at annual intervals, and provides for creditors in this respect only by requiring companies' annual accounts and reports to be filed at the Companies Registry. The Stock Exchange's requirements with which listed companies must conform are better in this respect, since they require half-yearly reports and the notification to the Stock Exchange (and often also to shareholders) of major events and transactions affecting the company immediately they occur. The law requires only major decisions of a constitutional character (such as alterations of the company's memorandum or articles of association, the issue of share capital and arrangements altering the rights of shareholders) and decisions involving the personal interests of directors or affecting the company substantially (such as substantial acquisitions or disposals of assets, dealings with directors and the payment to them of compensation for loss of office) to be approved by shareholders in general meeting. Again, the Stock Exchange's requirements supplement this in respect of listed companies by requiring shareholders' approval for acquisitions or disposals of assets over a certain size or involving large increases in the company's issued share capital.

Despite these arrangements to ensure that shareholders are kept informed and their consent obtained before major transactions are entered into, it cannot be said that either the law or the Stock Exchange's requirements provide for continuous supervision of directors. This would be possible only if a smaller body representative of shareholders were established to monitor the acts of the board of directors, to receive frequent (monthly or quarterly) reports from the board and to give or withhold its consent to an intermediate range of transactions by the board which were not large or important enough to call for the approval of the shareholders in general meeting, but which could have a substantial impact on the company's fortunes.

Such a system of supervision is provided in Germany by the obligatory establishment of a supervisory board (*Aufsichtsrat*) representative of both shareholders and employees of the company, and in the Netherlands and Italy by the appointment respectively of *commissarissen* and *sindaci*, whose role is no longer that of auditors as it was originally, but that of supervisors of and collaborators with the board of directors. To a lesser extent supervision of directors is provided in the United States by the appointment of audit committees of the board composed exclusively of non-executive directors. The increasing appointment of non-executive directors to the boards of British public companies may lead to the development of a supervisory role for them in time, but at present there are no legal requirements that any British company should establish a system for the continuous supervision of the board of directors.

12.07 Investigations and awards

The other alternative to litigation as a means of ensuring the fulfilment of directors' obligations is the provision of appropriate machinery for the investigation and redress of directors' alleged breaches of duty. British law provides such machinery by empowering the Secretary of State for Trade and Industry to appoint inspectors to investigate the affairs of a company, either generally or within the limits defined by the terms of their appointment, wherever the Secretary of State suspects that there may have been fraud in the conduct of a company's affairs or that its directors may have committed breaches of their duties, or wherever the Secretary of State accepts a request to appoint inspectors made by a certain fraction of the company's shareholders (Companies Act 1985, section 431(1) and (2) and section 432(1) and (2)). This power has been increasingly used in recent years, and many of the inspectors' reports which have been published reveal painstaking and thorough seeking out and examination of the available evidence and penetrating conclusions which match up well to judicial standards.

The defect of such investigations, however, is that the inspectors' reports are usually completed long after the events with which they deal have occurred. Moreover, although the Secretary of State is empowered to bring actions in the company's name to remedy breaches of duty by directors and other persons which a report reveals or, in appropriate cases, to apply to the court for the relief of minority shareholders from the conduct of the company's affairs which is or has been unfairly prejudicial to them (Companies Act 1985, section 438(1) and section 460(1)), the Secretary of State can do so only after the submission of the inspectors' report to him. By that time legal sanctions are often useless, because the company's assets have long been dissipated and the persons responsible are no longer available to be sued or have no assets to effect reparation.

This, of course, argues for an investigative procedure which is informal and speedy and carries with it the award of remedies which are appropriate in the circumstances. The model of the impartial, eminent and experienced referee or *ombudsman* which has been invoked in recent years as an extra-legal means for dealing with the citizen's complaints against public authorities, banks and practitioners in certain professions, readily suggests itself for this role.

It is very doubtful, however, whether an institution of this nature would prove useful, acceptable or effective. Companies are of the most diverse kinds in respect of their size, businesses and organisation, and do not lend themselves to a standardised system for the conciliation or settlement of allegations against their directors. Moreover, the expertise and wisdom which would be required of the referee or *ombudsman* – who would, like the early Chancellors presiding over the Court of Chancery, be exercising an unfettered power to devise fair and reasonable solutions (but here in respect of the intricate problems which often arise in the administration of companies) – would be more than could be expected of the small number of eminent people available for recruitment.

Furthermore, since a referee or *ombudsman's* recommendation could not be legally binding or conclusive without the prior agreement of the parties (when it would be equivalent to an arbitrator's award), it would most likely be only a precursor to litigation, and therefore would simply add to the total delay and cost of obtaining a solution. It would be possible to make reference to a referee or *ombudsman* available only if the parties agreed in advance to renounce their rights to litigate and to accept the referee's award as legally binding, but this would induce most complainants and respondents to decline because of the uncertainty of the outcome of a referee's hearing. Even if they agreed, it is doubtful whether there would be a substantial saving in time and cost in view of the volume and complexity of the evidence which would have to be produced to and examined by the referee. Unfortunately, palm tree justice is not as cheap or speedy as it is often imagined to be, if at the same time it is to be just.

12.08 Availability of litigation

If it is concluded that litigation is unavoidable as the ultimate means for enforcing directors' duties and obligations, the questions which necessarily follow are whether the present law affords proper facilities for companies, shareholders and creditors to initiate litigation, and whether the procedure by which they can do so is the most efficient and inexpensive that can be devised if justice is to be done.

The ability to bring an action in a company's name against directors alleged to be in breach of duty to the company is confined at present to the board of directors itself (which is unlikely to resolve to sue individual directors unless there has first been a complete change in the composition of the board) and the general meeting of shareholders, who may by passing an ordinary resolution resolve to sue in the company's name and appoint one or more of their number to conduct the litigation (*Marshall's Valve Gear Co. Ltd* v. *Manning, Wardle & Co. Ltd* (1909)). If either the board of directors or the shareholders in general meeting resolve that an action shall be brought by the company, the other of these two bodies cannot prevent the action from being instituted or contested by resolving that an action shall not be brought (*John Shaw and Sons (Salford) Ltd* v. *Shaw* (1935)).

The rule is both logical and workable, but it excludes the possibility that a substantial minority of shareholders (particularly those who have suffered most from the directors' alleged breach of duty to the company) may bring an action in the company's name. The only redress which minority shareholders have is to bring a derivative action in their own names (suing on behalf of themselves and all other shareholders of the company except the defendants), and as was shown in Chapter 11, this may be done under English law only if their allegation is that the directors' acts complained of are *ultra vires* the company or illegal, or that fraud or oppression has been practised on the plaintiffs, or that directors have breached their fiduciary duties (other than their duty of skill and care) and the defendants control the voting at general meetings. This limits the effectiveness of the derivative action as a means of redress for shareholders, and calls for artificial qualifications to be fulfilled by the plaintiff shareholders which have nothing to do with the merits of their complaint or the loss suffered by the company. In this respect the American rule is more just and practicable, that a derivative action may be brought by shareholders unless the board of directors or a general meeting has declined to sue in the company's name and has good business reasons for doing so.

The weak position of the minority shareholder in seeking redress for directors' breaches of duty to the company has been improved by the wider recognition by the courts in recent years of directors' duties to individual shareholders in addition to their duties to the company, and by the availability to minority shareholders of the statutory remedy for relief from the unfairly prejudicial conduct of the company's affairs. The position of creditors also has been improved by the recognition of wider common law duties owed by directors to them individually, and by the enactment of increasingly stringent statutory provisions imposing liability on directors to contribute to the assets of a company in liquidation to make good their defaults.

The question remains, however, whether the remedies of shareholders and creditors should be strengthened further, either by giving shareholders who hold a certain qualifying percentage of the company's issued share capital a statutory mandate to bring an action in the company's name, or by enabling shareholders and creditors individually to sue directors for loss suffered by them in consequence of the directors' breaches of duty to the company. The statutory mandate to sue in the company's name is extensively given to shareholders by the legislation of European countries, although the qualifying percentage of the company's issued share capital which must be held by the shareholders who initiate the action varies between different countries (in France it is the holders of 5 per cent of the issued share capital, and in Germany and Italy it is 10 per cent). France alone confers a statutory right on shareholders and creditors to bring individual actions for damages against directors in respect of the loss they have suffered by the fall in the value of their shares as the result of directors' breaches of duty to the company.

The conferment of a statutory mandate to sue in the company's name on the holders of a prescribed fraction of a company's shares has the disadvantage of artificiality, because a wrong done to a company causes it and its shareholders as much loss, whether the holders of 1, 5, 10, 25 or 51 per cent of its share capital complain of it. Nevertheless, the statutory mandate at least has the merit of simplicity when compared with the rules of English law governing the availability of derivative actions. Moreover, the requisite holding of issued share capital by shareholders who are given the mandate to sue can be made large enough to make it less likely that actions will be initiated by small shareholders by way of blackmail to coerce directors into buying out their shares at artificially enhanced prices.

The French provision conferring rights to sue on shareholders or creditors of a company who suffer individual loss in consequence of directors' breaches of the duties they owe the company, is more problematical, and would involve the abandonment of the principle recently re-affirmed by the Court of Appeal in *Prudential Assurance Co. Ltd* v. *Newman Industries Ltd (No. 2)* (1982), that no such actions may be brought under English law. The availability of such actions has not substantially increased the volume of corporate litigation in France, however. This is because individual actions are usually instituted in conjunction with actions brought in the company's name under the statutory mandate or otherwise, and all such actions are usually tried together. Moreover, it does not appear that individual actions by shareholders and creditors have been extensively used for improper coercive purposes.

12.09 Effectiveness and cost of litigation

The final question which a critique of litigation in respect of directors' duties and liabilities must deal with is whether the present forms of procedure are as effective and as economical in terms of time and cost as they could be. This is a wider question, since it involves a consideration of the bases and details of litigation procedure in general, and it is beyond the purpose of this book to undertake so extensive a task.

It may suffice, however, to observe that to be effective, litigation procedure must provide for the full exposition of the relevant facts alleged by each party in his pleadings, the identification at a pre-trial hearing of the relevant facts which are in dispute and the legal rules which the parties will respectively seek to have the court apply, the delimitation of the evidence upon which each party needs to rely for the proof of the facts alleged by him and the elimination of unnecessary evidence, the disclosure of documentary evidence by the parties to each other before the trial, and finally the limitation of the trial hearing to the presentation of essential conflicting evidence and arguments on the relevant points of law.

On the whole, the English forms of procedure and practice achieve this objective remarkably well, if not inexpensively. This is particularly so when the summary procedure for the enforcement of directors' liabilities in winding up proceedings is employed, and the contentions of the parties and the supporting evidence are initially (at least) contained in the affidavits filed in support of and against the summons which initiated the proceedings. The same is true to a lesser degree in proceedings by minority shareholders seeking relief from the unfairly prejudicial conduct of a company's affairs, where the proceedings are initiated by a petition setting out the complainant's allegations, and the evidence and arguments in support of and against the petition are contained in affidavits filed in the case. Nevertheless, it cannot be disputed that improvements in litigation procedure are always possible, but they are best introduced piecemeal when need is seen to exist. A radical revision of litigation procedure is needed only when the current system has ossified as the result of inertia, and this has not been the situation with English civil procedure during the last fifty years. It should always be remembered that properly structured civil litigation procedure unavoidably involves time, effort and expense. That is the price of justice.

Table of Cases

Note

The following abbreviations of the main Reports are used:

   AC – Law Reports Appeal Case Series
   All ER – All England Law Reports
   Ch – Law Reports Chancery Series
   ER – English Reports
   KB – Law Reports King's Bench Series
   QB – Law Reports Queen's Bench Series
   WLR – Weekly Law Reports

A Company, Re [1983] Ch 178 .... 12.03, 12.04
A Company (No 005287 of 1985), Re [1986] 1 WLR 281 .... 12.04
Aas v. Benham [1891] 2 Ch 244 .... 3.10
Aberdeen Rly Co. v. Blaikie Brothers (1854) 1 Macq; HL 461 ....
.... 3.06, 4.05
Abt v. Fraiman (1974) (unreported) 10.03
Adams v. Thrift [1915] 2 Ch 21 .... 9.05
Airways Ltd v. Bowen [1985] BCLC 335 .... 6.10, 11.05
Albion Steel and Wire Co. v. Martin (1875) 1 Ch D 580 .... 3.07
Alexander Ward & Co. Ltd v. Samyang Navigation Co. Ltd [1975] 2 All ER
   424 .... 11.05
Allen v. Hyatt (1914) 30 TLR 444 .... 9.03
Alpha Co. Ltd, Re [1913] 1 Ch 203 .... 11.05, 11.09
Ammonia Soda Co. Ltd v. Chamberlain [1918] 1 Ch 266, 278 .... 6.10
Anglo-French Co-operative Society, Pelly's Case (1882) 21 Ch D 492
   .... 11.06
Apperly v. Page (1847) 1 Ph 779 .... 11.11
Arenson v. Casson Beckman Rutley & Co. [1977] AC 405 .... 9.04
Armour Hick Northern Ltd v. Armour Trust Ltd [1980] 3 All ER 833 ....
   .... 8.07, 11.04

Table of Cases

Armstrong v. Jackson [1917] 2 KB 822 .... 4.05
Ashbury Rly Carriage and Iron Co. v. Riche (1875) LR 7; HL 653, 670 .... 11.12
Associated Tool Industries Ltd, Re (1963) 5 FLR 55 .... 12.04
Atherton v. Anderson (1938) 99 F 2d 883 .... 5.03
Atkins v. Wardle (1889) 5 TLR 734 .... 10.09
Attwool v. Merryweather (1867) LR 5; Eq 464n 11.11, 11.13
Automatic Self-Cleansing Filter Syndicate Co. Ltd v. Cunninghame [1906] 2 Ch 34 .... 1.15

B. Johnson & Co. (Builders) Ltd, Re [1955] Ch 634 .... 11.06
Bagot v. Stevens, Scanlon & Co. Ltd [1966] 1 QB 197 .... 3.03
Bainbridge v. Smith (1889) 41 Ch D 462 .... 1.15
Bamford v. Bamford [1970] Ch 212 .... 4.03, 11.12, 11.13
Banque de l'Indochine et de Suez S.A. v. Euroseas Group Finance Co. Ltd [1981] 3 All ER 198 .... 10.09
Barry and Staines Linoleum Ltd, Re [1934] Ch 227 .... 6.09
Barnes v. Andrews (1924) 298 F 614 .... 5.03
Beal v. South Devon Rly Co. (1864) 6 H & C 337, 341–2 .... 3.03
Bede Shipping Co. Ltd, Re [1917] 1 Ch 123 .... 4.03
Bell v. Lever Brothers Ltd [1932] AC 161 .... 2.08, 3.09, 9.02
Bellador Silk Ltd, Re [1965] 1 All ER 667 .... 12.05
Belmont Finance Corpn Ltd v. Williams Furniture Ltd (No 2) [1980] 1 All ER 393 .... 8.07, 11.04
Belmont Finance Corpn Ltd v. Williams Furniture Ltd [1979] Ch 250   11.06
Benjamin v. Elysium Investments (Pty) Ltd 1960 (3) SA 476 .... 12.04
Biggerstaff v. Rowatt's Wharf Ltd (1896) 2 Ch 93 .... 10.04
Birch v. Sullivan [1958] 1 All ER 56 .... 11.14
Black v. Fife Coal Co. Ltd [1912] AC 149 .... 8.05
Boardman v. Phipps [1967] 2 AC 46 .... 3.06, 3.08, 3.09, 3.10
Bondina Ltd v. Rollaway Shower Blinds Ltd [1986] 1 WLR 517 ...... 10.03
Boston Deep Sea Fishing Co. v. Ansell (1883) 39 Ch D 339 .... 3.07
Bray v. Ford [1896] AC 44 .... 3.06
Brazilian Rubber Plantations and Estates Ltd, Re [1911] 1 Ch 425 .... 5.01, 5.02, 6.04
Bridges and Salmon Ltd v. The Swan (Owner) [1968] 1 Lloyds Rep 5 .... 10.03
Briess v. Woolley [1954] AC 433 .... 9.03
British Airways Board v. Parish [1979] 2 Lloyds Rep 361 .... 10.09
British Murac Syndicate Ltd v. Alperton Rubber Co. Ltd [1915] 2 Ch 186 .... 1.04
British Thomas-Houston Co. v. Sterling Accessories Ltd [1924] 2 Ch 33 .... 10.01
Broadcasting Station 2GB (Proprietary) Ltd, Re [1964–5] NSWR 1648   4.02
Brooks Wharf and Bull Wharf Ltd. v. Goodman Brothers [1937] 1 KB 534 .... 10.01

Brophy v. City Services Co. (1974) 31 Del Ch 241 .... 3.10
Browne v. La Trinidad (1887) 37 Ch D 1 .... 1.15
Burland v. Earle [1902] AC 83 .... 4.05, 11.11, 11.12
Burt v. Irvine Co. (1965) 237 Cal App 5.03
Bushell v. Faith [1970] AC 1099 .... 1.05

C. Evans and Sons Ltd v. Spritebrand Ltd [1985] 1 All ER 415, [1985] 1 WLR 317 .... 10.01
C.H. Giles & Co. Ltd v. Morris [1972] 1 All ER 960 .... 1.04
Cameron's Coalbrook Steam Coal and Swansea and Lougher Rly Co., Re Bennett's Case (1854) 5 De G M & G 285 .... 4.03
Candler v. Crane Christmas & Co. [1951] 2 KB 164 .... 9.04
Carney v. Herbert [1985] AC 301 .... 7.01
Carriage Cooperative Supply Association, Re (1884) 27 Ch D 322 ..... 11.06
Caswell v. Powell Duffryn Associated Colleries Ltd [1940] AC 152 ..... 8.07
Charterbridge Corpn. Ltd v. Lloyds Bank Ltd [1970] Ch 62 ..... 2.08, 4.01
Cherry and McDougall v. Colonial Bank of Australasia (1869) LR 3; PC 24 .... 10.04
City Equitable Fire Insurance Co., Re [1925] Ch 407 .... 5.01, 5.02, 6.04
Claman v. Robertson (1955) 164 Ohio St 61 .... 11.15
Claridge's Patent Asphalte Co. Ltd, Re [1921] 1 Ch 453 .... 3.05, 6.09
Clark v. Urquhart [1930] AC 28 .... 9.05, 10.01
Clarke v. Henty (1838) 8 P & C Exch 187 .... 10.06
Clarkson v. Davies [1923] AC 100 .... 11.10
Coleman v. Myers [1977] 2 NZLR 225 .... 9.04
Continental Securities Co. v. Belmont (1912) 206 NY 7 .... 11.15
Conway v. Petronius Clothing Co. Ltd [1978] 1 All ER 185 .... 8.06
Cook v. Deeks [1916] 1 AC 554, 564 .... 3.08, 4.05, 6.10, 11.14
Coxon v. Gorst [1891] 2 Ch 73 .... 11.10
Cranleigh Precision Engineering Ltd v. Bryant [1964] All ER 289 3.08, 6.01
Craven-Ellis v. Canons Ltd [1936] 2 KB 403 .... 2.02, 2.03
Croydon Hospital v. Farley (1816) 6 Taunt 467 .... 10.09
Cuckmere Brick Co. Ltd v. Mutual Finance Ltd [1971] Ch 949 .... 9.03
Cuff v. London and County Land and Building Co. Ltd [1912] 1 Ch 440 .... 8.06
Cullerne v. London Suburban General Permanent Building Society (1890) 25 QBD 485, 490 .... 3.05
Customs and Excise Commissioners v. Hedon Alpha Ltd [1981] QB 815 .... 6.09, 10.10
Cutler v. Wandsworth Stadium Ltd [1949] AC 398 .... 8.05
Cyona Distributions Ltd, Re [1967] Ch 889, 902 .... 10.13

Daniels v. Daniels [1978] Ch 406 .... 11.14
Danish Mercantile Co. Ltd v. Beaumont [1951] Ch 680 .... 2.02, 11.05
Davidge v. White (1974) 377 F Supp 1084 .... 3.10

Table of Cases

Davidson v. Tulloch (1860) 3 Macq 783 ..... 11.11
Denham & Co., Re (1883) 25 Ch D 752 ..... 5.02
Derry v. Peek (1889) 14 App Cas 337 ..... 9.04
Devlin v. Slough Estates Ltd [1983] BCLC 497 ..... 8.06
Diamond v. Oreamuno (1969) 24 NY 2d 494 ..... 3.10
Dinsmore v. Jacobson (1928) 242 Mich 192 ..... 5.03
Dorchester Finance Co. Ltd v. Stebbings (1977) unreported but summarised in 1 *Company Lawyer*, 38 ..... 5.03
Dovey v. Cory [1901] AC 477, 490 ..... 3.05, 5.02, 8.07
Duck v. Tower Galvanising Co. [1901] 2 KB 314 ..... 2.03
Duncan Fox & Co. v. North and South Wales Bank Ltd (1880) 6 App Cas 7 ..... 10.06
Duomatic Ltd, Re [1969] 2 Ch 365 ..... 6.09
Durham Fancy Goods Ltd v. Michael Jackson (Fancy Goods) Ltd [1968] 2 QB 839 ..... 10.09
Dutton v. Marsh (1871) LR 6 QB 361 ..... 10.03

Edgington v. Fitzmaurice (1885) 29 Ch D 459 ..... 10.01
Elder v. Elder and Watson Ltd [1952] SC 49 ..... 12.04
Elliott v. Bax-Ironside [1925] 2 KB 301 ..... 10.03
Emmadart Ltd, Re [1970] Ch 540 ..... 4.02
England v. Curling (1844) 8 Bev 129 ..... 3.09
Estmanco (Kilner House) Ltd v. Greater London Council [1982] 1 All ER 437 ..... 11.13
European Central Rly Co., Re Syke's Case (1872) LR 13; Eq 255 ..... 4.01
Evans v. Brunner Mond and Co. [1921] 1 Ch 359 ..... 4.02
Evans v. Coventry (1857) 8 de G M & G 835 ..... 3.04
Exchange Telegraph Co. Ltd v. Gregory and Co. [1896] 1 QB 147 ..... 3.10
Exchange Telegraph Co. Ltd v. Central News Ltd [1897] 2 Ch 48 ..... 3.10

Ferguson v. Wilson (1866) 2 Ch App 77 ..... 9.02
Ffooks v. South Western Rly Co. (1853) 1 Sm & G 142 ..... 11.10
Fine Industrial Commodities Ltd v. Powling (1954) 71 RPC 253 ..... 3.08
Firbanks's Executors v. Humphreys (1886) 18 QBD 54 ..... 10.04
Five Minute Car Wash Service Ltd, Re [1966] 1 All ER 242 ..... 12.03
Forbes v. Jackson (1882) 19 Ch D 615 ..... 10.06
Forest of Dean Coal Mining Co., Re (1878) 10 Ch D 450, 451–2 ..... 3.02
Foss v. Harbottle (1843) 2 Hare 461 ..... 8.06, 11.09
Franchi v. Franchi [1967] RPC 149 ..... 6.02
Francis v. United Jersey Bank (1981) NJ 15 ..... 5.03

248 Table of Cases

Fraser v. Whalley (1864) 2 Hem & M 10 .... 4.03
Freeman and Lockyer v. Buckhurst Park Property (Mangal) Ltd [1964] 2 QB 480, 505 .... 1.12, 10.04

Gall v. Exxon Corpn (1976) 418 F Supp 1311 .... 11.15
Gaines v. Haughton (1981) 645 F 2d 761 .... 11.15
Gamble v. Brown (1929) 29 F 2d 366 .... 5.03
General Steam Navigation Co. v. Rolt (1858) 6 CBNS 550 .... 10.06
George Newman & Co. Ltd, Re [1895] 1 Ch 674 .... 6.10
Gerald Cooper Chemicals Ltd, Re [1978] Ch 262 .... 10.13
Gething v. Kilner [1972] 1 All ER 1166 .... 4.02
Gilt Edged Safety Glass Ltd, Re [1940] Ch 495 .... 6.09
Glassington v. Thwaites (1823) 1 Sim and St 124 .... 3.09
Globe Woolen Co. v. Utica Gas and Electric Co. (1918) 224 NY 483 .... 4.05
Gluckstein v. Barnes [1900] AC 240 .... 3.10
Gluckstein v. Barnes [1900] AC 240 .... 11.06
Gouriet v. Union of Post Office Workers [1978] AC 435 .... 8.05
Graham v. Allis-Chalmers Manufacturing Co. (1963) 41 Del Ch 78 .... 5.03
Gramophone and Typewriter Ltd v. Stanley [1908] 2 KB 89 .... 1.15
Grant v. United Kingdom Switchback Rlys Co. (1888) 40 Ch D 135 .... 11.12
Groel v. United Electric Co. of New Jersey (1905) 70 NJ Eq 616 .... 11.15
Groves v. Lord Wimborne [1898] 2 QB 402 .... 8.05

H.R. Harmer Ltd, Re [1958] 3 All ER 689 .... 12.03, 12.04
Hagell v. Currie [1867] WN 75 .... 11.10
Halprin v. Babbitt (1962) 303 F 2d 138 .... 11.15
Harben v. Phillips (1883) 23 Ch D 14 .... 1.15, 11.09
Hare v. London and Northwestern Rly Co. (1861) 2 J & H 80 .... 11.12
Harmer v. Cornelius (1858) 5 CB (NS) 236 .... 3.03
Harold Holdsworth & Co. Ltd v. Caddies [1955] 1 All ER 725 .... 1.07
Hawes v. Oakland (1882) 104 US 450 .... 11.15
Heald v. O'Connor [1971] 2 All ER 1105 .... 7.01
Hedley Byrne Co. Ltd v. Heller and Partners Ltd [1964] AC 465 .... 9.04
Hely-Hutchinson v. Brayhead Ltd [1968] 1 QB 549   1.12, 4.06, 7.10, 10.04
Heron International Ltd v. Lord Grade and Associated Communication Corpn plc [1983] BCLC 224 .... 4.03
Heyting v. Dupont [1964] 2 All ER 273 .... 3.08
Hirsche v. Simms [1894] AC 654 .... 3.07
Hivac Ltd v. Park Royal Scientific Investments Ltd [1946] Ch 169 .... 3.09
Hogg v. Cramphorn Ltd [1967] Ch 254 .... 4.03, 11.14

Table of Cases

Holme v. Brunskill (1878) 3 QBD 495 .... 10.06
Hoole v. Great Western Rly Co. (1867) 3 Ch App 262 .... 11.12
Horcal Ltd v. Gatland [1984] BCLC 549 .... 3.09
Horsley and Weight Ltd, Re [1982] 3 All ER 1045 .... 4.01
Howard Smith Ltd v. Ampol Petroleum Ltd [1974] AC 821 .... 4.03, 11.14
Hughes v. Metropolitan Rly Co. (1877) 2 App Cas 439 .... 6.10
Hun v. Carey (1880) 82 NY 65 .... 5.03
Hutton v. West Cork Rly Co. (1882) 23 Ch D 654 .... 4.01, 4.02
Hyundai Heavy Industries Co. v. Papadopoulos [1980] 2 All ER 29 .... 10.06

Imperial Hydropathic Hotel Company v. Hampson (1882) 23 Ch D 1, 12 .... 3.02
Imperial Hydropathic Hotel Co. Blackpool Ltd v. Hampson (1882) 23 Ch D 1 .... 11.12
Imperial Mercantile Credit Association v. Coleman (1871) 6 Ch App 558 .... 3.06, 3.07
Industrial Development Consultants Ltd v. Cooley [1972] 2 All ER 162 .... 3.08, 6.01
Island Records Ltd, ex parte [1978] Ch 122 .... 8.05

J E B Fasteners Ltd v. Mark Bloom Co. [1983] 1 All ER 583 .... 9.04
James v. Eve (1873) LR 6 HL 335 .... 1.04
Jermyn Street Turkish Baths Ltd, Re [1971] 3 All ER 184 ..... 12.03, 12.05
John Shaw & Sons (Salford) Ltd v. Shaw [1935] 2 KB 113 ..... 11.05, 12.08
John Wilkes (Footwear) Ltd v. Lee International (Footwear) Ltd [1985] BCLC 444 .... 10.09
Joint Stock Discount Co. v. Brown (1869) 8 Eq 381 .... 3.05, 5.02

Kavanaugh v. Commonwealth Trust Co. (1918) 223 NY 103 .... 5.03
Kaye v. Croydon Tramways Co. [1898] 1 Ch 358 .... 4.05
Kerry v. Maori Dream Gold Mines Ltd (1898) 14 TLR 402 .... 11.13
Kettle v. Dunster and Wakefield (1927) 138 LT 158 .... 10.03
Kingston Cotton Mills Co. (No 2), Re [1896] 1 Ch 331 .... 3.05, 8.07

LPTB v. Lupson [1949] AC 155 .... 8.07
Lagunas Nitrate Co. v. Lagunas Syndicate [1899] Ch 392 .... 5.01, 5.02
Lake v. Brutton (1856) 8 de GM & G 440 .... 10.06
Land Credit Co. of Ireland v. Lord Fermoy (1869) LR 8; Eq 7 .... 3.04, 3.05, 5.02
Landes v. Marcus and Davids (1909) 25 TLR 478 .... 10.03
Law v. Law [1905] 1 Ch 140 .... 9.02
Lawson v. Financial News Ltd (1917) 34 TLR 52 .... 11.05
Leeds and Hanley Theatre of Varieties Ltd, Re [1902] 2 Ch 809 .... 7.07
Leeds Estate Building and Investment Co. v. Shepherd (1887) 36 Ch D 787, 801 .... 3.05

Levin v. Clarke [1962] NSWR 686 .... 4.02
Lindgren v. Land P Estates Co. Ltd [1968] Ch 572 .... 9.02
Litvin v. Allen (1940) 25 NYS 2d 667 .... 5.03
Lloyds Bank Ltd v. Bundy [1975] QB 326 .... 9.04, 10.06
Loch v. John Blackwood Ltd [1924] AC 783 .... 12.01
London and General Bank Ltd, Re [1895] 2 Ch 166 .... 11.06
London and Mashonaland Exploration Co. v. New Mashonaland Exploration Co. [1891] WN 165 .... 3.09
London, Bombay and Mediterranean Bank Ltd, Re [1866] WN 407 .... 11.10
London Financial Association v. Kelk (1884) 26 Ch D 107 .... 3.05
London School of Electronics Ltd, Re [1985] BCLC 273 .... 12.03, 12.05
Lonrho Ltd v. Shell Petroleum Co. Ltd (No 2) [1982] AC 173, 185 ..... 8.05
Lord v. Copper Miners Co. (1848) 2 Ph 740 .... 2.02, 11.09
Lucas v. Fitzgerald (1903) 20 TLR 16 .... 3.05
Lynde v. Nash [1928] 2 KB 93, [1929] AC 158 .... 7.07

Mahony v. East Holyford Mining Co. (1875) LR 7 HL 869 .... 2.03
Maidstone Building Provisions Ltd, Re [1971] 3 All ER 363 .... 10.13
Marine Insurance Co., Rance's Case (1870) 6 Ch App 104 .... 3.05
Marshall's Valve Gear Co. Ltd v. Manning, Wardle & Co. Ltd [1909] 1 Ch 267 .... 6.10, 8.06, 11.05, 12.08
Mason v. Harris (1879) 11 Ch D 97 .... 11.13
Maxform Sp. A. v. Mariani and Goodville Ltd [1981] 2 Lloyds Rep 54 10.09
Mayer v. Adams (1958) 37 Del Ch 298 .... 11.15
Measures Brothers Ltd v. Measures [1910] 2 Ch 248 .... 6.01
Meltzer v. Atlantic Research Corpn (1964) 330 F 2d 956 .... 11.15
Menier v. Hoopers Telegraph Works Ltd (1874) 9 Ch App 350 .... 11.13
Merryweather v. Moore [1892] 2 Ch 518 .... 6.02
Michelson v. Duncan (1979) 407 A 2d 211 .... 11.15
Mitton, Butler and Priest Co. Ltd v. Ross (1976) *The Times*, December 22 .... 10.12
Minister of Housing and Local Government v. Sharp [1970] 2 QB 222, 267 .... 8.07
Morison v. Moat (1851) 9 Hare 241 .... 6.02
Morris Ltd v. Gilman (BST) Ltd (1943) 60 RPC 20 .... 3.10
Morris v. Kanssen [1946] AC 459 .... 2.02, 2.03
Moschi v. Lep Air Services Ltd [1973] AC 331 .... 10.06
Moseley v. Koffyfontein Mines Ltd [1911] 1 Ch 73 .... 11.12
Mozley v. Alston (1847) 1 Ph 790 .... 2.02, 11.09
Multinational Gas and Petrochemical Co. v. Multinational Gas and Petrochemical Services Ltd [1983] BCLC 461 .... 10.01
Munster v. Cammell Co. (1882) 2 Ch D 183 .... 1.15

National Westminster Bank Ltd v. Morgan [1983] 3 All ER 85   9.04, 10.06

Table of Cases

New British Iron Co., ex p. Beckwith, Re [1898] 1 Ch 324 .... 1.15
New Mashonaland Exploration Co., Re [1892] 3 Ch 577 .... 5.02
Newhart Developments Ltd v. Co-operative Commercial Bank Ltd [1978] QB 814 .... 11.05
Nocton v. Lord Ashburton [1914] AC 932 .... 9.04
Nordisk Insulinlaboratorium v. Gorgate Products Ltd [1953] Ch 430 .... 6.01
North West Transportation Co. v. Beatty (1887) 12 App Cas 589 .... 4.05

Overend Gurney & Co. v. Gibb (1872) LR 5; HL 480 .... 5.01, 5.02
Oxford Benefit Building and Investment Society, Re (1886) 35 Ch D 502 .... 3.04

Parke v. Daily News Ltd [1962] Ch 927 .... 4.01, 4.02
Parker v. McKenna (1874) 10 Ch App 96 .... 3.07, 11.06
Pasmore v. Oswaldtwistle UDC [1898] AC 387 .... 8.05
Patent Agents Institute v. Lockwood [1894] AC 347 .... 8.05
Patent Wood Keg Syndicate Ltd v. Pearse (1906) 50 Sol Jo 650 .... 7.05
Patrick and Lyon Ltd, Re [1933] Ch 786 .... 10.13
Pavlides v. Jensen [1956] Ch 565 .... 11.13, 11.14
Pedley v. Inland Waterways Association Ltd [1977] 1 All ER 209 .... 1.05
Pender v. Lushington (1877) 6 Ch D 70 .... 11.05
Penkivil v. Connell (1850) 5 Exch 381 .... 10.03
Penrose v. Martyr (1858) EB & E 499 .... 10.09
Percival v. Wright [1902] 2 Ch 421 .... 9.02
Performing Rights Society v. Ciryl Theatrical Syndicate [1924] 1 KB 1 10.01
Peso Silver Mines Ltd v. Cropper (1966) 58 DLR (2d) 1 .... 3.08
Philips v. Astling (1809) 2 Taunt 206 .... 10.06
Pickering v. Stevenson (1872) LR 14; Eq 322 .... 3.05
Piercy v. Mills & Co. Ltd [1920] 1 Ch 77 .... 4.02, 11.13, 11.14
Plantations Trust Ltd v. Bila (Sumatra) Rubber Lands Ltd (1916) 85 LJ Ch 801 .... 1.04
Pledge v. Buss (1860) John 663 .... 10.06
Pollitz v. Wabash Railroad Co. (1912) 207 NY 113 .... 11.15
Preston v. Grand Collier Dock Co. (1840) 11 Sim 327 .... 11.11
Price v. Rhondda UDC [1923] WN 228 .... 11.10
Prudential Assurance Co. Ltd v. Newman Industries Ltd (No 2) [1982] Ch 204, 221 .... 9.01, 11.11
Prudential Assurance Co. Ltd v. Newman Industries Ltd (No 2) [1982] Ch 204, 222 .... 11.14, 12.08
Puddephatt v. Leith [1916] 1 Ch 200 .... 1.04

Queensland Mines Ltd v. Hudson (1978) 52 ALJR 399 .... 3.08

Table of Cases

R.A. Noble and Sons (Clothing) Ltd, Re [1983] BCLC 273 .... 12.05
R. v. Grantham [1984] QB 675 .... 10.13
Rainham Chemical Works Ltd v. Belvedere Fish Guano Co. Ltd [1921] 2 AC 465, 475–6 .... 10.01
Rama Corpn Ltd v. Proved Tin and General Investments Ltd [1952] 2 QB 147 .... 1.12
Ramskill v. Edwards (1885) 31 Ch D 100 .... 5.02, 11.06
Read v. Astoria Garage (Streatham) Ltd [1952] Ch 637 .... 1.15
Regal (Hastings) Ltd v. Gulliver [1967] 2 AC 134, 150 .. 3.07, 3.08, 6.10, 11.12
Reid v. Explosives Co. (1887) 19 QBD 264 .... 6.01
Rely-a-Bell Burglar and Fire Alarm Co. Ltd v. Eisler [1926] Ch 609 .... 11.04
Robb v. Green [1895] 2 QB 315 .... 6.02
Roberts, Re [1905] 1 Ch 704 .... 11.05
Rolled Steel Products (Holdings) Ltd v. British Steel Corporation [1985] 3 All ER 52; Ch 246 .... 2.08, 4.01
Rosenblum v. Judson Engineering Corpn (1954) 99 NH 267 .... 3.09
Rouse v. Bradford Banking Co. Ltd [1894] AC 586 .... 10.06
Royal British Bank v. Turquand (1855) 5 E & B 248 .... 10.04
Russell v. Wakefield Waterworks Co. (1875) LR 20; Eq 474, 481 .... 11.11, 11.12

Said v. Butt [1920] 3 KB 497 .... 9.01
Salmon v. Quin and Axtens Ltd [1909] 1 Ch 311 .... 11.12
Salomons v. Laing (1859) 12 Beav 377 .... 11.12
Saltman Engineering Co. Ltd v. Campbell Engineering Co. Ltd (1948) 55 PRC 203 .... 3.09, 3.10
Scottish Co-operative Society Ltd v. Meyer [1959] AC 324 .... 12.03, 12.04
Scott v. Scott [1943] 1 All ER 582 .... 1.15
Seaton v. Grant (1867) 2 Ch App 459 .... 11.10
Selangor United Rubber Estates Ltd v. Cradock (No 3) [1968] 2 All ER 1073 .... 3.04, 5.02, 6.09, 7.01, 8.07, 11.04, 11.06
Sequois Vacuum Systems Inc. v. Stransky (1964) 229 Cal App 2d 281 .... 3.09
Services Club Estate Syndicate Ltd, Re [1930] 1 Ch 78 .... 11.10
Sharpe, Re [1892] 1 Ch 154, 165 .... 3.05
Shaw v. Holland [1900] 2 Ch 305 .... 3.07
Shindler v. Northern Raincoat Co. Ltd [1960] 2 All ER 239 .... 1.09
Shuttleworth v. Cox Brothers & Co. (Maidenhead) Ltd [1927] 2 KB 9 . 1.08
Silber Light Co. Ltd v. Silber (1879) 12 Ch D 717 .... 11.05
Simpson and Miller v. British Industries Trust Ltd (1923) LT 699 .... 11.05, 11.10
Simpson v. Westminster Palace Hotel Co. (1860) 8 HL Cas 712 .... 11.12
Singer v. Carlisle (1941) 26 NYS 2d 320 .... 3.09
Smith v. Brown Borhek Co. (1964) 414 Pa 325 .... 11.15
Smith v. Croft [1986] 1 WLR 580 .... 11.10

Table of Cases

Smith and Fawcett Ltd, Re [1942] Ch 304 .... 4.01
Smith v. Sparling (1957) 354 US 91 .... 11.15
South American and Mexican Co., Re Exp p. Bank of England [1895] 1 Ch 37 .... 11.05
South of England Natural Gas and Petroleum Co. Ltd, Re [1911] Ch 573 .... 7.07
Southern Foundries (1926) Ltd v. Shirlaw [1940] AC 701 .... 1.05, 1.07
Spink (Bournemouth) Ltd v. Spink [1936] Ch 544 .... 7.01
Spokes v. Grosvenor Hotel Co. [1897] 2 QB 124 .... 11.10, 11.12, 11.13
Stevens v. Hoare (1904) 20 TLR 407 .... 9.05
Studdert v. Grosvenor (1886) 33 Ch D 528 .... 3.05

Taupa Totara Timber Co. Ltd v. Rowe [1978] AC 537 .... 9.08
Teck Corpn v. Millar (1972) 33 DLR (3d) 288 .... 4.03
Terrapin Ltd v. Builders Supply Co. (Hayes) Ltd [1960] RPC 128 ...... 3.10
Thomas v. Drysdale (1925) SC 311 .... 12.01
Thomas Marshall (Exports) Ltd v. Guinlé [1979] Ch 227 .... 3.08, 6.01
Tiessen v. Henderson [1899] 1 Ch 681 .... 4.05
Torquay Hotel Co. Ltd v. Cousins [1969] 2 Ch 106 .... 8.05
Transvaal Lands Co. v. New Belgium (Transvaal) Land and Development Co. [1914] 2 Ch 448 .... 4.05
Trimble v. Goldberg [1906] AC 494 .... 3.10

United Copper Securities Co. v. Amalgamated Copper Co. (1917) 244 US 261 .... 11.15
Untermeyer v. Fidelity Daily Income Trust Inc (1978) 580 F 2d 22 ... 11.15

Victor Battery Co. Ltd v. Curry's Ltd [1946] Ch 242 .... 7.01
Viola v. Anglo-American Cold Storage Co. [1912] 2 Ch 305 .... 11.05

W. and M. Roith Ltd, Re [1967] 1 All ER 427 .... 4.01
Wallersteiner v. Moir [1974] 3 All ER 217 ....
.... 3.04, 4.01, 8.07, 11.04, 11.05, 11.12, 11.14
Walsham v. Stainton (1863) 1 De G J and S M 678 .... 9.02
Walton v. Mascall (1844) 13 M & W 452 .... 10.06
Weeks v. Propert (1873) LR 8; CP 427 .... 10.04
West London Commercial Bank Ltd v. Kitson (1883) 12 QBD 157 ... 10.04
Westbourne Galleries Ltd, Re [1970] 3 All ER 374, [1971] Ch 799 .... 12.03
Westminster Property Group plc, Re [1985] 2 All ER 426 .... 9.08
White v. Bristol Aeroplane Co. Ltd [1953] Ch 65 .... 4.01
White Star Line Ltd, Re [1938] Ch 458 .... 4.01
Whitwood Chemical Co. Ltd v. Hardman [1891] 2 Ch 416 ...... 3.09, 11.04
William C. Leitch Brothers Ltd [1932] Ch 71 .... 10.13
William C. Leitch Brothers Ltd (No 2), Re [1933] Ch 261 .... 10.13
Williams v. Lister (1913) 109 LT 699 .... 11.05
Wilson v. Lord Bury (1880) 5 QBD 518 .... 10.01

Wincham Shipbuilding, Boiler and Salt Co., Re Poole, Jackson and White's Case (1878) 9 Ch D 322 .... 4.01, 10.01
Windsor Steam Coal Co. Ltd, Re [1929] 1 Ch 151 .... 6.09
Windsor Steam Coal Co., Re (1901) Ltd [1929] 1 Ch 151 .... 11.06
Wright *v.* Simpson (1802) 6 Ves 714, 734 .... 10.06

Table of Statutes

Business Names Act 1985 .... 7.02

Civil Liability (Contribution) Act 1978
   s.1(1) 10.07, 10.10, 11.07
   s.2(1) 10.07, 10.10, 11.07
   s.2(2) 10.10, 11.07
Companies Act 1862
   s.79(5) 12.01
Companies Act 1928
   s.78 .... 6.05
Companies Act 1929
   s.45(1) 7.01
Companies Act 1948 .... 1.05
   s.54 .... 7.01, 8.07
   s.210(1) 12.03
   s.210(1)-(3) 12.01
   s.222(f) 12.01
Companies Act 1980
   s.75 .... 12.02
Companies Act 1985
   s.9 .... 1.04
   s.10(2) 1.03
   s.13(1) 9.01
   s.13(3) 9.01
   s.14 .... 1.15
   s.17(1) 1.04
   s.22(2) 10.08
   s.24 .... 10.08
   s.32(1) 7.02
   s.34(7) 7.09
   s.35(1) 10.04
   ss.43-47 .... 7.01
   s.46(1) 11.01

s.46(2)	11.01
ss.53-55	7.01
s.56(1)	7.07, 9.05
s.56(2)	7.07
s.56(4)	7.07
s.56(5)	7.07
s.58(1)	7.07, 9.05
s.58(2)	7.07, 9.05
s.59(1)	7.06, 9.04
s.60(1)	7.06, 9.04
s.60(3)-(6)	7.06
s.63	11.06
s.64(1)	7.07
s.64(2)	7.07
s.64(5)	7.07
s.66(1)	7.07
s.67	9.04
s.67(1)	9.05
ss.67-69	7.07
s.68(1)	9.05
s.68(2)	9.05
s.68(3)	9.05
s.80(1)	7.05, 11.04
s.80(1)-(4)	7.06
s.80(2)	7.06
s.80(8)	7.06
s.80(10)	7.06
s.81(1)	7.06
s.81(2)	7.06
s.81(3)	7.06
ss.83-85	7.07
s.83(1)	9.06, 11.04
s.83(4)	9.06
s.83(5)	9.06
s.83(7)	9.06
s.84(1)	9.06, 11.04
s.84(2)	9.06
s.84(3)	9.06
s.85(1)	9.06
s.85(2)	11.04
s.85(3)	9.06
s.86(1)	9.06
s.86(2)	9.06
s.86(4)	9.06
s.86(5)	9.06
s.89(1)	7.06
s.89(4)	7.06

s.91(1)	7.06
s.92(1)	7.06, 9.07
s.92(2)	9.07
s.95(1)	7.06
s.95(2)	7.06
s.99(1)	7.01
s.99(2)	11.04
s.101(1)	10.07
s.102(1)	11.04
s.103	7.01
s.103(1)	11.04
s.104(4)	11.04
s.104(5)	11.04
s.108	7.01
s.114	7.01
s.117(1)-(3)	10.07
s.117(7)	10.07
s.117(8)	10.07
s.118(1)	10.07
s.125(6)	7.05
s.141(1)	7.05
s.142(1)	7.05
s.142(2)	7.05
s.143	7.01
s.143(1)	3.10, 11.04
s.143(3)	11.04
s.151	7.01
s.151(1)	3.04, 8.07, 11.04
s.151(2)	8.07
ss.151-158	7.01
s.153	3.04
s.155	3.04
s.155(6)	7.13
s.156(2)	7.13
s.156(3)	7.13
s.156(4)	7.13
s.156(7)	7.13
s.169(4)	7.14
s.169(5)	7.14
s.169(8)	7.14
ss.171-176	7.01
s.173(3)	7.13
s.173(4)	7.13
s.173(5)	7.13
s.173(6)	7.13
s.185(1)	11.01
s.185(6)	11.01

s.185(7)	11.01
s.191(1)	7.14
s.191(2)	7.14
s.191(5)	7.14
s.192(2)	6.10
s.221(1)	7.04
s.221(2)	7.04
s.222(1)	8.06
s.223(1)	7.04
s.224(1)	7.04
s.224(3)	7.04
s.224(4)	7.04
s.224(6)	7.04
s.225(1)	7.04
s.225(4)	7.04
s.227(1)	7.04
s.228(1)	7.04
s.228(2)	7.04, 8.06
s.229(1)	7.04
s.230(1)	7.04
s.230(2)	7.04
s.231(1)	7.04, 7.09
s.231(2)	7.04, 7.09
s.231(4)	7.09
s.232(1)-(3)	7.04
s.235	7.01
s.235(1)	7.04
s.235(2)	7.04
s.235(3)	7.04, 7.09
s.235(7)	7.04, 7.09
s.236	7.04
s.237(3)	8.06
s.238	7.01
s.238(1)	7.04
s.238(3)	7.04
s.239	7.01, 7.04, 7.05
s.240(1)	7.04
s.240(4)	7.04
s.241	7.01
s.241(1)	7.05
s.241(2)	7.05
s.242(1)	7.04
s.242(2)	7.04
s.243	7.01
s.243(1)	7.02
s.243(3)	7.04
s.243(4)	7.04

s.244(1)	7.04
s.245(1)	7.04
s.245(2)	7.04
s.263(1)	8.07
s.263(3)	8.07
s.277	7.01
s.282(1)	1.03, 1.14
s.282(3)	1.03
s.285	2.03
s.288(1)	7.14
s.288(3)	7.14
s.288(5)	7.14
s.303	1.01, 1.05
s.303(2)	1.05
s.303(5)	1.05
s.304(1)	1.05
s.304(2)	1.05
s.304(3)	1.05
s.304(4)	1.05
s.306(1)	10.12
s.309(1)	4.02
s.309(2)	4.02
s.310(1)	4.05, 6.05
s.310(2)	6.05
s.310(3)	6.07
s.312	8.03, 9.08, 11.04
s.313	8.03, 9.08, 11.04
s.314(1)	9.08
s.314(2)	9.08
s.314(3)	7.10
s.315(1)	7.10, 9.08
s.316(3)	9.08
s.317	2.05
s.317(1)	4.06, 7.10
s.317(2)	4.06
s.317(3)	4.06, 7.10
s.317(4)	4.06, 7.10
s.317(5)	4.06, 7.10
s.317(7)	4.06
s.318	2.05
s.318(1)	7.14
s.318(7)	7.14
s.318(9)	7.14
s.319(1)	1.10, 7.05
s.319(3)	1.10, 7.05
s.319(5)	1.10
s.319(6)	1.10, 8.04

Table of Statutes

s.320	2.05
s.320(1)	4.06, 7.05, 8.01
s.320(2)	4.06, 7.05, 8.01
s.320(3)	4.06, 8.01
s.322(1)	4.06, 8.01
s.322(2)	4.06, 8.01
s.322(3)	4.06, 8.01
s.322(4)	8.01
s.324	7.09
s.325	7.09
s.325(1)	7.14
s.325(5)	7.14
s.326(6)	7.14
s.328	7.09
s.330	2.05, 7.01
s.330(2)-(4)	8.02
s.330(5)	8.02
ss.330-342	2.08
s.331(3)	8.02
s.331(7)	8.02
s.341(1)	8.02
s.341(2)	8.02
s.342	2.05, 7.01
s.342(1)	8.02
s.342(2)	8.02
s.342(4)	8.02
s.346	4.06
s.349(4)	10.09
s.356(1)	7.14
s.356(3)	7.14
s.356(4)	7.14
s.356(6)	7.14
s.359(1)	11.01
s.359(2)	11.01
s.366	7.01
s.366(1)-(3)	7.05
s.366(4)	7.05
s.367(1)	7.05, 8.04
s.367(3)	7.05
s.368(1)	1.05
s.368(2)	1.05, 7.05
s.368(4)	7.05, 8.04
s.368(6)	7.05
s.369(1)	7.05
s.369(2)	7.05
s.372(1)-(3)	7.05
s.372(4)	7.05

s.372(6)	7.05
s.372(7)	7.05
s.376(1)	7.05
s.376(2)	7.05
s.376(3)	7.05
s.376(7)	7.05
s.377(1)	7.05
s.377(2)	7.05
s.377(3)	7.05
s.379(1)	1.05
s.379(2)	1.05
s.382(1)	4.02
s.384(1)	7.05
s.384(5)	7.05
s.425(1)	7.11
s.425(2)	7.11
s.426(2)	7.11
s.426(7)	7.11
s.431	7.12, 11.02
s.431(1)	12.07
s.431(2)	12.07
s.432	7.12, 11.02
s.432(1)	12.07
s.432(2)	12.07
s.434(1)	7.12
s.434(3)	7.12
s.434(4)	7.12
s.435(1)	7.12
s.436(2)	7.12
s.436(3)	7.12
s.438(1)	11.02, 12.07
s.440	11.02
s.442	11.02
s.444	11.02
s.445	11.02
s.447	11.02
s.447(1)	7.12
s.447(2)	7.12
s.447(6)	7.12
s.450(1)	7.12
s.450(3)	7.12
s.451	7.12
s.454	11.02
s.458	10.13
s.459	12.02
s.459(1)	11.01, 12.02, 12.03
s.460(1)	11.02, 12.07

s.461	12.02
s.461(1)	12.02
s.461(2)	12.02
s.503(1)	10.12
s.503(2)	10.12
s.504(1)-(3)	7.13
s.517(1)(*e*)	10.08
s.545	6.10
ss.577-582	7.13
s.584	7.13
s.585	7.13
s.659(1)	4.02
s.659(2)	4.02
s.659(3)	4.02
s.713(1)	7.04
s.719(1)	4.02
s.719(2)	4.02
s.719(3)	4.02
s.719(4)	4.02
s.727	6.09
s.727(1)	6.08, 10.10
s.727(2)	6.08
s.727(3)	6.08
s.730(1)	7.02, 7.05
s.730(2)	7.02
s.730(3)	7.02
s.730(4)	7.02
s.730(5)	7.02
s.733(2)	7.02
s.736(1)	2.07, 10.08
s.736(1)-3	2.07
s.736(4)	2.07
s.741(2)	2.04, 4.06, 6.01, 10.13, 11.07
s.741(3)	2.04
s.744	2.07, 6.08, 9.04
sched. 3	7.07, 9.05
sched. 4	7.04
sched. 5	7.04
sched. 6	7.04
sched. 7	7.04, 7.09
sched. 24	7.02, 7.05
Companies Consolidation (Conseqential Provisions) Act 1985	7.02
Companies (Tables A to F) Regulations 1985	1.01
sched.	4.05
Company Directors Disqualification Act 1986	
ss.1-6	11.02
s.2	10.10

Table of Statutes

ss.2-6	1.03
s.6	10.10
s.8	10.10, 11.02
ss.8-10	1.03
s.10	10.10, 11.02
s.11	1.03
s.11(1)	10.10
s.13	10.10
s.15	10.10
Company Securities (Insider Dealing) Act 1985	6.09, 7.02
s.1	6.03
s.1(1)	3.10
s.1(3)	3.10
s.1(4)	3.10
s.1(8)	3.10
s.4	6.03
s.8(3)	3.10
s.9	6.03
Criminal Penalties etc. (Increase) Order 1984	7.02
Insolvency Act 1986	7.08
42(1)	11.05
s.89(1)	7.13
s.89(2)	7.13
s.89(4)	7.13
s.89(5)	7.13
s.112(1)	11.08
s.126(1)	11.08
s.130(2)	11.08
s.131(1)	7.13
s.131(2)	7.13
s.131(4)	7.13
s.131(7)	7.13
s.132(1)	7.13
s.165(3)	11.05
s.167(1)	11.05
s.210(1)	7.13
s.210(4)	7.13
s.210(5)	7.13
s.212(1)	11.06
s.212(3)	11.06
s.212(5)	11.06
s.213	10.13
s.213(2)	10.13
s.214(1)	10.13
s.214(2)	10.13
s.214(3)	10.13

s.214(4)	10.13
s.214(5)	10.13
s.214(6)	10.13
s.214(7)	10.13
s.215(4)	10.13
sched. 1 para 5	11.05
sched. 4 para 4	11.05

Magistrates' Courts Act 1980
s.32 .... 7.02

Perjury Act 1911
s.2 .... 7.13
Prevention of Fraud (Investments) Act 1958 .... 6.09

Stock Exchange (Listing) Regulations 1984 .... 7.04, 7.07
   para. 7(1)(b) 7.07, 9.05
   para. 7(7) 7.07
Supreme Court Act 1981
s.50 .... 11.04

Theft Act 1968
s.19(1) 7.04

Index

accounts, *109–13*
  annual, 109–10
  criminal offences, 112–13
  circulation of, 112
  disclosure obligations, and, 129–30
  group, 109–10
  notes to, 109–10
  periodical, 109–13
  signing of, 112
acquisitions by directors,
  statutory remedies, and, 137–8
agency,
  directors' liability to shareholders, and, 153–7
American law
  derivative actions, and, 224–7
  British law, contrast with, 227
  business judgment exception, 226–7
  non-ratifiability exception, 226–7
  preliminary demands, rule requiring, 225–6
annual general meetings, *115–16*
  circulation of shareholders' opinions, and, 119
  proxy appointments, 120–21
  requisition in respect of resolutions at, 118–19
appointment of directors, *3–8*
  contractual arrangements, 6–8
    enforcement of, 7–8
    form of, 7–8
    voting agreements, 8
  normal method, 3–6
  prescriptions of Companies Act 1985, 3–4
  private companies, 6
  public companies, 4–6
arrangements,
  disclosure obligations, and, 130–31
articles of association,
  removal of directors, and, 9–11

bank directors,
  negligence by, 89
bill of exchange,
  liability of signatory of, 185–7
breach of statutory duty,
  award of damages for, 201–202
  litigation in company's name, and, 201–202
breach of warranty of authority, *177–80*
  enforcement of contract, and, 179
  measure of damages, 178

capital, *121–128*
  initial,
  inadequacy of, 183–4
  loan, *see* loan capital
  principal disclosure obligations on issue of, 121–8
  share, *see* share capital
Companies Acts, duties under, *103–35*
  accounts, *see* accounts
  criminal offences under Companies Act 1985, 105–108, *see also* criminal offences
  criminal sanctions, prevalence of, 103–104
  examples of, 105
  disclosure obligations on issue of capital, *see* capital
  inspection rights, 135
  interim reports, 114
  meetings of shareholders, *see* shareholders
  methods of enforcement, 103–109
  modes of enforcement, 197–8
  nature of obligations, 103–109
  principal disclosure obligations, *see* disclosure obligations
  reports, *see* directors' report
  statutory obligations, 103–105
  method of analysis, 108–109
  statutory prohibitions, 103–105

Index

compensation,
  liabilities to shareholders, and, 171–2
compensation for loss of office,
  statutory remedies, and, 140
competition, *51–3*
  American decisions, 51–2
  contractual provisions, 51–2
  directors' right to compete, 51
compromises,
  disclosure obligations, and, 130–31
contracts of company, *75–80*
  directors' interests in, *75–80*
  directors' statutory obligations, 78–80
  approval by general meetings, 79–80
  notification of interests, 78–9
  rescission, company's right of, 75–8
  rights of company when director has interest, 75–8
confidential information,
  termination of directorship, and, 94
conflicts of interest, *41–2*
corporate information, *53–8*
  American decisions, 56–7
  confidentially communicated, 54
  extraneous purposes, use for, 57–8
  property, as, 53–4
  share dealings, 54–6
  use of, *53–8*
costs,
  indemnity against, 97
creditors, *173–95*
  duties to, 173–195
  interests of, 69
  liabilities to, 173–95
  breach of warranty of authority, 177–80
  contracts by directors personally, 176–7
  exclusive personal liability of directors, 175–6
  general immunity, 173–5
  guarantees, *see* guarantees
  immunity of directors as regards company's creditors and contractors, 173–5
  inadequacy of public company's initial capital, 183–4
  liquidation, in, 189–95, *see also* liquidation
  negotiable instruments, signatories of, 185–7
  persons prohibited from being or acting as directors, 187–9
  situations where directors are concurrently liable, 180–83
  situations where directors liable but company not, 175–80
  sole member of company, 184–5
creditors,
  litigation by, 208–10
  form of, 208–10

criminal offences, *105–108*
  accounts, in respect of, 112–13
  Companies Act 1985, under, 105–108
  penalties, 106–107
  persons who may be convicted of, 107–108
  reports relating to, 112–13

damages,
  breach of warranty of authority, and, 177–80
  enforcement of directors' statutory duties, and, 141–4
  litigation by shareholders, and, 218–19
de facto directors, *25–8*
  protection of outsiders, and, 26–8
  status of, 25–6
  transactions entered into by, 26–8
debentures,
  public offerings of, 124
declaration of solvency, 133–4
derivative action, *211–16*
  American law, 224–7
  character, 211–12
  circumstances in which may be brought, 214–16
  costs, 213
  independence of plaintiff shareholder, 213–14
  injunction, for, 217
  lie only where company can sue, 212–13
  origins, 211–12
  restrictive view of scope of, 215–16
appointment of, *see* appointment of directors
functions of, *see* functions of directors
legal status of, *see* legal status of directors
powers of, *see* powers of directors
removal of, *see* removal of directors
skill and care, duty of, *see* skill and care, duty of
directors' reports
  criminal offences, 112–13
  disclosure obligations, and, 129–30
  notes to, 111
discharge of directors' duties, *92–102*
disclosure obligations, *128–35*
  accounts, and, 129–30
  arrangements, 130–31
  company transactions, interests in, 130
  compromises, 130–31
  declarations in connection with share purchases and liquidations, 132–4
  directors' reports, and, 129–30
  furnishing of information, 128–9
  investigation of company's affairs 131–2
  share purchases, 132–3

Index

disposals to directors,
  statutory remedies, and, 137–8
duties under Companies Acts, *103–35, see also*
  Companies Acts, duties under
duty not to exceed powers, *37–41*
  absolute liability, whether, 39
  delimitation of directors' powers, 37–9
    breach of law, and, 37–8
    transaction beyond delegated powers, 38–9
    transactions unconnected with objects of company, 38
  negligence, and, 40
duty not to make personal profit, *41–58*
  conflicts of interest, 41–2
  direct personal interest, and, 42–6
  exploitation of business opportunities, 46–50
  incidental profits, 45–6
  opportunities not available to company, 48–9
  profits obtained by director controlled companies, 46–7
  profits obtained from transactions within scope of company's business, 47–8
  profits obtained indirectly, 44–5
  rejection of opportunity by company, and, 49–50
  share issues, 43–4
  duties to shareholders, 148–72
  advice, 157–65
  common law duty of care, 157–9
    application of, 160–63
    future cases, 163–5
  fiduciary duty of care, 159–60
    application of, 160–63
    future cases, 163–5

employees, 66–68
  interests of, *66–8*
    extent of duty to consider, 66–7
    power to make provision for, 67–8
enforcement of directors' statutory duties, *136–47*
  acquisitions by directors, 137–8
  breaches of statutory obligations, 142–4
    judicial evasion of question, 144–6
  claims for damages, 140
  compensation for loss of office, 140
  conclusions as to, 146–7
  damages, actions for, 141–4
  disposals to directors, 137–8
  financial accommodation for directors, 138–40
  injunctions, 141–4
  loans for directors, 138–40
  remedies in absence of statutory provision, 140–47
  restitution, 140
  statutory remedies, 137–40
exoneration provisions in constitution of company, 95–7
  indemnity against costs, 97
  insurance against directors' liability, 95–6
  invalidity of, 95–6
  legality of, 95
extraordinary general meetings, *116–17*
  requisition of, 117–18
  shareholders' rights, 117

false statements,
  prospectuses, in, 128
fiduciary duties, *33–58*
  achieving fulfilment of company's interests, 73–5
  breaches of directors, 221–4
    director control, necessity of, 223
    limiting factors, 223–4
    negligence, and, 221–2
  cessation of directorship, and, 93–4
  common law duties, and, 36–7
  competition, *see* competition
  corporate information, *see* corporate information
  directors ceasing to be subject to, 92–4
  duty not to exceed directors' powers, 37–41
    see also duty not to exceed powers
  duty not to make personal profit, *see* duty not to make personal profit
  duty to use powers in interests of company and for proper purposes, 59–75
  extension to company directors, 34–6
  group transactions, 63–4
  initiation of breach of, 92–3
  interests of company and shareholders as a whole, 59–75
  judicial extension of, 59–80
  nature of, 33–4
  statutory extension of, *59–80*
  termination of, *see* termination of directors' duties
  trustees, and, 34–5
financial accommodation for directors
  statutory remedies, and, 138–40
fraud or oppression of minority shareholders, *219–21*
  control of company by defendants, 220
  infringement of shareholders' personal rights, 220–21
fraudulent trading, *191–5*
  criminal offence, 191–2
functions of directors, *1–2*

Index

general meetings,
   approval of contract or arrangement, by, 79–80
   approval of service contracts by, 16
group transactions,
   fiduciary duties of directors, and, 63–4
groups of companies,
   shadow directors, and, 29–30
   significance of relationship, 31–2
guarantees, *180–83*
   discharge of surety, 182
   extent of liability on, 181
   fiduciary nature of, 182–3
   personal, 180–83

holding company,
   definition, 30–31
incomplete share subscriptions, 168–9
injunction,
   derivative action for, 217
   enforcement of directors' statutory duties, and, 141–4
   litigation by shareholders, and, 216–18
insider dealing, *54–6*
   termination of directorship, and, 94–5
insurance,
   directors' liability, against, 96–7
interim reports, 114
investigation of company's affairs, 131–2, 238–9
   awards, and, 238–9

legal status of directors, *1–23*
   British pragmatism, 2–3
   decisions of courts, 21–2
   enforcement of membership rights, 22–3
   ideal categorisation, 21
   non-interference with shareholders' wishes, 23–4
   office holders or employees, 20–24
liabilities to shareholders, *148–72*
   agency, and, 153–7
   compensation for loss of office, and, 171–2
   directors negotiating sale of shareholders' shares, 155
   general immunity, 148–53
      agency, and, 150–51
      examples, 150–53
      misrepresentation, and, 152–3
      negligence, and, 151
      reason for, 148–50
   incomplete share subscriptions, 168–9
   individual shareholders, to, 153–65
   listing applications, 169–70
   pre-emption provisions, 155–6
   preferential subscription rights, 170–71
   prospectuses, *see* prospectuses
   statutory, 165–72

liquidation, *189–95*
   contribution, 189–90
   directors' liabilities in, 189–95
   fraudulent trading, 191–5, *see also* fraudulent trading
   orders made by liquidator, 194–5
   personal liability by memorandum of company, 190–91
   wrongful trading, 192–5, *see also* wrongful trading
   proceedings against directors, and, 206–207
   prospectuses in respect of, 126–8
litigation, *196–227*
   availability of, 240–42
   breaches of company's constitution, and, 216–19
   company by, 199–208
   company's name, in, 199–202
      authorised by board or general meeting, 203–204
      breach of statutory duty, 200–201
      compromises, 204–205
      contribution, 207–208
      costs, 204
      defendants, 207–208
      indemnity, 207–208
      liquidation, and, 205
      nature of relief sought, 199–200
      receivership, 205
      settlement of actions, 204–205
   cost of, 242–3
   creditors, by, 208–10
   effectiveness of, 242–3
   illegal acts, and, 216–19
   modes of enforcement, by, 196
   power to sue in company's name, 203–205
   proceedings against directors in company's liquidation, 206–207
   shareholders, by, 208–210, 210–27
      American solution, 224–7, *see also* American law
      breaches of fiduciary duties by directors, 221–4
      compensation, and, 218–19
      damages, and, 218–19
      derivative action, 211–16, *see also* derivative action
      enforcement of liabilities to company, 210–27
      fraud or oppression of minority shareholders, 219–21
      injunctive relief, 216–18
      restitution, 218–19
   ultra vires acts, 216–19
loan capital, 121–4
loans for directors,
   statutory remedies, and, 138–40

Index

management, functioning of, *17–20*
  board, decisions of, 17–18
  delegation, 18–19
  formality, 19–20
  informality, 19–20
managing directors, *11–14*
  appointment of, 11–12
  functions, 13–14
  removal of, 12
meetings, *114–21*
  annual general, *see* annual general meetings
  extraordinary general, *see* extraordinary general meetings
  shareholders, of, 114–21
memorandum of association,
  personal liability of directors in liquidation, and, 190–91

negligence, 40
  bank directors, by, 89
  duty of skill and care, and, 84–6
negotiable instruments,
  liabilities of signatories of, 185–7

parent companies,
  definition, 30–31
persons prohibited from being or acting as directors,
  liability to creditors, 187–9
powers of directors,
  abuse of, 60–61
  misuse of, 61–2
  purpose expressed in memorandum or articles, 70–71
  use for proper purpose, 70–73
    purpose not expressed, where, 71–3
    rule, nature of, 73
private companies,
  appointment of directors, 6
profit,
  duty of directors not to make personal profit, 41–58
prospectuses, *124–8*
  listed securities, in respect of, 126–8
  material false statements in, 128
  obligatory contents, 125–6
  ommissions, 167–8
  untrue statements, 165–7
proxy appointments, *120–21*
public company,
  appointment of directors, 4–6
  inadequacy of initial capital, 183–4
public interest, 69–70

release from liability,
  resolution of shareholders, 100–102

relief from liability, *98–102*
  court, power of, 98–9
  instances of, 99–100
removal of directors, *9–11*
  articles, and, 11
  statutory power, 9–10
    weaknesses of, 10–11
remuneration,
  fixing, 62
rescission,
  company's contracts, and, 75–8

Secretary of State,
  remedial powers, 197–8
service contracts, 14–16
  approval by shareholders in general meeting, 16
  mandatory, not, 14–15
  terms of, 15–16
shadow directors, *28–32*
  definition, 28–9
  groups of companies, 29–30
  statutory provisions applicable to, 29
share capital, *121–4*
share dealings,
  corporate information, and, 54–6
share issues,
  duty not to make personal profits, and, 43–4
share purchases,
  disclosure obligations, and, 132–3
shareholders, *114–21, 148–72*
  adverse treatment of certain classes, 64–6
  approval of service contracts by, 16
  class meetings, 120
  directors' duties to, *see* duties to shareholders
  directors' liabilities to, *see* liabilities to shareholders
  interests of, 59–75, 233–5
  member, as, 233–4
  liabilities for directors' acts, 157
  litigation by, 208–10
    form of, 208–210, *see also* litigation
  meetings of, *see* meetings
  preferential subscription rights, 122–4
    liability of directors, and, 170–71
  release of directors' liability by resolution of, 100–102
  remedies for unfair treatment, 228–43
    capacity in which wrongdoers act, 235
    conduct of petitioning shareholder, 236
    petitioner need not be minority shareholder, 235–6
  statutory relief form, 228–36
    conduct by directors meriting, 230–33
    conduct not unfairly prejudicial, 232–3

270 Index

shareholders, *(cont.)*
  statutory relief form, *(cont.)*
    present legislation, 229–30
    statutory jurisdiction of courts, 228–9
    unfairly prejudicial conduct, 230–32
shares,
  authorisation to issue, 121–2
  incomplete subscriptions, 168–9
  public offerings of, 124
skill and care, duty of, *81–91*
  absence of professional standard, 83–4
  American case law, comparison of, 87–91
  bank directors, 89
    non-banking directors, 89–91
  examples of, 84–6
  illustrative decisions, 86–7
  judicial decisions, 86–7
  judicial dicta, 82–3
  negligence, and, 84–6
  personal character of, 81–4
  standard of, 81–91
sole member of company,
  liability to creditors, 184–5

statement of company's affairs, 134
Stock Exchange,
  listing applications,
  liabilities to shareholders, and, 169–70
supervision of directors, 237–8

termination of directors' duties, *92–102*
  cessation of directorship, and, 93–4
  confidential information, and, 94
  initiation of breach of duty, and, 92–3
  insider dealing, and, 94–5
  when ceasing to be subject to fiduciary duties, 92–4
trustees,
  fiduciary duties of, 34–5

ultra vires, 60–61
unfairly prejudicial conduct, 230–32

wrongful trading, *192–5*
  defences, 193
  Insolvency Act 1985, and, 192–3